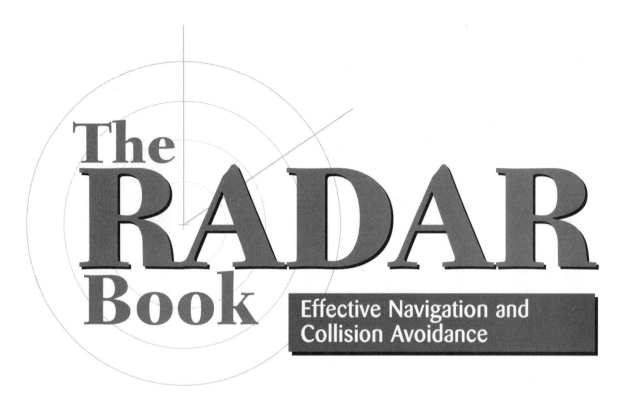

The RADAR Book

Effective Navigation and Collision Avoidance

Kevin Monahan

FineEdge.com

Important Legal Disclaimer

This book is designed to acquaint the mariner with techniques and methods of using nautical radar systems for coastal and offshore navigation. It is not for navigation. A prudent navigator does not rely on any single technique or piece of equipment for navigation in critical situations. The user of this book must accept full responsibility for all consequences from its use. There may well be mistakes, both in the typography and in content; therefore this book should be used only as a general guide, not as an ultimate source of information. No warranty, expressed or implied is made by FineEdge.com LLC as to the accuracy of the diagrams and related material, nor shall the fact of publication or personal use constitute any such warranty. No responsibility is assumed by FineEdge.com LLC or the author in connection therewith. The author, publisher and any governmental authorities mentioned herein assume no liability for errors or omissions, for any loss or damages incurred from using this information.

The views expressed in this book are those of the author's, alone, and, do not reflect any policy, written and unwritten, of the Canadian Coast Guard.

Edited by Réanne Hemingway-Douglass
Book design by Melanie Haage
Original drawings by Kevin Monahan were rendered into digital graphics by Shawn O'Keefe.
Image enhancements by Augustine Torres
Cover photos courtesy of Furuno and Nobeltec

Figures I-1, 10-5, and 10-12 were first published in *The Use of Radar at Sea*, 2nd Edition (1954), by FJ Wylie, published by Hollis and Carter for the Institute of Navigation and reproduced here with the permission of the Royal Institute of Navigation.

All photos and screen captures in the text by the author, Kevin Monahan, unless otherwise credited.

Address requests for permission to:
FineEdge.com LLC, 14004 Biz Point Lane,
Anacortes, WA 98221
www.FineEdge.com

Library of Congress Cataloging-In-Publication Data
Monahan, Kevin, 1951–
The radar book : effective navigation and collision avoidance / by Kevin Monahan.— 1st ed.
p. cm.
ISBN 1-932310-05-3
1. Radar in navigation I. Title.
VK560.M593 2003
623.89'33—dc22   2003021881

Dedication

This book is dedicated to Jon Martin Churchill—friend and mentor,
who retired from the Canadian Coast Guard in October 2003 after 35 years of service.

Acknowledgements

Although writing is often a solitary pursuit, it is not an isolated one. It would have been impossible to put together a technical book of this magnitude without the help of many people. I would like to extend my deepest appreciation to those who have helped me, both in large and small ways, and in particular to:

Mark Bunzel of FineEdge.com, my publisher, for his vision, and his unfailing encouragement and faith in the outcome of this project; Réanne Hemingway-Douglass, my editor, for her insightful contributions. Don Douglass of the Research Vessel *Baidarka*—without whom I would not have been able to obtain the radar photographs in this book—for his advice, inspiration and good humour. I also want to thank Helmut Lanziner of Xenex Navigation Inc. for his kind contributions of images, advice, critical review, and sidebar material.

The following were extremely helpful fulfilling my requests for technical assistance and images for this book, I would like to thank; Group Captain David Broughton and Heather Leary, the Royal Institute of Navigation; Lauren Banerd, Offshore Systems International; Jeff Kauzlauric and Larry Till, Furuno USA; Art Ubalde and Grace Short, Pharos Marine Electronics; Shepard Tucker, J. Mark Barrett, and Josh Harman, Nobeltec Corporation; Cynthia Cagle-Garza, Si-Tex Marine Electronics; Nancy Baumgartner, RayMarine; and Alfred Chiswell, Puget Sound Coast Artillery Museum.

For their support, interest and critical review of the original manuscript, I am indebted to; Robert Hale, publisher of Waggoner Cruising Guide; Terry Patten of Compass Rose Nautical Books in Sidney B.C.; Tyler Brand, Specialized Mariner; Bruce Everts, MV *Tapawingo;* Jack and Linda Schreiber, MV *Sanctuary*; and my brother Pat Monahan, who carefully checked my mathematics.

I wish to express my appreciation to the countless mariners and fishermen with whom I have shared life at sea, and from whom I learned so much, including my numerous friends and colleagues in the Canadian Coast Guard and Coast Guard Auxiliary and the United States Coast Guard.

Last, but by no means least, I would like to express my appreciation to my wife Nancy, who unselfishly encouraged me to devote the time and effort necessary to complete this book, who kept our life and home together while I did so, who supported me emotionally and whose faith in this project was unsurpassed.

Contents

RAdio Detection And Ranging

Radar is an acronym for RAdio Detection And Ranging. In its simplest form, radar uses microwave radio signals (similar to the frequencies used in your microwave oven) to **detect** objects at a distance, and to obtain information about the distance (**range**) and direction (**bearing**) to those objects.

Using a modern radar set, you can observe your surroundings in daylight or darkness, through fog, snow and rain, 24 hours a day, 365 days a year.

Other navigation systems, such as GPS and Loran C interfaced with chart plotters, will tell you immediately where you are in relation to land and other permanent features, but they do not tell you about transient phenomena, such as other boats, barges, floating obstructions, etc. *Radar is the only navigational aid that not only helps you find out where you are, but shows you where everyone else is too.*

Using radar you can observe a dynamic, changing situation in real time in zero visibility and darkness, yet navigate with confidence and safety. In other words, having a radar set is almost like having x-ray vision.

Yet many boaters find radar displays hard to interpret and, consequently they fail to use their equipment anywhere near its full potential. Of all the navigational aids available to the recreational and small commercial boater, radar requires the most interpretation in order to be used successfully; but once mastered, radar is the most valuable of them all.

This book will help you understand how your radar works, so you can properly control and interpret the information it provides, as well as teach you the techniques for navigation, blind piloting, and collision avoidance, *so you can get absolutely the most out of your set.*

History

Radar was developed by the British and German military during the Second World War in order to detect enemy aircraft. Early radar antenna installations were not mobile, so they were camouflaged for safety, and they were directional—able to scan only a certain portion of the sky.

> "We knew . . . where we were, but the trouble was, we didn't know where any place else was."
>
> —Ezra Meeker, *Pioneer Reminiscences of Puget Sound*

Nonetheless, the new technology played an important part in the Battle of Britain, enabling ground crews to obtain early warning of enemy bomber attacks and to direct British fighter aircraft to intercept the approaching threat.

Later versions of this equipment utilized rotating aerials, which were not only mobile, but could also scan the entire sky; and the ancillary equipment was reduced in size enough to allow it to be packed into the back of a large truck.

Under the impetus of war, radar equipment evolved rapidly and, by 1945, virtually every naval ship and submarine was equipped with a rotating radar antenna. For the first time in maritime history, seamen could pierce through the curtains of fog and darkness and literally see unlighted and invisible objects at great distances. *Navigators tend to view other ships as potential enemies, ready to collide with their own ships given the right circumstances.* In keeping with this tradition, mariners still refer to objects viewed on radar as "targets." Radar, then, is the mariner's last defense against these enemies.

Once seamen began to use the new technology for collision avoidance in peacetime, they believed that collisions at sea would become a thing of the past. [See **Sidebar**.] They were surprised to find that collisions at sea still occurred between ships fitted with radar.

By the early 1970s, the average small-vessel radar was compact enough to fit in the pilot-house of a small fishing vessel or workboat and cost less than $10,000. Its advantages being so clear, many small commercial operators began to install radar sets on their vessels. These radars were not the "daylight" radars of today. They were analog sets with little capability for brightness and, consequently, in order to observe the

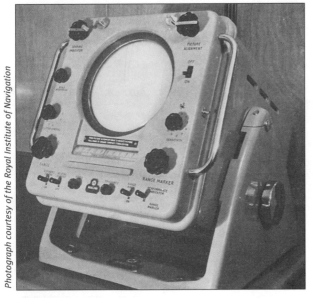

Photograph courtesy of the Royal Institute of Navigation

Fig. I-1
The Old and the New
A Marconi Radiolocator IV using a cathode ray tube (CRT) and analog technology, circa 1952.

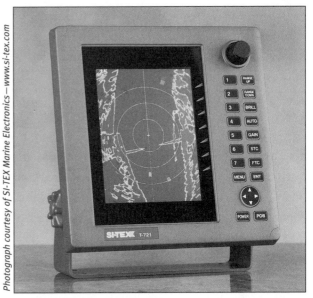

Photograph courtesy of SI-TEX Marine Electronics — www.si-tex.com

A modern Si-Tex T-721 colour raster-scan radar with Liquid Crystal Display (LCD).

Though the modern radar set to the right can far outstrip the 1952 model to the left in performance and ease of use, the two radars share many of the same basic functions.

radar screen in daylight, the user was forced to view the screen under a shaded hood. This limited its usefulness for daytime, because the operator would have to allow his eyes to readjust to the daylight every time he removed his eyes from the hood.

In the late 1980s a revolution took place in small-boat radars—the raster-scan radar or "day-

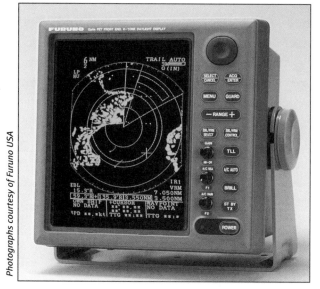

Photographs courtesy of Furuno USA

Fig. I-2
Modern Small-Boat Daylight (Raster-Scan) Radars
One uses a Liquid Crystal Display (LCD), the other a more traditional cathode ray tube (CRT), but both provide the necessary functions for full navigation capability.

The *Andrea Doria*

It is said facetiously that, with the introduction of radar to commercial shipping, came the first radar-assisted collisions, such as the collision of the *Andrea Doria* and the *Stockholm* near Nantucket Light in 1956. The two ships observed each other on radar for twenty-nine minutes, but still managed to collide. The Italian luxury liner *Andrea Doria* was struck amidships by the Norwegian liner and, after struggling to remain afloat for eleven hours, the magnificent ship turned her bottom to the sky and sank.

How could such a tragedy happen, when both ships were equipped with Loran A and radar? These miracles of twentieth century technology were poorly understood in the early days of commercial use. The ships had been observing each other on radar, but neither had systematically plotted the other. Radar should have made it possible to avoid the collision, but instead, both crews made incorrect assumptions from the available information and poor decisions followed. The *Andrea Doria* made a last-minute turn to port, intending to pass what her captain assumed to be a fishing trawler. As the *Stockholm* turned to starboard to avoid the other ship, the *Andrea Doria* turned directly across her path, presenting her vulnerable midship section, and the two ships came together with disastrous results.

Forty-nine passengers and crew lost their lives that night. Though more than 1600 survived the disaster, they would never forget its tragedy and pathos or their role in one of the most spectacular sea rescues in history.

light radar." Because a new raster-scan radar actually processed the signals it received, it could generate an image on a standard video monitor, allowing the operator to view the radar screen in full daylight conditions without having to duck under a hood or into a darkened room. Small-boat operators began to use their radars regularly for collision-avoidance and navigation in the daytime, in good visibility, and they found it significantly added to their confidence and safety.

But probably the most important feature of the modern raster-scan radar was that it actually *processed information*—allowing it to display that information in a number of different ways, and permitting the radar to interface with other electronic equipment.

Today, boat owners can superimpose a radar display on an electronic chart and interface a GPS navigator to show the location of a waypoint on the radar display, thus incorporating the radar and electronic chart display into a completely integrated "electronic bridge."

You need no longer wonder exactly where you are. You can view your vessel moving on the chart background and see, against the same background, the images of other vessels and their exact positions in relation to your own.

Where this technology will go next is anybody's guess. It appears that the only limits are those of the imagination—not only of the manufacturer, but also of the boater who uses the equipment.

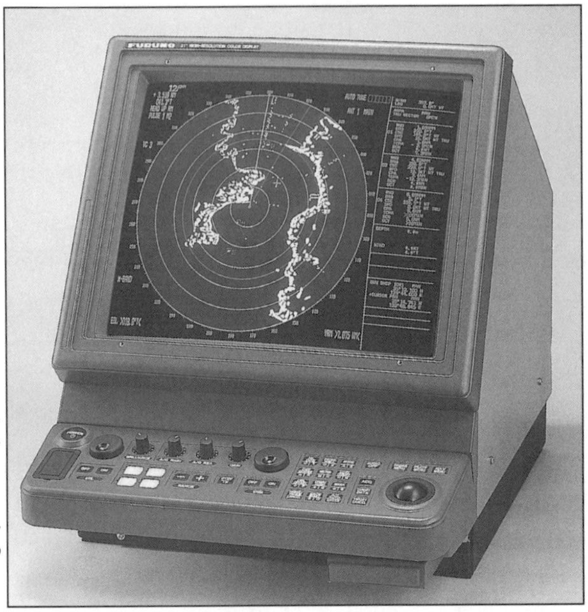

Fig. I-4
Nobeltec Insight Radar Overlay on Electronic Chart
A Nobeltec Insight radar image overlaid on an electronic chart and displayed on a laptop PC. Using this combination of charting and navigational technology, operators can see their own position in relation to the chart, as well as the movement of other vessels and transient features superimposed on the chart.

Photograph courtesy of Furuno USA

Fig. I-3
A Furuno ARPA (Automatic Radar Plotting Aid)
This radar combines a clear daylight display with target-processing capability that allows the operator to see the movements of other vessels at a glance.

Tuning Your Eye

To the untutored eye, a marine radar display bears no resemblance to the real world. The images displayed there seem to be nothing but slowly changing patterns of light and dark. They certainly do not look like a map or a picture of the surrounding waters and land.

You have been told that radar is the best technology ever; radar will help you navigate at night and in fog; radar will help you avoid collisions. But when you look at the screen with its rotating patterns of light and dark, it makes no sense. And if it does not make sense, how can it be of any help at all?

I have seen intelligent, sensible people go into a state of panic on first introduction to a radar display because they cannot understand the images they find there. This isn't their fault. Of all the navigation technologies, radar requires the most interpretation. Most books and user manuals will tell you how to tune your radar set, but they fail to help you tune-up your own eyes and perceptions so you can focus on the relevant parts of the image.

So how do you figure out these patterns; and how will this help you navigate?

The Searchlight Principle

Imagine that your radar antenna is actually a very powerful searchlight. Also imagine that you are rotating the searchlight through 360°, and illuminating all the land and ships around you. It is the reflected light from the land and ships that enables you to see them in exactly the same way the reflected radar beam enables your radar to see through darkness and fog. However, you must remember this key concept—any object that is behind another, such as in a valley behind a hill, is not only invisible to your eyes, it is also invisible to your radar.

Objects or land areas that are hidden from your radar are said to be in a ***Radar Shadow***. Consequently, only the land that is actually illuminated by the radar beam will appear on the radar display. The radar can see only those objects that are in direct line of sight.

To measure the distance of a target, the radar actually measures the time it takes for its beam to travel to an object and for the reflected echo to return to the antenna. Knowing the time taken, and the direction of the radar beam at the time, the radar determines the range and bearing to the object, and then projects a "pip" in the appropriate location on the display. In this manner it builds up a representation of every object it can see in the area. The result is an image that is presented in plan view, as if it were a map to be viewed from overhead. But this map view shows only those areas that are actually illuminated by the radar beam; areas in the radar shadow are missing from view.

This type of display, showing the *position* of radar visible targets in *plan* view is known as a **Plan Position Indicator** (**PPI**). Every radar set uses a **PPI** display; and understanding the **PPI** view is fundamental to interpreting the wealth of information your radar can provide.

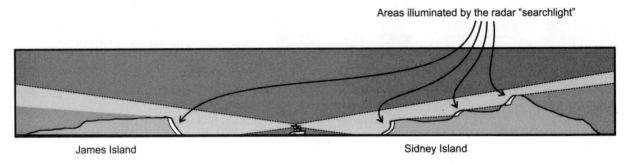

▲ **Fig. 1-1**
Imagine that your radar is a very powerful searchlight illuminating the land around you.

▲ **Fig. 1-2**
When your radar illuminates the land around you, some areas remain in shadow. As the highlighted surfaces in the photograph indicate, only the land that is actually in the direct line of sight of the radar beam will be illuminated, and only those areas will show up on the display.

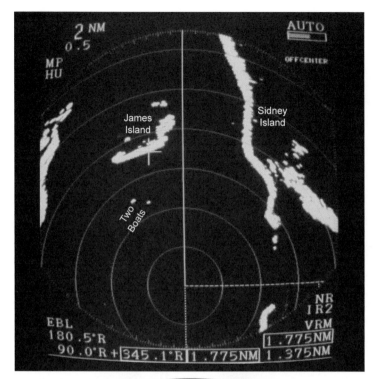

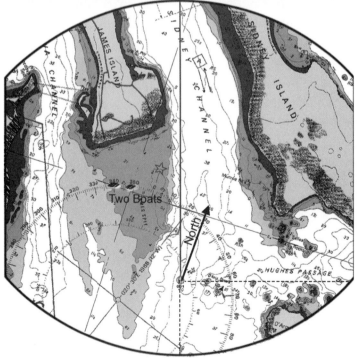

◄ Fig. 1-3 The Plan Position Indicator (PPI)
The Plan Position Indicator (PPI) displays in plan view (as if from above) only what is in your line of sight. Radar shadow areas do not appear on the display.

Note the range scale is indicated in the upper left corner of the display, as is the interval between range rings. Also note that the image has been shifted so that the point representing the vessel's location has been shifted toward the bottom of the display, thus bringing the shore of Sidney Island onto the display.

If you superimpose the radar image over a chart of the area, it is easy to see how the radar image coincides with geographic features on the chart. The cliffs on Sidney Island and James Island are clearly illuminated and return strong images. Behind the cliffs, the flat areas of the island do not appear on the radar display, but the hills beyond the cliffs are visible because they project upwards out of the radar shadow and into the radar beam. [See **Fig. 1-1.**]

The Look of the Display

The next thing you will notice is that each echo slightly changes every couple of seconds, and that the images undergo this subtle change in regular clockwise sequence. This rotating zone of change represents the sweep of the radar beam in the real world. *If you think of the front edge of this rotating zone of change as updating the latest radar image on the display, you may find it easier to understand.*

For reasons we will discuss later, this rotating line of updated information is known as the **time base**. The center of the PPI, around which the time base rotates is known as the "**sweep origin**" or "**time base origin**" and represents the position of your own vessel.

Some echoes wink in and out of existence. They may be the echoes of birds or they may simply be transient electronic noise; generally they do not last beyond a single revolution of the time base. Larger images on the display which are usually the echoes of landmasses, do not change significantly with each revolution of the time base.

Whenever the time base rotates through the "straight up" position, it appears to "paint" a vertical line originating at the center of the display. This is the **heading flash** and it indicates the direction the bow is pointing (the vessel's heading). This type of display is known as a "**Head-up**" presentation. (There are other ways to view a radar image, which we will discuss later.)

Understanding the Radar Display

Of course, the image on your display will remain static only as long as your vessel remains in the same place and headed in the same direction. *Once on the move, you must deal with a dynamic situation.*

When your vessel is in motion the radar displays a dynamic, changing image, centered on your own position. It stands to reason that in order to understand what landforms are being displayed by the radar, you must simultaneously figure out where you are in relation to those landforms. This task is made more complex by the nature of the radar image, which displays only the land surfaces that are illuminated by the rotating beam. As you move in relation to the land, the images change significantly.

Let's imagine you are behind the wheel in your boat. In spite of its being a bright sunny day

---

Ranges and Range Rings

In Chapter 2 we discuss how to set up your radar. When you have set the radar up properly, the image will resemble **Fig. 1-3**.

Notice that the range scale is indicated in the upper left corner of the figure. The range scale indication on your radar may be located elsewhere, but international standards require that it be displayed prominently. Your user manual will tell you where to look on your particular set.

The range scale is the distance from the center of the display to its edge (whether or not the sweep origin is offset). In Fig. 1-3, the range scale is 2.0 Nm.

Also note, there is another number below the range scale indication. In **Fig. 1-3** 0.5 Nm represents the distance between the range rings. You can use the range rings to roughly estimate distances.

Range rings can be turned off in most radars, but it is normally best to leave them on, until you have developed a good facility with the radar. Range rings provide a rough indication of distance, and the different range ring patterns on each range scale provide a hint as to the scale in use.

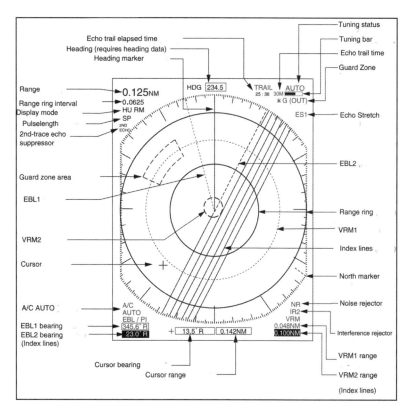

Fig. 1-4 ▶
Display Indications for the Furuno FR7062
This is the model used to capture many of the images in this book.

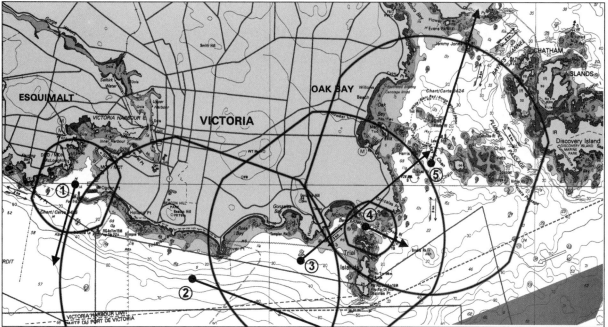

▲ Fig. 1-5
The Voyage of the MV *Baidarka*
As you proceed out of Victoria Harbour toward Sidney, you collect a series of screencaptures of your radar display. (See pages 11 to 21) the chart in this figure and in **Fig. 1-6** shows the areas covered by the screencaptures, and the direction of travel at the time.

you have decided to start your radar operating so you can become familiar with its operation. This turns out to be a wise choice because, as you leave the harbour breakwater and turn the corner to head up the channel, you find that a fog is blanketing the entire area.

You have a couple of choices—either turn around and wait for the fog to clear, or go ahead and navigate using your radar. You decide to go ahead, using your new radar. After all, what is the point in spending several thousand dollars, if you are not going to use the radar when you need it.

Your radar is about to become a new set of eyes, peering through the fog to help you navigate and to show you what vessels and other hazards lie ahead. Let's watch the radar image as you navigate through these waters.

(continued on page 25)

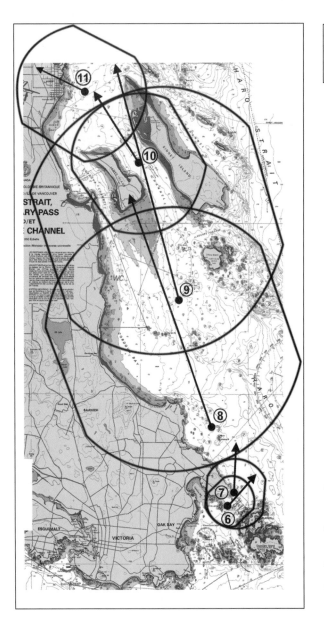

> A large-scale chart covers a small area.
> A small-scale chart covers a large area.

◀ **Fig. 1-6**
The Voyage of the MV *Baidarka* (*continued*)
In the following figures, note that the position of the vessel in relation to the contours of the land determines the shape of the radar images. Also note that though the shapes of the illuminated areas change dramatically, certain features continue to be recognizable so long as they are in sight.

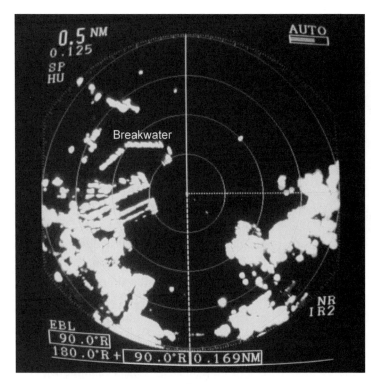

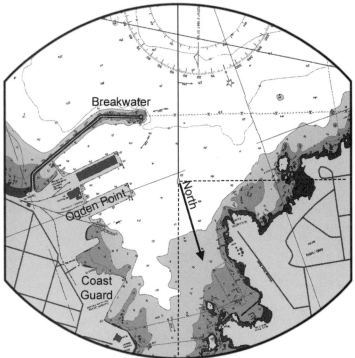

◄ Fig. 1-7
Position 1

Ahead and to port is the Ogden Point
Breakwater at the entrance to Victoria
Harbour; directly abeam to port is the Ogden
Point shipping terminal. Some of the ships at
the terminal are masking the shore end of the
breakwater so it appears disconnected from
the shore. But you can instantly recognize
the breakwater by the dog-leg in its structure. You are heading approximately 190°T,
and the image is oriented so that the direction ahead is at the top of the screen. This
style of presentation is known as **Head-up
display**.

The range scale is set at 0.5 Nm
because the waterway is relatively narrow
and congested. If the radar range scale were
set to see farther ahead, the image of the
harbour entrance would be too small to be
useful.

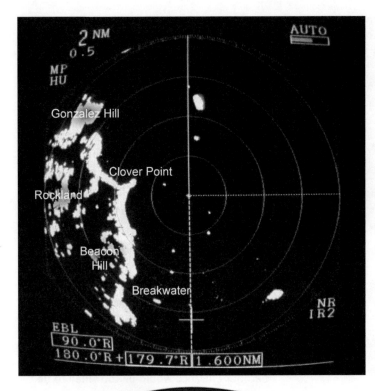

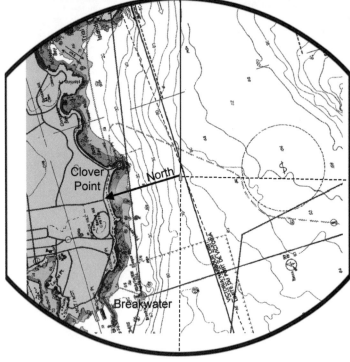

◀ **Fig. 1-8**
Position 2

Now that you have cleared the harbour entrance, it makes sense to increase the range scale to 2 miles. You are now nearly abeam Clover Point, which is clearly identifiable approximately 3/4 Nm away (as shown by the range rings). Ahead are two small boats and one large ship—a second large ship can be seen astern and to starboard. These ships could be mistaken for islets, except that the chart shows no land in those positions, and the ships move differently on the display than land targets do.

Note that behind the shoreline, Beacon Hill, Rockland, and Gonzales Hill are very clearly visible, but the lower lying neighbourhoods of Fairfield are in radar shadow.

The best way to identify specific points is to look for their characteristic features. For instance, you can instantly recognize Clover Point by its prominence from the general trend of the coast. Once you have identified Clover Point, other features begin to fall into place.

By now you have altered your heading to approximately 110°T and the new heading is at the top of the display. When you turned to the east after leaving the harbour, the image on the display rotated to keep the direction ahead in the 12:00 position.

A "pip" is the smallest target echo—usually the echo of a buoy, vessel or a small isolated rock.

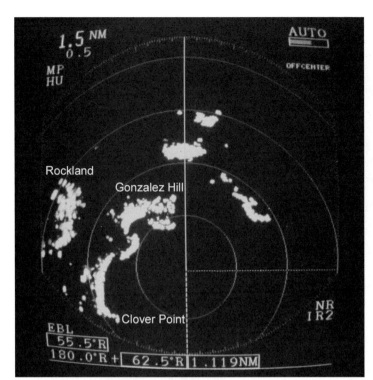

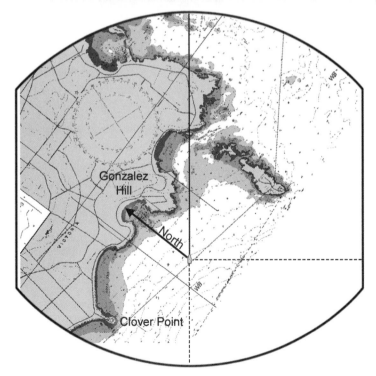

◄ Fig. 1-9
Position 3

Prior to entering Enterprise Channel, you shifted the sweep origin of the PPI from the center to the lower portion of the display. This provides a longer view forward, while maintaining the same level of detail inherent in the current range scale.

Ahead and to the right is Trial Island and to the left, Gonzales Hill and Rockland can be seen beyond the shore. Clover Point is still visible astern, and though its appearance has changed somewhat, it still stands out from the general trend of the coast serving as an ideal landmark.

Also, you can now see land beyond Hartling Point; this land was previously hidden by the point itself. On the other hand, land which was previously visible can no longer be seen.

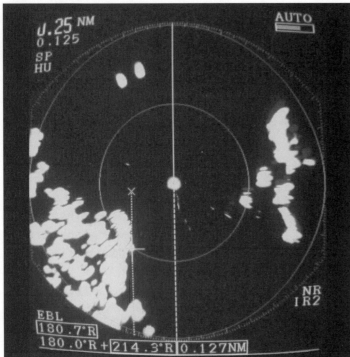

◄ Fig. 1-10
Position 4
On entering Enterprise Channel, you reduced range scale to 0.25 Nm, to make the detail of the narrow channel more readily apparent. You also shifted the sweep origin back to the center of the display. *Baidarka* has turned 45° to starboard, causing the image of the land mass to rotate 45° to port (counter-clockwise).

Ahead and to port are two targets. One is the south cardinal buoy marking Mouat Reef. The other is not Mouat Reef, because the reef dries only at a 0.9 meter tide and, at the present time, the tide is higher than that, so the second target must be something not marked on the chart. Sure enough, as you get closer to the target you can see that the second target is a fishing boat at anchor near the buoy.

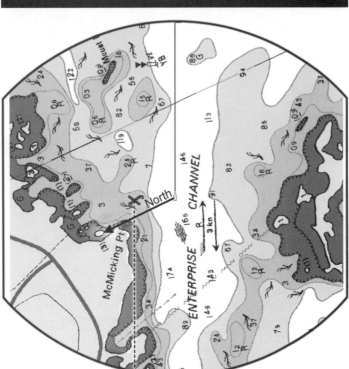

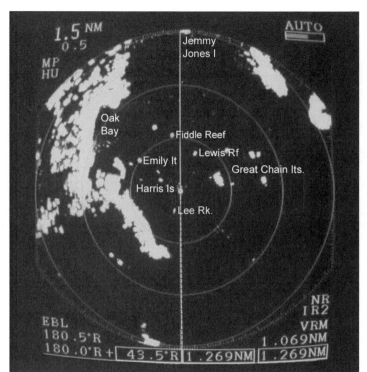

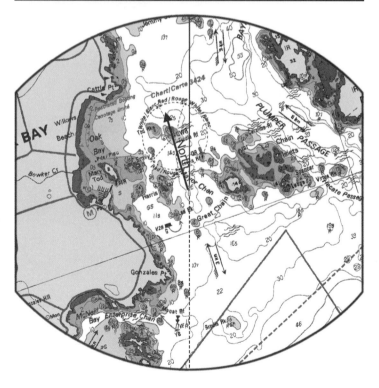

◀ **Fig. 1-11**
Position 5

You have now entered Baynes Channel, which is encumbered by a number of reefs and islets. The first thing you must do is identify each target on the display. To do so, you have increased the range to 1.5 Nm. In this case, all the targets on the display can be matched to specific rocks or islets, so it is safe to assume there are no other vessels in the immediate area.

Here, you are heading directly for Jemmy Jones Island, (which is only just now appearing at the top of the display) between Fiddle Reef and Lewis Reef.

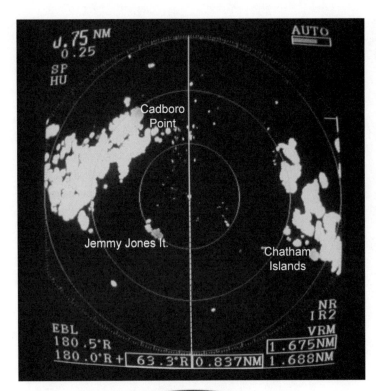

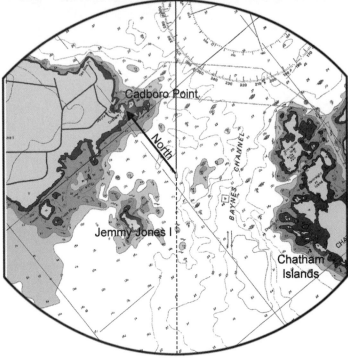

◄ **Fig. 1-12**
Position 6

Once past Jemmy Jones Island, *Baidarka* is now heading approximately 045°T and you have reduced the range scale to 0.75 Nm to show more detail while rounding Cadboro Point.

Note the clutter near the point. This is due to wind waves opposing the tidal currents (which creates an uncomfortable chop). However, you should not try to eliminate this clutter at the present time. If it is a local phenomenon, the clutter will disappear when you have rounded the point.

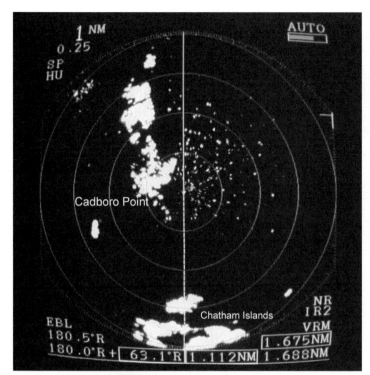

◀ Fig. 1-13
Position 7

On rounding Cadboro Point, the clutter due to the choppy conditions is still present and therefore is probably not just a local effect. Notice that the clutter extends farther to the northeast than to the south. This is because the faces of waves to windward are steeper and return a better radar echo than the backs of waves lying downwind. You have turned *Baidarka* 45° to port, causing the image of the land mass to rotate 90° to starboard (clockwise).

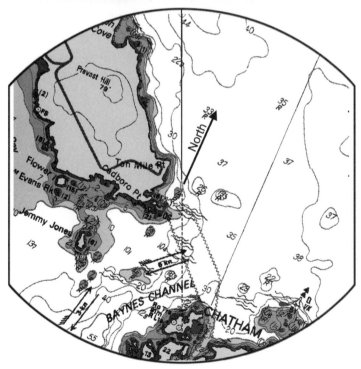

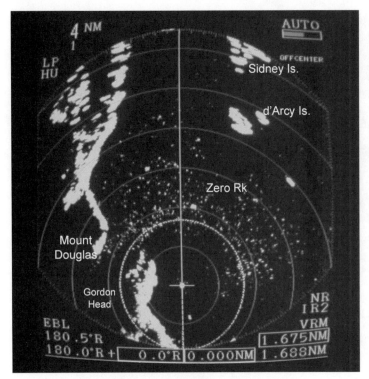

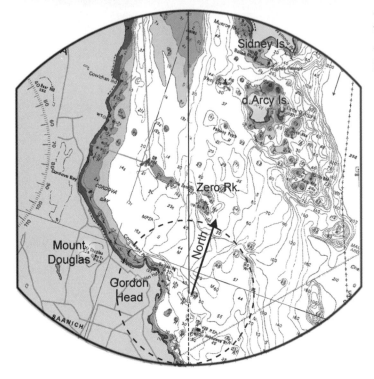

◀ **Fig. 1-14**
Position 8

Now that you are in open water, it is time to raise the range scale again. In this case, in order to see far enough ahead, you have again shifted the center of the PPI (sweep origin) to the bottom portion of the display, and set the range scale to 4 Nm.

The southern shore of Cordova Bay is not visible because it lies in the shadow of Gordon Head, but Mount Douglas rises above the shadow and is clearly visible. Also, the northern shore of Cordova Bay is visible, as is d'Arcy Island and the southern extreme of Sidney Island.

Notice, too, that a strong northeast wind is blowing, and there is a lot of sea clutter present. The "anti-Sea Clutter" control has been engaged, suppressing the clutter close to the sweep origin (the position of *Baidarka*), but Zero Rock (your next navigation point) is almost overwhelmed by the clutter, and Little Zero Rock is completely invisible.

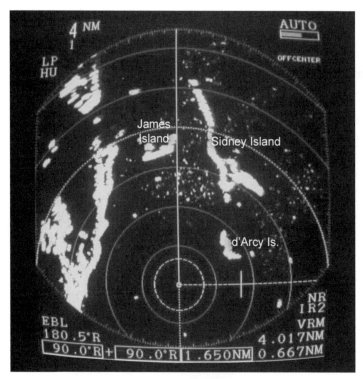

◄ **Fig. 1-15**
Position 9
The cliffs on James Island and Sidney Island are now very clearly visible. Very little of the interior of these island is visible, because the flat country above is in the radar shadow of the cliffs. [See **Fig. 1-2.**]

The northeast chop continues, and consequently, the "anti-Sea Clutter" control is still engaged, which reduces the clutter at close range.

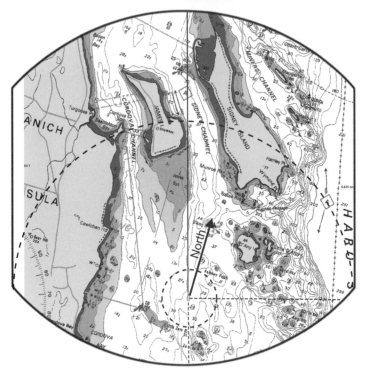

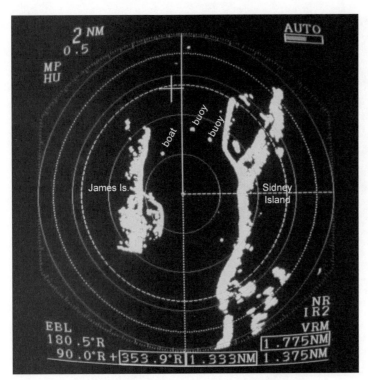

◄ **Fig. 1-16**
Position 10

Now in Sidney Channel the chop has moderated, so you have reduced the "anti-Sea Clutter" control. To port is the low-lying portion of James Island, and behind that, the high ground. The line of cliffs on the island is clearly identified. To starboard is Sidney Island. Again, sand cliffs return a very strong echo. Also, the first spit is visible approximately 45° to starboard. This spit is composed of low-lying sand, but because the western face is scoured to a steep smooth surface, it shows well on radar.

Ahead, two buoys are visible to starboard, and a vessel (of some sort) to port.

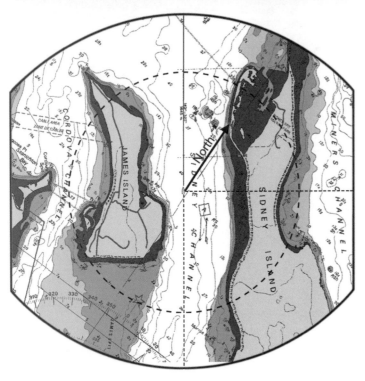

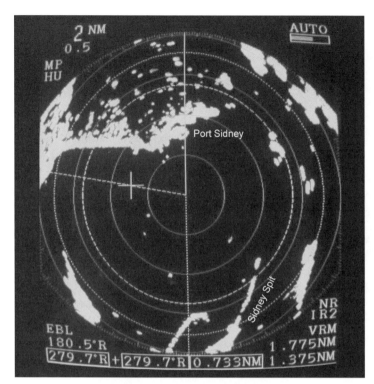

◄ **Fig. 1-17**
Position 11

The final approach to Port Sidney Marina. Directly astern is the southern-most of the two spits on Sidney Island. Ahead is the Port Sidney Marina breakwater. Close examination shows a small radar shadow behind the breakwater, but also a group of targets within the rock breakwater. These targets are the masts of boats that rise above the breakwater and which, consequently, show as separate targets on the radar display.

As you approach the marina, the image will become clearer, especially as you switch to a shorter range scale.

Other vessels are ahead and to port— watch their movements closely to make sure they do not come into conflict with your own.

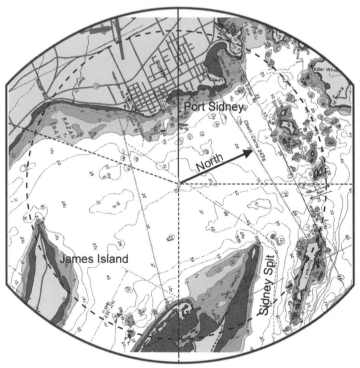

Use your radar both day and night! This will help you develop familiarity with the equipment and then, when you are forced to depend on it at night or in poor visibility, you will trust your own skills.

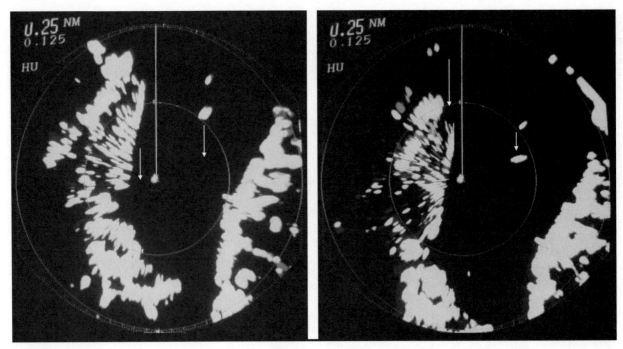

▲ Fig. 1-18
Head-Up Display
The heading of your vessel is always at the top of the display. When you are on a steady heading, targets move toward the bottom of the display.

Head-Up Relative Motion Displays

When the heading flash points to the top center of the display, the radar is said to be in **Head-up mode** because the vessel's heading (direction the bow is pointing) is toward the top of the screen. All the figures in this chapter show radars in Head-up mode.

Beginners should always choose this type of presentation mode, because it is the most intuitive type of display. In the Head-up mode, the position of objects on the screen is represented as being essentially the same as your perception by eye. The heading flash will always point toward objects that are dead ahead. An object seen on the starboard bow will appear to the right of the heading flash. Objects abeam will appear to either side of the display, and objects astern will appear in the lower half of the display.

This presentation mode is also a **relative motion mode.** In relative motion, the land-masses move from the top to the bottom of the display as the vessel moves forwards; and when the vessel turns, the land masses (and other objects) rotate around the screen opposite to the direction the vessel turns. When a turn is completed, the heading flash still points toward objects that are dead ahead, and objects abeam are still to either side of the display. In a Head-up display, your own vessel is represented at the sweep origin facing toward the top of the display.

As you learn to use the radar, you will realize that this is a tremendously important feature of the Head-up display.

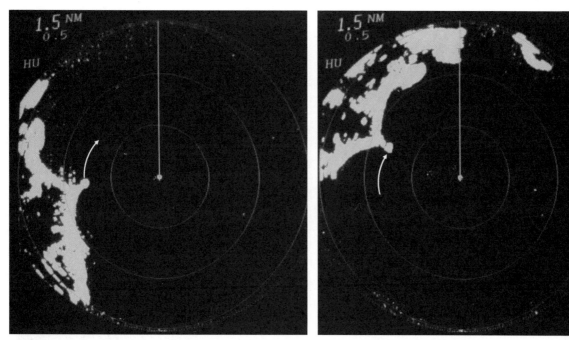

▲ Fig. 1-19
Head-Up Display
When you turn, all targets turn in the opposite direction. Here your vessel has turned toward the shore; on the Head-up display the shore has rotated toward the heading flash. Since the second image was taken a short time after the first, some new areas are now visible ahead.

Heading Flash

You can describe the location of every echo on the display by its relationship to the heading flash in the same way you would describe an object sighted visually. A target is to the right or the left of the heading flash, and less than 90° (forward of the beam) or more than 90° (aft of the beam). Thus an object could be described as 120° to port, or 85° to starboard. (These are known as **"relative" bearings**, because they are relative to your own ship's heading.) Practically though, relative bearings to objects are measured clockwise from the heading flash; thus the bearing to an object 120° to port would be described as 240°R (for "relative").

Because the heading flash is intended to represent the heading of the vessel, it is synchronized to the scanner position, when the scanner is facing directly ahead.

You should be able to temporarily turn off the heading flash, in order to see if it is hiding any small echoes; it should reappear as soon as you let go of the switch. You should not be able to turn it off permanently—the heading flash is a vital aspect of the display.

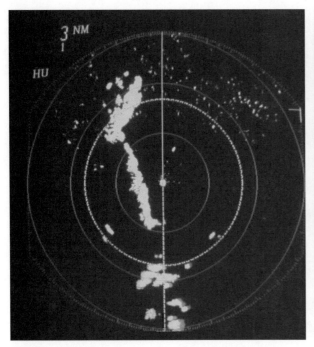 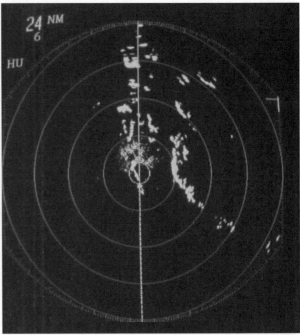

▲ **Fig. 1-20**
Short Range vs Long Range
The same location viewed on short range (3 Nm) and long range (24 Nm) displays. Obviously the short-range view provides far more information for close navigation.

A Tragedy

One moonless and rainy night, a 24-foot pleasure craft equipped with radar and GPS ran into a cliff face at high speed, unfortunately with fatal results for two occupants. This incident took place in a lake that was less than 2 miles wide—in fact, the tragic voyage ended less than a mile from where it started. No one could understand how the operator got so far off course when he had the latest radar and GPS installed, so I was asked to evaluate the navigational situation prior to the collision.

The accident had taken place in a fresh water lake, so I knew the electronics were salvageable. I recovered the radar and GPS and sent them to technicians who could obtain the last data from the equipment. The result was not what I expected; it appeared that the radar had been set to long range. In fact, the last time it was used it had been set to operate at 72-mile range, which would admirably display the tops of mountains a significant distance away, but which would provide no detail about the waters of the lake the vessel was on. The entire width of the lake would have been shown in an area less than 1/4 inch wide. Obviously this range scale would not have provided the operator with any useful information.

The radar should have been set to 3-mile range or less, in order to show the opposite side of the lake in the outer 1/3 of the display and to show the features on the near side of the lake.

(continued from page 10)

Choosing the Appropriate Range Scale

Working with radar is the art of interpreting images. In fact, the operator who can best interpret the image will get the most from his or her radar. The logical conclusion, then, is that the better definition you can obtain from an image (thus reducing ambiguity), the more information you will obtain. Choosing the appropriate range scale is critical to obtaining the most from the radar.

When you use a large-scale harbour chart, you do so specifically in order to observe greater detail than was available in smaller-scale charts. In exactly the same way, you must chose a larger-scale (shorter range) display in order to see more detail in the objects you are observing. [See **Fig. 1-10**]. When you chose a shorter range, any specific object will appear farther and farther from the sweep origin until, at some point, the range is so short that the object no longer appears on the screen at all.

Obviously, you must strike a balance between obtaining adequate detail, keeping the desired object in the display, and keeping a long-range lookout.

- Most observers agree that you should keep the object of interest in the outermost ⅓ of the display.

- This may not be possible where there are two or more objects of interest, and in fact, you may wish to alternate between long and short range in order to observe two separate objects. Or, you may have to compromise and accept a certain loss of detail.

> **The rotating time base and range rings are centered on the sweep origin—the bright spot at the center of the Plan Position Indicator (PPI). However, you can shift the entire PPI up, down or side to side. When you do so, the sweep origin is no longer at the center of the radar display. (See Figures 1-9, 1-14, and 1-15.)**

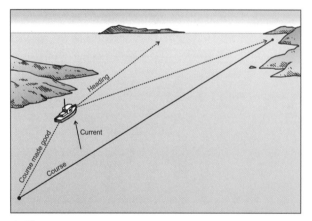

▲ **Fig. 1-21**
The Difference between Course Made Good (CMG) and Heading

The Difference Between Course and Heading

The heading flash points in the direction the bow is pointed (the heading, or the course steered), which is not necessarily the same as the direction the vessel is travelling. Wind, seas, and currents acting at an angle to the vessel's heading can push a vessel off its intended course line. The greater the strength of these outside forces, the greater the discrepancy between the course steered (or heading) and the actual track or course made good (CMG). In an extreme example, a vessel travelling at six knots across a river in which the current was also running at six knots, would find itself set off course by 45°.

When using radar, you must remember that the heading flash is not necessarily pointing in the direction of travel. Later you will see how significant this may be.

▲ **Fig. 1-22**
Radar-Conspicuous Targets
Cliffs are highly "conspicuous" because their surfaces are perpendicular to the radar beam. Most of the area above the cliff is in shadow, except for the church spire, which is also a good reflector of the radar beam.

▲ **Fig. 1-23**
The Effect of Tide Level
A rocky foreshore appears much different at low water than it does at high water. Consequently it will appear different on radar. Sometimes these differences are very significant.

- If you are observing nearby objects on short range, you should switch to long range on a regular basis to see if other vessels are approaching.

- *Unless you monitor long ranges at regular intervals, approaching vessels may get dangerously close before you are aware of them.* When your radar is set to the 0.5 Nm range scale, and you are making ten knots through the water, another vessel travelling at ten knots on a reciprocal course appears at the upper edge of the display only 1½ minutes before it collides with you. If either vessel is travelling faster than 10 knots, the time is even less.

Identifying Radar-Conspicuous Objects and Features

Sometimes it is difficult to match up the image of the land on the display with the landforms shown on the chart. While we deal with this subject in detail in a later chapter, you need to understand a little of what makes some radar targets conspicuous, while others are almost undetectable.

In general, landforms that present a flat face toward the radar antenna will reflect radar energy back to the antenna quite efficiently. Other features, especially smooth beaches, mudflats and the like will deflect the radar energy away from its source. (This is one of the principles behind the stealth bomber's invisibility to radar.) Buildings and bridges, especially when made of metal, reflect radar energy efficiently, but small fiberglass or wooden boats do so poorly—which is why they are advised to carry radar reflectors.

Your biggest challenge will be to identify the various geographic features on the display—such as points and headlands. Beginners often find radar displays confusing, and even if you have an intuitive understanding of radar shadows and the appearance of land on a display, looks can often be deceiving.

Consequently, you must look for rocky islands, headlands, etc. to use as references when plotting a position. In **Fig. 1-8**, Clover Point is easily identifiable because of the manner in which it projects from the general trend of the shore.

As a result you should track your progress throughout the voyage by keeping a mental tally of major points and islands as you pass them, and comparing them to the chart. At each major stage of the trip [Figures 1-5 and 1-6], there are landmarks you can use to assist in locating your approximate position. At each stage, you can actually identify a new landmark ahead before the previous landmark disappears off the display astern. In this way, you will be able to identify various points of interest as you progress on your voyage, as well as being certain of where you are, should your radar suddenly quit (as all electronic devices are capable of doing).

Be sure that you can always identify major features in your vicinity. You will need all the cues you can get from the radar and not base your decision purely on the *shape* of a feature. Remember that some parts of the feature may be in radar shadow. Instead, use other cues to assist you in identifying particular features:

- The positions of other features such as islands, off-lying rocks, etc. in relation to the major feature of interest.

- The general trend of the coastline (it is difficult to see this trend when viewing the coast from close up, but from a distance the general nature of the coastline is often obvious).

- When attempting to identify a bay by its shape, wait until you are sure that its entire shoreline is within line of sight. Otherwise you may conclude that radar shadow areas form part of the

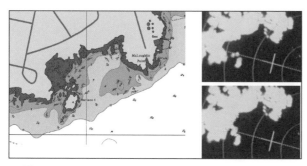

▲ **Fig. 1-24**
Harrison Island
Left: At high water, Harrison Island is identifiable by the two rocks lying close to shore, and an open bay behind the island.

Right: But at low water, the two rocks have merged with the shoreline and the open bay has disappeared.

When looking for radar prominent features, take the height of the tide into consideration and, when possible, use points and headlands that are steep and bold.

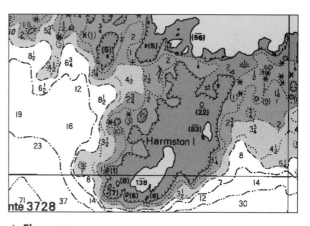

▲ **Fig. 1-25**
Harmston Island
At low water the appearance of Harmston Island on radar will be considerably different than at high water.

bay, leading you to mis-identify the bay as a result.

♦ Try to focus on prominent features—in **Fig. 1-8** Clover Point is the easiest to identify.

♦ Look only at the leading (inner) edges of land areas—closest to the center of the display. The outer edges probably represent the leading edges of radar shadows.

♦ Make allowance for the height of the tide. If the point or headland has extensive rocky foreshore, its appearance on radar will differ, depending on the tide. In general it is best to use landmarks that are steep and bold and are not associated with extensive drying areas.

Chapter Two

Early Successes from Simple Techniques

In the last chapter we focused on training your eye to recognize landforms when your vessel is in motion. This chapter is aimed at early successes: simple techniques for obtaining instant satisfaction with a minimum of preliminaries. However, first you must set-up your radar in order to take advantage of its capabilities as an aid for:

1. Navigation and pilotage
2. Collision avoidance.

How to Set Up Your Radar

On most radar sets, the controls discussed below can be found on the front panel. However, on smaller units, especially those designed for outdoor use, a number of these controls may be available only as menu choices. Whatever the case may be, adjusting them in the proper sequence is critical to obtaining the best picture.

Some control functions may be set automatically by the radar; so for now, allow the radar to set the automatic functions for you. However, in the future, you should override the automatic control, to develop skill at setting up the radar image yourself. Once you have learned to control these functions manually you will find that, in extreme circumstances, you can do a better job

of getting a clear radar picture than the automatic functions possibly can.

Before starting, make sure that the Brilliance, "anti-Sea Clutter" and "anti-Rain Clutter" controls are turned off or down to minimum.

1. Turn the power **On.**

   ◆ Most radars must warm up before being ready to transmit. This may take three minutes or more. A count-down to "Standby" mode should appear on the display.

   ◆ Once in "Standby" mode, the radar is powered up and ready to transmit but it is not actually transmitting.

2. Press **Tx/Stby.** This control toggles between "Standby" and "Transmit" modes.

   ◆ When the radar is in "Standby" mode, pressing this control begins the transmission of radar pulses. When you are moored alongside other vessels or when someone is near the radar scanner you may want to warm up the radar, without actually transmitting. In this case you would press the **Tx/Stby** control only when clear of people and other vessels.

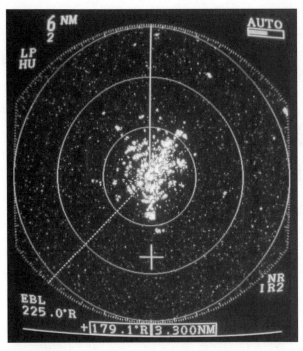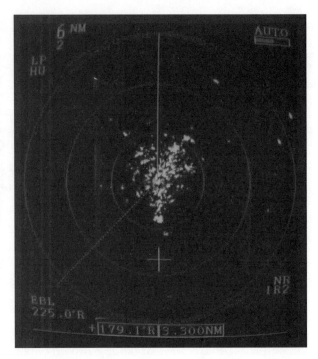

▲ **Fig. 2-1**
Brilliance Adjustment
The brilliance adjustment should not be so high that
it blurs the image on the display (left) nor so low that
you have trouble seeing the image or distinguishing
the rotating time base (right).

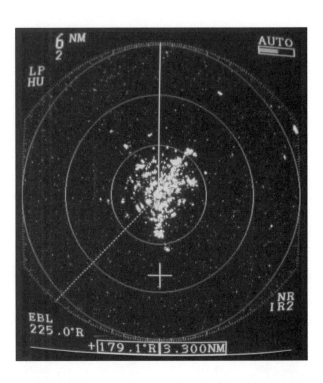

Fig. 2-2 ▶
Brilliance Properly Adjusted
In this figure, the brilliance is properly adjusted. The
exact setting will depend on ambient light conditions. At night it may be difficult to turn the brilliance
low enough. Most radars are equipped with a tinted
plexiglas cover which helps reduce the brilliance further than is possible with the brilliance control alone.

- When the radar is in "Transmit" mode pressing this toggle control returns it to "Standby" mode.

- When turning the radar off, most sets require that you press the **Power On/Off** and the **Tx/Stby** controls at the same time.

3. Once the radar is transmitting (and receiving), switch it to **6-mile range scale**.

4. Set the **Brilliance** control. If the control is a knob, turn it fully off (normally counterclockwise), then slowly increase the brilliance until you can clearly see the time base rotating around the center of the display.

5. Set the "**Gain**" control.

- The Gain control (also known as "sensitivity") is like the volume on a stereo or a radio. When it is turned down, you will not see anything on the display, but when it is turned fully up, the screen is filled with white "noise".

- Turn the Gain control fully off and then slowly increase the "volume".

- At first you see only a few echoes close to the center of the display; but as you turn up the Gain, you will see more echoes farther from the center. As you continue to turn up the Gain, these echoes take on clearer and clearer definition.

- At some point, small speckles of noise begin to show against the blank background. Turn the Gain down until these speckles (or grass) almost disappear.

- You may observe that the area near the center of the screen is cluttered with echoes. Do not worry about this for now.

6. Set the "**Tuning**" control. In most modern radars, tuning is set automatically, and there is no manual override. However, if your set is equipped with tuning control, simply turn it either way until you get the best image of a long range contact. If you are in a marina, you may have to wait until you depart and have distant targets on your display.

7. Reduce the range to 1 Nm or less. You will notice that when the radar is properly set up for 6 Nm range scale, a significant amount of clutter appears around the sweep center. As soon as you reduce the range to 0.5 Nm or less, this clutter may dominate the entire display. [**Fig. 2-5**]

8. Set the "**anti-Sea Clutter**" control. ("anti-Sea Clutter" is also known as **STC—Sensitivity Time Control—or A/C Sea**.) [**Fig. 2-6**]

- Turning up the "anti-Sea Clutter" control reduces sensitivity near the center of the screen.

- In order to get the best long range image, you increased the "Gain" setting to the point where the center of the screen became cluttered with light. Now that you have established a good background level of "Gain", reduce the sensitivity near the center of the screen by using the "anti-Sea Clutter" control.

- As you increase the "anti-Sea Clutter", you will find that the clutter and ghost images disappear, and much more detail emerges near the center of the screen. Adjust the "anti-Sea Clutter" control for the maximum definition at close range.

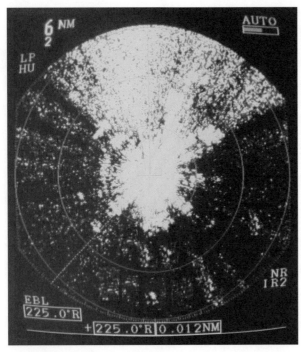 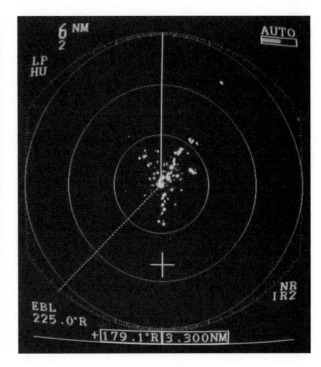

▲ **Fig. 2-3**

Gain Adjustment

Left: Too much gain results in a large amount of speckling in the background or, as in the figure above, it may completely overwhelm the displayed image.

Right: Too little gain results in the radar failing to detect distant targets.

Fig. 2-4 ▶

Gain Properly Adjusted

A properly adjusted radar at 6-mile range scale. Note that the center of the display is cluttered with "noise", and that there is still some speckling in the background. This image was taken in Victoria Harbour, so numerous pips representing the tops of many nearby buildings are visible.

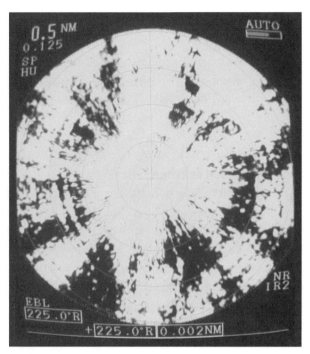

▲ Fig. 2-5
Clutter and Noise at Reduced Range Scale
Now that the radar has been set up properly at medium range, reduce the range to 0.5 Nm. The clutter that was near the sweep center on 6 Nm range scale, now dominates the entire display.

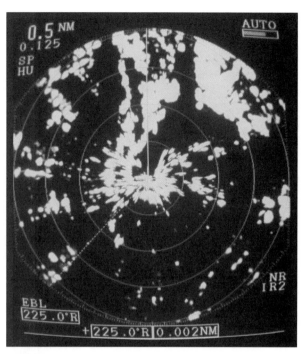

▲ Fig. 2-6
Clearing up the Image with "anti-Sea Clutter" Control
Increase the "anti-Sea Clutter" control (which reduces sensitivity at close range), until you get the clearest image. The open water of the harbour can clearly be seen ahead and to the right of the heading marker.

◆ Be careful not to turn it up so high that you eliminate weak echoes from nearby small boats which will have the same effect as if you turned the "Gain" too low. Also note that as you turn it up, the "Gain" suppression effect moves farther away from the sweep origin.

◆ When you think you have it just right, turn it down a tiny amount. It is always better to see a few ghost images than it is to miss small objects close by.

Congratulations—you have set up your radar to show the best image. Later we will discuss the working of these controls in more detail, and how you can use them to achieve surprising results; but for now, you have done well.

In general, most non-automatic controls on a radar set will "drift" away from their optimum settings. So, unless you have significant experience with your specific radar set and can be assured that these settings will not drift, *you should go through this set-up process every time you turn on your radar.* You should also repeat steps 5 to 8 at regular intervals as long as your radar is operating—especially when you change from long range to short range and back again.

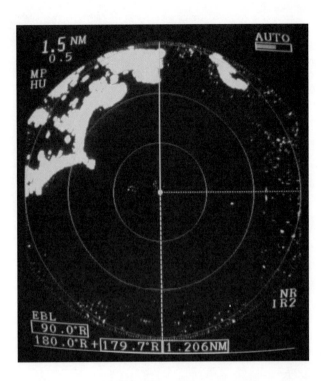

Estimating Position Using Range Rings

If you know your approximate heading, and you know the distance off a prominent feature, then it is easy enough to estimate your approximate

◄ **Fig. 2-7**

Rough Estimation of Range

Your vessel is travelling northeast near the Victoria waterfront in Juan de Fuca Strait. You have chosen to use Clover Point as your reference shoreline abeam because it is so unmistakable. The radar image of the peninsula intrudes approximately halfway into the middle range circle which, according to the indication at the top left, is bracketed by range rings at 0.5 Nm and 1.0 Nm, therefore the distance to Clover Point is approximately 0.75 Nm.

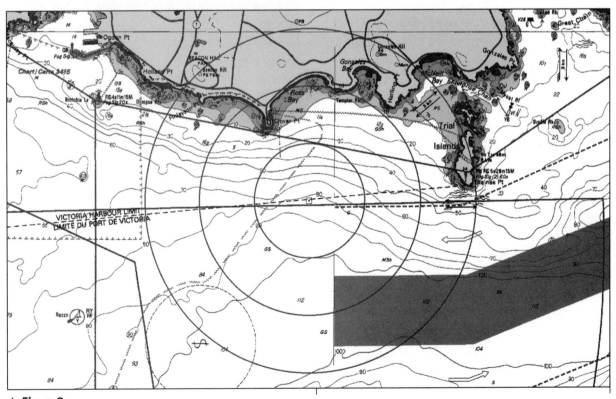

▲ **Fig. 2-8**

Range Rings on the Chart

If you drew the range rings on your chart, it would look like this.

Fig. 2-9 ▶
Estimating Position
Using your thumb and index finger (or dividers—if you want more accuracy) measure 0.75 Nm from the latitude scale at the side of the chart, then transfer that measurement to the chart, placing your index finger on the reference shoreline (Clover Point). You can obtain a fairly good estimate of your position this way—in this case near the tip of your thumb.

position. To do this properly, though, you must estimate the distance to a feature that is abeam. If you are not confident of your ability to identify a particular feature abeam, you may have to wait a while for a suitable target.

Once you are satisfied with the identification of the feature abeam, simply "guesstimate" the approximate distance to the point, headland, or island, using the fixed range rings. Next, transfer this distance to your chart, using dividers or, if your "guesstimate" is very rough, simply use your fingers.

If you do not need a highly accurate position and just want to know your approximate position, simply estimate the distance to two radar-conspicuous features, using the permanently displayed range rings on your display. Once you have done

so, roughly translate the distances to your chart to determine approximately where you are.

> If the tide is low and you have used a reference shoreline with extensive rocky foreshore, you must plot the position on the chart, using the seaward extent of the foreshore as the reference shoreline.

Variable Range Marker (VRM)

While using the fixed range rings is acceptable in making very rough approximations of distance, it is not acceptable for precise navigation. That is why each radar set is equipped with one or more **Variable Range Markers (VRM)** for precise measurement of distances. (It is actually surpris-

Using Paper Charts

Many of the navigation procedures in this book rely on paper charts. If your vessel is equipped with an electronic chart system (ECS) or GPS chart plotter, you may think you do not need to know how to use radar for navigation because your ECS or GPS performs all your navigational tasks for you.

But some day, your ECS or GPS will certainly fail. If you want to be able to navigate precisely with your radar you must have charts available and practice the procedures. Only then will you develop the habits that will see you through when your ECS or GPS lets you down.

ing how precise the VRM can be!) While it depends on the range scale in use, you can typically obtain distance measurements accurate to within +/- 50 feet at short ranges. As a result, you will find the VRM to be one of the most valuable features of your radar set.

The VRM is simply an adjustable range ring which you can shrink to disappear at the center of the display or which you can expand to the extreme outer edge of the display and beyond. Somewhere on the display, you will find the VRM symbol and beside it an indication of the distance from the VRM to the center of the display.

Some radars utilize a trackball to adjust the VRM, while others are equipped with knobs or keys. Whatever the method used, you should practice with the adjustment until you can operate it with a fine degree of control. To

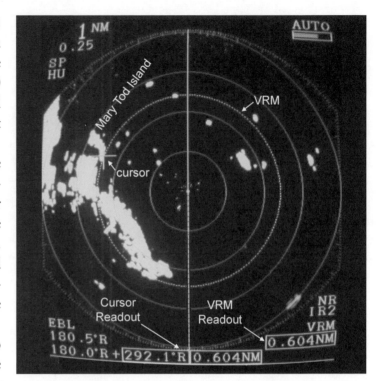

Fig. 2-10 ▶

Using the VRM to Find your Position (near Victoria, British Columbia)

This radar uses a trackball to move the cursor to drag the VRM range ring in and out. Using the cursor, place the moveable range ring so that it just touches the inner edge of the image of Mary Tod Island. The readout at the bottom of the display indicates the VRM is at 0.604 Nm. The cursor also indicates the same distance because you used the cursor to drag the VRM ring into place.

Note that the VRM is brighter than the fixed range rings and uses short dashes instead of a solid line.

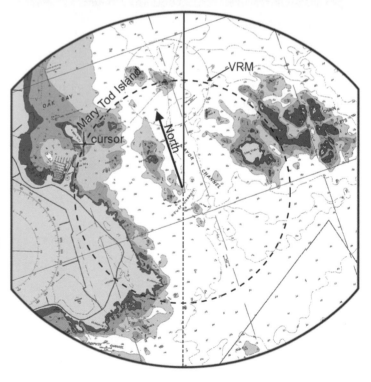

measure the distance to a feature on the display, *move the VRM outward until the outer edge of the VRM just makes contact with the leading edge (inner edge) of the target you are measuring.* The target could be another vessel, an isolated rock, or a conspicuous point of land.

Finding Position Using the Variable Range Marker (VRM)

If you know the distance to a specific geographic feature, then you know that your vessel must be located somewhere on a circle that is centered on the position of that feature. In other words, you have obtained a **circle of position (COP)**.

If you obtain two or more circles of position, your vessel's position must be on both circles of position—where the two circles intersect.

In classical navigation, the navigator learns to use bearings to geographic features because bearings can be measured easily and accurately with a compass. However, for reasons that will become apparent later, a bearing taken from radar is not

nearly as accurate as a range (distance). This is why you must learn to measure distances accurately and quickly with the VRM.

1. Identify two radar-conspicuous features. (You may have to increase or reduce the range scale.) *Remember:* For best results, adjust the range scale so that the feature of interest is in the outer third of the display.

2. Measure the range (distance) to one of the two features using the VRM.

3. Using a compass (the kind that holds a pencil, not the kind that finds direction) measure the distance on the latitude or distance scale on the chart.

4. Once you have adjusted the compass, place the point on the feature you measured on the radar display and, as accurately as possible, scribe a circle around that feature. This circle is your first circle of position.

5. Make allowance for the tide level. If the headland has extensive rocky foreshore,

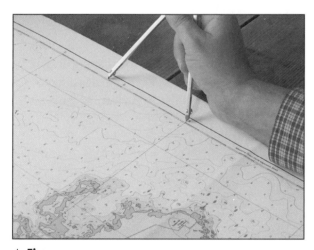

▲ **Fig. 2-11**
Measuring Distance on the Chart
Using the latitude scale on the side of the chart set the compass to 0.604 Nm. (One minute of latitude equals one nautical mile.)

▲ **Fig. 2-12**
Finding the First Circle of Position
Then place the point of the compass on the point you measured with the VRM, and scribe a portion of a circle to represent the circle of position. Your vessel must be on this circle of position.

you must place the point of the compass on the portion of the foreshore that, in your opinion, represents the location of the shoreline at the time. In the example above, the tide is high, so you do not have to make allowance for the foreshore.

6. Repeat steps 2, 3, 4 and 5 for the second geographic feature.

7. Your vessel's position will be at the place where the two circles intersect. However, as you will discover that when circles intersect, they do so at two points, not just one.

8. Most of the time you will have no trouble determining which point of intersection is the true position; but sometimes you will have to measure the range to a third object, repeating steps 2, 3, 4, & 5 again.

9. You will find that it isn't necessary to draw the full circle of position on the chart. Instead, just draw the portion of the circle that passes through the portion of the chart

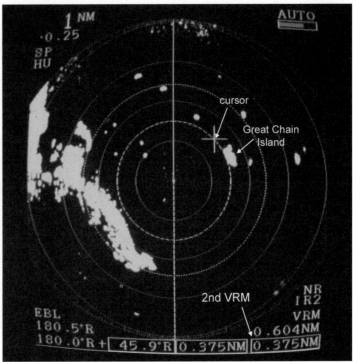

▲ **Fig. 2-13**
Measuring Distance to Two Points of Land with the VRM
Using a second VRM (if you have one), measure the range to a second radar-conspicuous feature—in this case the closest point of Great Chain Island.

Sometimes it is difficult to find a suitable point in the outer third of the display. In this case you have chosen to use a target in the middle third; this isn't wrong, but you should avoid doing so if possible.

◀ **Fig.2-14**
Finding the Second Circle of Position
When two circles intersect, they do so at two points, not one. In most cases, you can easily tell which point of intersection represents your true position; here it is clearly the lower point of intersection.

containing your approximate position. Comparing the display with the chart will help you decide where that area lies on the chart.

10. If you have plotted three circles of position based on three points of reference, the result will be a triangle, known as a "cocked hat". Your vessel's position will be in the exact center of the triangle.

Congratulations, you have just plotted your position on a chart, using the unique features of radar navigation. As you develop familiarity with the technique, you will get faster at the process and more confident with the results. One way to estimate the quality of your position fixing is to use three ranges whenever possible. As a general rule, the smaller the "cocked hat", the more confident you can be in the resulting position. If you are careful to obtain the best measurement possible using the VRM and if you are very careful with the compass, you will be able to obtain positions that are accurate to less than 2% of a nautical mile (120 feet) when using range scales less than three miles.

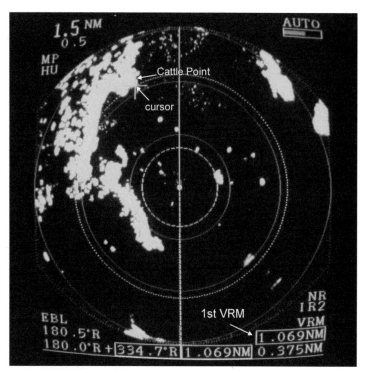

Fig. 2-15 ▲
Resolving Ambiguity with a Third Range Measurement
In order to resolve the ambiguity of position, you select a third reference point (Cattle Point) for measurement, using the first VRM.

Cocked Hat

Fig. 2-16 ▶
When you use three circles (or lines) of position, they will form a triangle known as a "cocked hat". Your position will be in the center of the "cocked hat".

The triangle gets its name from the resemblance to the three-cornered hats that gentlemen and captains wore in the eighteenth century.

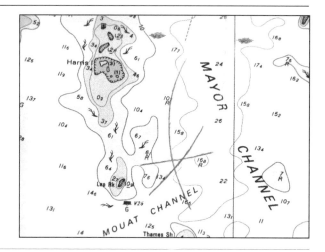

◀ Fig. 2-17
Resolving Ambiguity with a Third Circle of Position
When taking a position using only two points you should always try to use reference points that are approximately 90° apart. In this case, you are using a point approximately 90° away from the other two to resolve the ambiguity of position.

Choosing Radar-Conspicuous Points for Position Fixing

In order to avoid ambiguity, and to ensure that you get the most accurate position, follow these guidelines when choosing reference features for position fixing:

- Choose prominent points with as little foreshore as possible
- When using two reference points, choose two that are nearly 90° apart
- When using three reference points, chose three that are nearly 60° apart
- Avoid choosing features that are closely grouped, or features that are nearly 180° apart

Constant Bearing / Decreasing Range Means Collision Course

If you observe another vessel on a constant bearing with decreasing range, it will surely collide with you unless either you or the other vessel changes course or speed. (This holds true whether you observe it by radar or with the naked eye; in bright daylight or fog; small boat or supertanker.) This maxim is not difficult to remember, but strangely enough, vessels collide on a regular basis. The cause of these collisions is usually a lack of knowledge or a failure to recognize the warning signs.

If you suspect another vessel may be on a collision course, in order to determine whether the bearing of the other vessel is constant, *you must maintain your own heading for the length of time it takes to obtain bearings.*

It takes time to determine whether or not you're on a collision course. You cannot tell with just one glance for the simple reason that the other vessel may *appear* to be headed away from your boat, when it is actually on a collision course. In fact, it is safe to say that as long as your boat is in motion, *you will never collide with a vessel that is headed directly for you unless you are also heading directly for it. By the time it reaches your present position, you will have moved elsewhere.* This is why you must systematically observe the bearings of all other vessels that are in close proximity, or of larger ships that are at a distance.

The *Collision Regulations* require that all vessels act in certain predictable ways when operating near other vessels. This is because both vessels need time to assess the developing situation in order to determine whether there is a risk of collision and, if there is, they need to know what to expect of one another.

A vessel that changes headings frequently, when in proximity to other vessels, will never have the opportunity to systematically observe another vessel's bearings to assess the risk of collision. And, conversely, operators of the vessels around him will not have a clue as to his future movements either. That operator is creating a hazard for all the vessels around him.

Electronic Bearing Line (EBL)

Fortunately radar manufacturers realized very early that mariners would need to take bearings of radar targets. (In **Fig. I-1** the knob on the upper left corner of the radar set is the "Bearing Indicator".) The Electronic Bearing Line is simply a line that originates at the **sweep origin** that can be rotated through 360° by manipulating a knob, trackball or digital control. Elsewhere on the display you will find an EBL symbol, and beside it an indication of the bearing of the EBL. On a Head-up display, the EBL will indicate the relative bearing (the number of degrees from the heading flash to the EBL, measured in a clockwise direction). Relative bearings are indicated in **°R**.

The EBL is graduated in 0.1 degree increments, but since radar bearings often incorporate an error of one degree or more, this precision is not really useful. When you use the EBL for collision avoidance purposes you will not care about the actual readout of the number of degrees in any case; your primary concern will be the consistency of the measurement.

Avoiding Collisions

If you are steering a steady course and you observe another vessel at a constant bearing, it will appear in exactly the same location relative to the structure of your boat.

On the radar display, however, it will appear to move directly toward the center of the screen from the edge.

Extracts from the INTERNATIONAL REGULATIONS FOR PREVENTING COLLISIONS AT SEA, 1972 (*Collision Regulations*)

Rule 7
Risk of Collision

(a) Every vessel shall use all available means appropriate to the prevailing circumstances and conditions to determine if risk of collision exists. If there is any doubt such risk shall be deemed to exist.

(b) Proper use shall be made of radar equipment if fitted and operational, including long-range scanning to obtain early warning of risk of collision and *radar plotting* or *equivalent systematic observation* of detected objects.

(c) *Assumptions shall not be made on the basis of scanty information, especially scanty radar information.*

(d) In determining if risk of collision exists the following considerations shall be among those taken into account:

   (i) *such risk shall be deemed to exist if the compass bearing of an approaching vessel does not appreciably change,*

   (ii) such risk may sometimes exist even when an appreciable bearing change is evident, particularly when approaching a very large vessel or a tow or when approaching a vessel at close range.

[Italics are author's own.]

There are a number of different Collision Regulations (COLREGS).

♦ The International Regulations for Preventing Collisions at Sea apply in international waters, and to seaward of the various COLREGS demarcation lines on US charts.

♦ The US Inland Navigation Rules apply to the inland waters of the United States.

♦ In the United States, landlocked lakes or lakes that cannot be navigated from one State to another do not fall under the US Inland Navigation Rules. Instead, they fall under State or local jurisdiction.

♦ In Canada, the International Rules apply, with some Canadian modifications, especially in the Great Lakes where the rules are fully consistent with the US Inland Navigation Rules.

The basic steering and sailing rules quoted in this book are drawn directly from the International Rules. There is no conflict between the basic steering and sailing rules in these or any other COLREGS.

If you rotate the EBL until it is directly over the target echo on the display, the target echo will follow the EBL toward the center of the display. If it falls away to either side of the EBL, you will know that the other vessel will pass either ahead or behind you and that there is no risk of collision.

But, if the target echo remains on the EBL, you are involved in a potential collision situation. How you resolve the issue depends on whether or not you are in restricted visibility and whether or not you are the stand-on or the give-way vessel. [See **Chapter 9.**]

Successful avoiding action can consist of any of the following:

♦ Alteration of course

♦ Decrease in speed

♦ Increase in speed (there are very rare occasions when this would be appropriate)

♦ A combination of a change in course and speed.

According to Rule 8 of the Collision Regulations, any action you take should be taken early and should be substantial so that observers on the other vessel will be able to see

Proper Lookout

Under Rule 5 of the *Collision Regulations* (COLREGS) all vessels must "maintain a proper look-out by sight and hearing as well as by all available means appropriate in the prevailing circumstances and conditions so as to make a full appraisal of the situation and of the risk of collision". The reference to "all available means" includes radar, if you have it on your boat.

Again, Rule 7 [see above] requires that if your vessel is equipped with radar, you must use it in any condition of visibility or weather. Numerous court decisions have held that the person who has radar on board must use the radar and must be familiar with its characteristics and limitations.

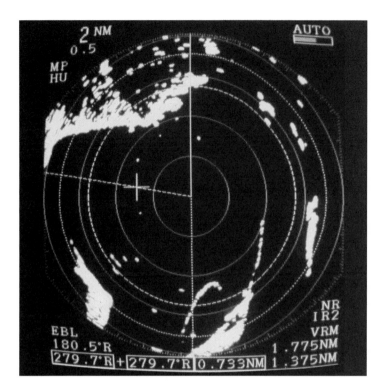

Fig. 2-18 ▶
Electronic Bearing Line (EBL)
On this display, two EBLs are shown at the lower left. One is set at 279.7ºR, and the other at 180.5ºR (almost directly astern).

The EBL is easily controlled by a knob and reads out in tenths of a degree. Some radar sets are equipped with "offset EBLs" which can measure the range and bearing between any two targets on the display.

◀ **Fig. 2-19**
Vessel on a Constant Bearing
Instead of taking compass bearings, you can eyeball another vessel against the structure of your own, to determine if it is on a constant bearing.

You must maintain course and speed or this eyeball method will not work.

Even though the ship does not appear to be heading toward you, since it maintains a constant bearing and a decreasing range, it becomes apparent that it is on a collision course.

that you have taken action. You should monitor the situation until you are finally past and clear of the other vessel.

Once you have made your move, you should be able to see the results of the maneuver on the radar display.

Since a collision course is defined as one on which the other vessel maintains a steady bearing/decreasing range, after successful avoiding action, the target will no longer follow the EBL toward the center of the display.

Instead, the target will follow a new relative course; this will occur even if the target ship did not actually alter course. The target's relative course is the combination of both your own course and speed and the other vessel's course and speed. Alter any one of the four factors that combine to produce the collision course, and the relative track on the display will change.

In crowded waters you may observe many other targets on the display. So far, the examples we have used focus on a single target, but when a number of targets appear, you will have to *allocate top priority to the targets that threaten you the most*. In general, these will be the closest

targets. Some radars are fitted with two EBLs. If yours is one of these, you can plot two targets at the same time. However, there will inevitably be occasions when the number of targets is greater than the number of EBLs.

In good visibility, you will be able to rule out a number of targets, because they will be heading in predictable directions. For instance, in the entrance to a crowded harbour, large ships and tugs will normally follow a traffic lane. If you are familiar with the ferries and other vessels that frequent the area, you may recognize these vessels and be able to predict their movements. *However, when numerous targets surround you, you should always try to identify each one—both on the display and visually.* At night it is especially important to identify the navigation lights of every target you see on the radar. Some of the targets may be buoys or isolated rocks or structures—the rest are vessels and may present risk of collision.

Remember: ***Do not become so fixated on the images on the display that you forget there is a real world outside the wheelhouse windows.*** Always resist the temptation to fixate and con-

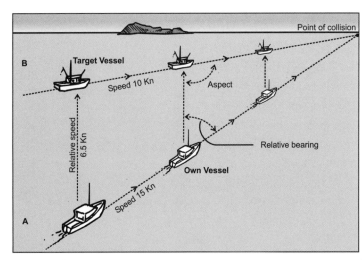

◀ **Fig. 2-20**
A Collision Situation
Rule 7 (d) (i) states that risk of collision exists if the compass bearing of an approaching vessel does not appreciably change.

tinue to maintain a good visual lookout. When the pip on the radar suddenly appears as a real ship looming out of the fog, you will be satisfied you knew exactly when and where to look for it. Never let the radar completely replace your visual awareness of the world around you.

Echo Trails

As soon as the rotating time base "paints" an image on the radar display, the image slowly fades until it is painted again. If the image is not refreshed by the time base, it disappears. Thus the displayed images are said to have a degree of "persistence."

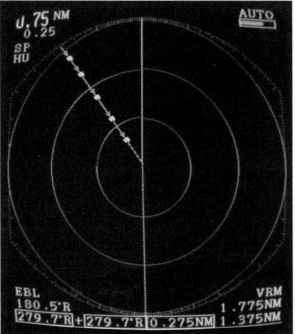 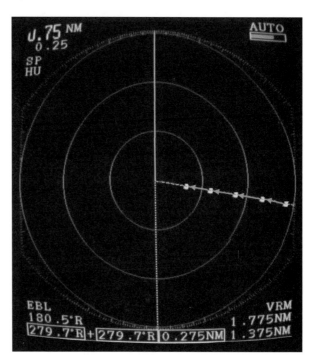

▲ **Fig. 2-21**

A Collision Situation on Radar

Even though the two vessels in **Fig. 2-20** are not heading toward each other, they are both on courses that will ultimately result in a collision. This is revealed by radars on both boats that show the situation developing over time. Each target is shown as a series of "pips" on a steadily decreasing range and bearing.

Left—from point of view of vessel A (your own vessel)

Right—from point of view of vessel B (the target vessel)

The speed with which the range reduces is the "relative speed". The "relative bearing" is the angle between the heading flash and the target on each radar. Thus each vessel sees the other at a different "relative bearing".

Closest Point of Approach (CPA)

As shown in **Fig. 2-22,** the point of minimum distance between the projected relative track of the other vessel and the center of the PPI is known as the Closest Point of Approach (CPA). Here it is possible to estimate the CPA using the fixed range rings. However, you can also obtain a much more accurate estimate of the CPA by plotting the approach of the other vessel as shown in **Appendix A.**

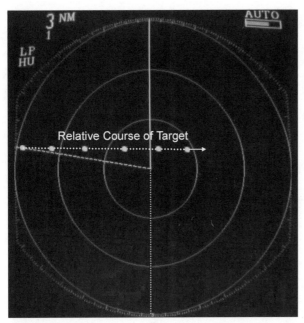 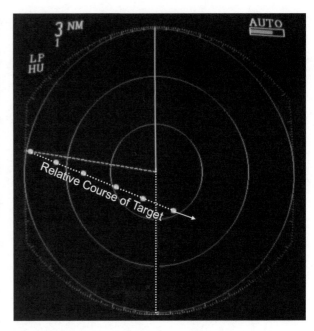

▲ Fig. 2-22
Targets Passing Clear
Left
A series of echoes from a target does not advance down the EBL. Instead it falls off to the forward side of the EBL, indicating it will pass ahead less than .5 mile distant.

Right
A series of echoes from a target does not advance down the EBL. Instead it falls off toward the stern, indicating it will pass astern of you at approximately .5 mile distance.

In any potential collision situation, there are two types of vessel. The **Stand-on Vessel** is required to maintain its course and speed. The **Give-way Vessel** is required to stay out of the way of the other. Though the terms "privileged" or "burdened" are not specifically used in the COLREGS, you may encounter them. A privileged vessel is essentially a stand-on vessel and a burdened vessel is a give-way vessel. There are, however, degrees of privilege. The exact responsibilities between different types of vessel are specified in Rule 18.

Fig. 2-24 ▶
Avoiding Action—By Turning to Starboard
Instead of reducing your own speed, you turn to starboard when you reach position A. Since this is a head-up display, the target rotates to port as your own vessel turns to starboard, until you have steadied up on your new course at position B. The target is now ahead and to port of your heading marker.

Relocate the EBL so it lies over the new target position.

The target now follows a new relative course line which does not follow the EBL toward the center of the display. Instead, it moves off to port, clearly no longer on a collision course.

(The turn to starboard must be significant—30° or more—in order for it to be readily apparent to the other vessel on radar.)

Avoiding Action

Target approaching from forward starboard quadrant. The target is on a collision course, following the EBL toward the center of the display. There are two different ways to deal with this situation. You can instantly see the effects of the maneuver on the display.

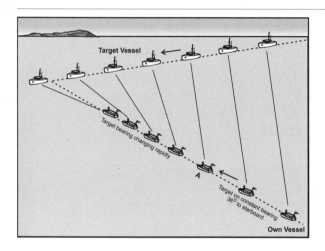

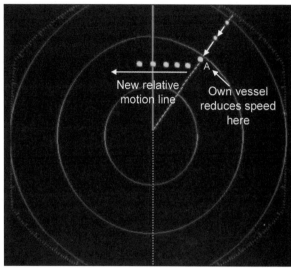

▲ **Fig. 2-23**

Avoiding Action—Reduce Your Own Speed

As the target moves down the EBL directly toward the center of the screen it is clear that it is on a collision course. Once you have tracked it to position A, you reduce your own speed. This reduction of speed results in the target following a new relative course line, and passing to port ahead of you. Note that on the radar display, once you reduce your own speed, the distance between the target "pips" has decreased, because the relative speed of the other vessel is lower.

(An increase in speed would result in the target passing behind you. NOT A GOOD IDEA since it results in your vessel crossing ahead of the other, contrary to Rules 15 and 19.)

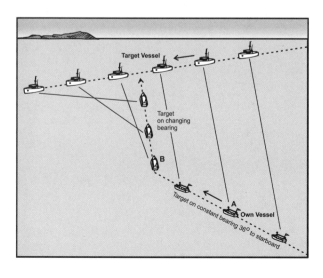

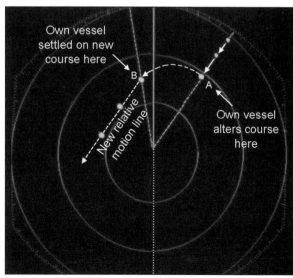

> "Scanning the horizon and instrument panel regularly is a must for safe boating. A short-handed skipper or navigator fascinated by electronic charts, radar, or GPS can easily become fixated and experience a total loss of situational awareness. It's happened to me; it could happen to you."
> —Don Douglass, author of the "Exploring" series of west coast Cruising Guides

The Echo Trail feature on your radar allows you to extend the "persistence" of the images for a number of revolutions of the time base. The result is that targets with a component of relative motion, in moving across the display, will lay down ghostly images behind them. From the direction of these echo trails, you can infer the relative course of any target on your display and determine whether a risk of collision is developing.

Fixed objects move down toward the bottom of the display, 180° opposite to the heading flash. However, objects in real motion move across the display at some other relative course and speed. You can instantly rule out fixed objects and focus on the targets that concern you the most and identify the objects with the greatest relative speed by the length of their echo trails.

Some radar sets permit you to extend the persistence of images to a number of pre-selected times. For instance, you may select echo trails of 15 seconds, 30 seconds, 1 minute or even more.

After an echo trail is older than the selected time, the older portions are deleted. As a result, the trails do not clutter the entire display.

Before making a large alteration of course, turn off the echo trails. After you have completed the turn, you can restart the function.

The echo trail feature will reset itself if you change range scale. (If it did not, the display would become cluttered with information that was no longer valid.) However, you should keep the radar on a consistent range setting while you are assessing targets for risk of collision, otherwise your echo trails will be erased when you change range scales.

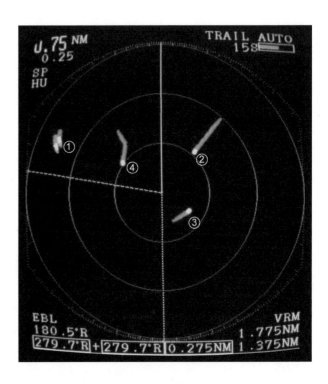

Fig. 2-25 ▶

Echo Trails, Including Fixed Targets

Note that the length of the echo trails is proportional to the relative speed.

1. A fixed target—probably an isolated rock
2. A target on a collision course
3. A target slowly crossing behind
4. A target previously on a collision course, which has altered course and will now pass astern

You will have to take avoiding action for target 2. You may turn to starboard or slow down and let target 2 pass ahead.

Fig. 2-26 ▶

Echo Trails After a Turn

A target on the starboard bow was on a collision course, so you turned to starboard. Once you started the turn, the trail of the target, plus every other target on the display, was smeared counter-clockwise across the display, to the point that it is almost useless. However, since the trail function is set to 15 seconds the radar will soon correct itself.

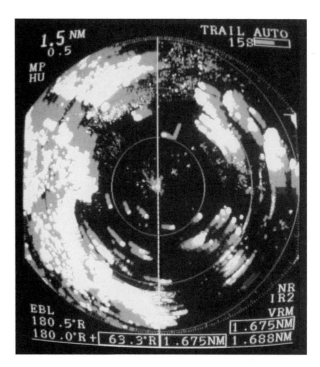

When no longer using the echo trail feature, turn it off!

Caution: *Everything on the display will set down echo trails, even land echoes, so if you make a large alteration of course, all the images will paint a broad swath of ghost trail on the screen, rendering it almost useless. If you ever needed a graphic demonstration of the reasons for maintaining course and speed while assessing risk of collision, this is it.*

Chapter Three

The Equipment

Radar Components

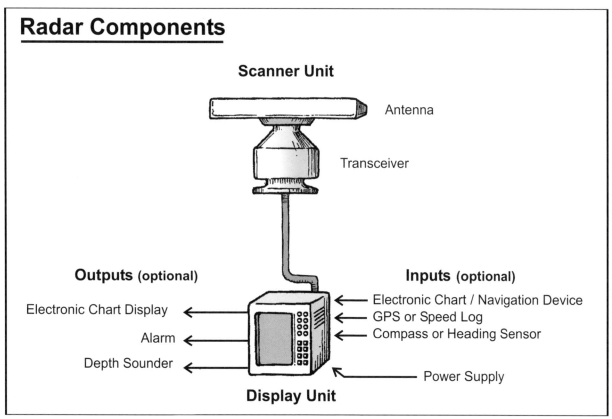

Scanner Unit

Antenna

Transceiver

Outputs (optional)

Electronic Chart Display ←

Alarm ←

Depth Sounder ←

Inputs (optional)

→ Electronic Chart / Navigation Device
→ GPS or Speed Log
→ Compass or Heading Sensor

→ Power Supply

Display Unit

▲ **Fig. 3-1**
Radar Components

RADAR Components

A radar installation consists of two main components, the **scanner unit** and the **display unit**.

Scanner Unit

The Scanner Unit consists of a rotating **antenna** and a **transceiver** (transmitter / receiver)

◆ The **transceiver** generates pulses of microwave energy using a magnetron which is located at the base of the **antenna**. The microwave pulses are then passed to the **antenna** through a **waveguide** where they are broadcast in a discrete beam.

◆ Once the **antenna** has transmitted the microwave pulse, it switches to "receive" mode. In "receive" mode, the **antenna** captures reflections of the same microwave pulse (the echoes) reflected by boats, land, and other objects in the vicinity, then passes these echoes to the **transceiver** where they are processed and routed to the **display** unit.

Two types of scanner units are used in small boat radars; open array antenna and radome.

◆ The essential difference between the two is the "radome" that houses the antenna and the transceiver in a single waterproof enclosure. The rotating antenna inside the radome simply broadcasts the microwave energy through the plastic housing.

◆ An "open array antenna" is housed in a separate waterproof housing from the transceiver and can be seen rotating.

▲ Fig. 3-2
An Open Array Antenna
The open array uses a slotted-waveguide antenna. The magnetron and transceiver are located in the housing at the base of the antenna.

▲ Fig. 3-3
A Radome Antenna

Fig. 3-4 ▶
Internal Components of a Radome Antenna
A radome contains the same type of slotted-waveguide as an open array antenna. The only difference is that the magnetron and antenna are housed in a single water-proof enclosure.

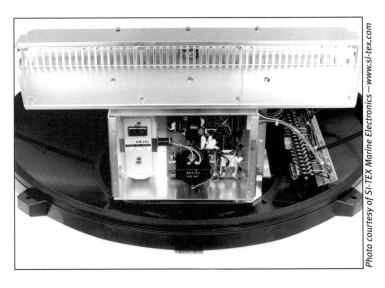

▲ Fig. 3-5
A Radome Mounted High on the Mast of a Sailboat
With its radome mounted at this height, the radar
can "see farther over the horizon." At approximately
22 feet off the water, the horizon for this scanner is
about 6 nautical miles away.

♦ *The wider the antenna unit, the narrower the horizontal beam-width.* (This is important.)

Generally the use of **radomes** is limited to smaller, short-range radars. It is simply not practical to enclose a 48- or 60-inch rotating antenna inside a single housing. Most sailors prefer radomes over open-array scanners, because a rotating open-array can foul sails and lines, leading to needless risk and damage. Radomes are also significantly cheaper than open array antennas; but because they come in smaller sizes only, sailors cannot take advantage of the narrow beam-widths of larger open array antennas.

> *Never paint the sides of a radome or the radiating surface of an open array antenna. The paint blocks transmission and reception of microwave signals.*

Replacing the Magnetron

Radar magnetrons have been with us for almost 60 years now, but their time has come to an end. The problem is that magnetrons are unable to confine their emissions to a specific frequency. Instead they produce a large amount of "spurious" or "out of band" emissions which interfere with users of other radio frequencies adjacent to the microwave radar band (such as cellular telephones).

In the increasingly crowded radio spectrum, marine radars have become a problem, and so the International Telecommunications Union has mandated that marine radars must confine their emissions to a tightly controlled band. This means the end of the magnetron as we know it.

As of January 1, 2003, all newly installed radars on large commercial vessels must comply with the new standard. Existing ships will not have to replace their old magnetron-driven sets until 2012.

At this time it is unclear if, or when, small vessel radars will be required to incorporate the new technology. However, it is likely that the new technology will become available in the near future and eventually it will become the standard.

Scanner Installation

The scanner should be mounted as high as practical, with an all-round view of the horizon, and level to the operating waterline of the vessel. Keep obstructions to a minimum; obstructions that are unavoidable should be kept as small as possible.

The open construction of a lattice mast allows the radar beam to pass through [see **Fig. 5-23**, **Chapter 5**] and return to the scanner. However, it may interfere with the radar beam and cause "ghosting effects". [See **Chapter 5**]

Fig. 3-6 ▶

A Poor Installation

By mounting this radome on the forward side of the flying bridge, the owner has ensured that it is effectively blind to any targets astern. The operator will not be able to detect high-speed vessels overtaking and will loose track of any overtaken vessels. Also, the operator will be able to see only half the picture when navigating.

As if this isn't enough, if the radar is accidentally left on while the operator is on the flying bridge, he or she will be irradiated by microwaves.

Fig. 3-7 ▶

An Effective Installation

Mounted high above all other obstructions, this scanner will have an almost totally unobstructed view of its surroundings. The small antenna and light-pipe astern of the scanner have no appreciable effect on its performance.

At 16 feet off the water, the horizon for this antenna is approximately 5 nautical miles away.

Fig. 3-8 ▶

A Canadian Coast Guard Auxiliary Rescue Vessel

The radome has been mounted as high as possible in order to detect targets at the greatest possible distance. For a scanner mounted 8 feet off the water, the horizon is only 3.5 nautical miles away.

Frequencies

There are two types of radar in common use, X Band, and S Band. The difference is in the particular microwave frequencies used.

X Band

- ◆ Wavelength = 3 cm
- ◆ Commonly used in recreational and small commercial applications
- ◆ Greater ability to resolve objects close together at short and medium ranges
- ◆ More sensitive to interference from rain and snow

S Band

- ◆ Wavelength =10 cm
- ◆ Used in large commercial applications
- ◆ Greater ability to detect small objects at long ranges

The nature of the microwave frequency and the pulse length imposes some fundamental limits and constraints on your radar's performance.

For instance:

- ◆ An S Band radar is able to detect targets at longer ranges than an X Band radar, but most small boats are unable to mount their radar scanners high enough to take advantage of the superior long range detection capabilities of the S Band sets.
- ◆ A radar with a wide beam is unable to resolve separate images from objects that are close together. In that case there will be no point in fitting a wide beam antenna with a fine resolution display unit.

Thus large commercial ships generally use both X Band and S Band radars, whereas small vessels almost never use S Band radars.

Display Unit

The display unit further processes the incoming echoes and plots them on a Plan Position Indicator (PPI) display [see **Chapter 1**]. Display units may use the familiar CRT (cathode ray tube) common to computer monitors, or an LCD (Liquid Crystal Display) common to flat-screen computer monitors and laptop computers.

CRT Displays

- CRT displays offer substantially clearer images and a degree of resolution that, until recently, was unmatched by LCD counterparts. CRT displays also offer a variety of image-brightness levels that can help you differentiate strong echoes from weak ones.

- Modern TFT displays have higher resolution and can be viewed in almost any lighting conditions. However, when direct sunlight falls on the screen, you may have difficulty with reflected glare (as you would watching a TV in direct sunlight), but most display units come with a viewing shade that surrounds the screen on three sides, reducing glare problems.

- Viewing an older analog set requires using a viewing hood that excludes almost all light.

- CRT radar displays are bulky, so you may have difficulty finding an appropriate location to mount your CRT radar display unit.

- CRT displays are more expensive and consume more power than LCD displays.

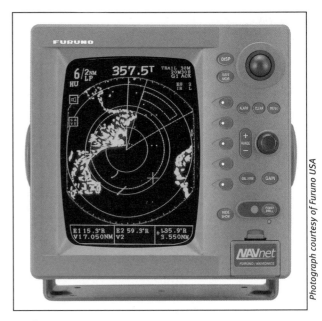

▲ Fig. 3-9
A Furuno Cathode Ray Tube (CRT) Radar

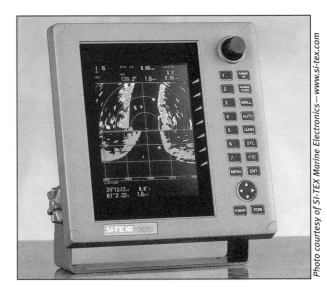

▲ Fig. 3-10
A Liquid Crystal Display (LCD)

The most recent advance in liquid crystal display technology—thin film transistor (TFT)—closes the gap between LCD and CRT displays. Modern TFT displays have higher resolution and can be viewed from a much wider angle than previous liquid crystal displays.

LCD Displays

- Most inexpensive radars are equipped with LCD display units.

- The primary advantages are the physical depth of the unit, water-resistance, and price.

- Because of the minimum depth, LCD display units offer an ease of mounting that may, alone, make the choice worthwhile.

- Water resistant LCD display units are the only appropriate type for installation on open boats.

- LCD displays can be viewed in direct sunlight and they consume less power.

- Until recently, LCD displays offered lower resolution than CRT displays, but the new thin film transistor (TFT) displays are giving the Cathode Ray Tube serious competition.

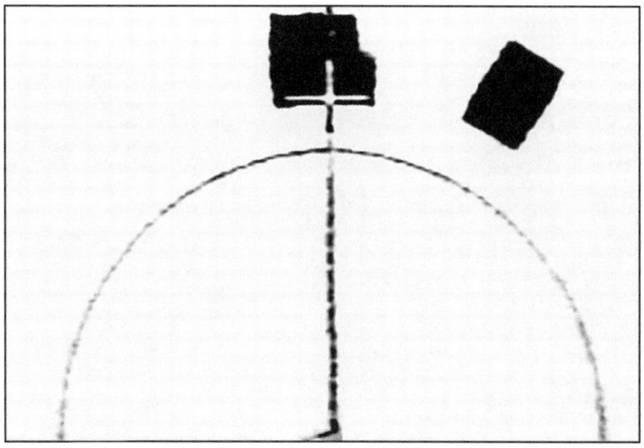

▲ **Fig. 3-11**

Detail of a Highly Pixelated LCD Display

Two groups of targets are visible, but the display is not capable of fine enough resolution to determine whether the right-hand target is composed of one or two smaller targets.

Pixels and Image Resolution

The image on your radar display is assembled from thousands of small squares called pixels. In any individual image a pixel may be light or dark or a shade of colour in between to represent different echo strengths. Brighter pixels represent stronger echoes; dimmer pixels represent weaker echoes.

In order to display a high-resolution image, the display must utilize more pixels in a given space—in other words, the pixels must be smaller. An inexpensive radar may show relatively few pixels, and consequently the resulting image will be very coarse. Large features will appear to have "blocky" edges. Small echoes will be composed of, at most, one or two pixels and will give no indication of the echo shape. In addition, there may only be one colour of echo strength available to the display.

High-end radar displays are capable of a high degree of resolution. The pixels on such sets are tiny, resulting in detailed images; even small targets are composed of many pixels and thus give an indication of echo shape. Finally, the display is able to discriminate between targets that are closely grouped, showing each as a separate echo. In general, CRT radars offer the highest image resolution.

In early analog radar sets, magnetrons were installed below deck in order to protect them from the elements. As a result, the microwave pulses were ducted through a **waveguide**—a hollow tube of specific dimensions that channelled the microwave energy to the antenna. This was not a flexible arrangement. Most small boat radars now fit the magnetron at the base of the antenna unit, thus making a composite "scanner" unit. The result is that installers can use multi-wire cables instead of rigid tubing—a very flexible arrangement that allows numerous installation options.

Controls

- The display unit is also fitted with numerous controls, which are used to regulate the transmitted pulses, manipulate the received echoes and assist in interpretation of the display.

- Controls may be individual control buttons and/or rotary knobs, or they may be menu-driven through software, or a combination of the two.

- In many radars, you may be able to directly control the most common features using rotary

Radar Safety

Radar uses microwave frequencies similar to those used in your microwave oven. In the early days of radar, apocryphal stories were circulated about the steward who cooked a chicken by suspending it from a scanner in such a way that it rotated with the antenna and was continuously immersed in the microwave radiation. Conventional wisdom holds that the low-power units on small vessels are incapable of burning skin even at close range. But the same conventional wisdom recommends that you keep your distance, and especially do not expose your eyes to the radar beam. Without doubt, other people would resent it if you exposed them to your radar beam.

▲ **Fig. 3-12**
Radar Etiquette
Part safety, part etiquette—never leave your radar transmitting when close alongside a wharf or another boat. *Remember:* Radar uses microwave frequencies very similar to those used by your microwave oven. You should never stand close to an operating scanner.

- In "Standby" mode, the antenna may or may not be rotating, but it is *not* transmitting.
- Only when you switch your radar to "Transmit" mode does it begin emitting microwave radiation.
- All radar manufacturers equip their sets with a "Standby" function. In "Standby" mode the radar is warmed up and is ready to transmit at the flip of a switch without having to be warmed up again.
- Because it is enclosed, you cannot tell if a radome scanner is in standby mode or transmitting just by looking at it.

Consequently you must follow a few simple safety procedures:

- Whenever you go alongside another boat or a dock, place your radar in "Standby" mode to avoid exposing yourself and other people to the microwave radiation.
- Never work around the scanner when it is operational. To be safe, make sure the radar is "off," and place a sticky note on it indicating you are working near the scanner. If you leave the radar in "Standby," someone may switch it to "Transmit" mode without realizing you are near the scanner.
- Mount the radar scanner high enough that the beam is well clear of your head when you operate the boat from the flying bridge.

knobs and buttons, but for less-frequently-used features and set-up functions, you will have to resort to menu trees.

♦ In general it is safe to state that ***the more functions you can directly control, the more user-friendly the radar set.***

Knobs and Switches vs Menus and Soft-Keys

As the capabilities and functions of radar equipment become more complex, and more choices are offered to the operator, the problem of how

commands should be entered arises—by menus or by special-function controls, or by both?

Knobs, keys and switches are bulky; they take up significant amounts of space on the face of any electronic equipment and, when installed in weather-resistant units, they must be individually sealed. Consequently manufacturers prefer to use menus and sub-menus instead. This allows them to produce smaller and less expensive display units. Users navigate the menus using a trackball or a multi-arrow key, to control the various functions of the radar set. Although the reduced size (and price) is an advantage, it can be

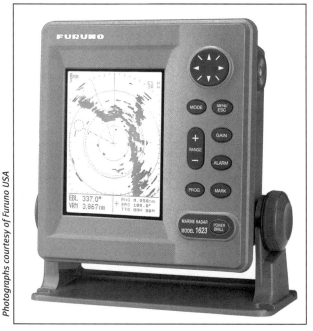

Photographs courtesy of Furuno USA

▲ **Fig. 3-13**
Radar Control Panels
Left
This display unit is equipped with only nine keys, one of which is a "menu" key. All functions except for range scale must be controlled through the manipulation of a menu tree using the multi-arrow key at the top of the panel.
Right
The control panel on this radar is very similar to the panel on the left. However, this radar is also equipped with five soft-keys directly to the right of the display. These soft-keys take on different functions depending on the software "page" that is open. In addition the unit has a menu function that permits the operator to access the lesser-used functions of the radar.

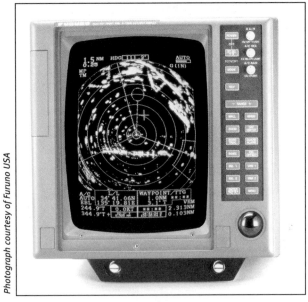

▲ **Fig. 3-14**

A Furuno Control Panel with Dedicated Controls

In this control panel, virtually every common function (and some uncommon functions) have their own dedicated controls. However, there is also a menu button at the lower right to provide access to the least frequently-used functions and set-up options.

a frustrating experience to change a frequently-used function, such as range scale or gain.

Thus the menus in the software structure work well for set-up processes and for less-commonly-used functions.

The ideal system uses a combination of the above in a manner that is easily understandable and that allows the user to operate the unit with little reference to a manual. Commonly-used functions such as range scale and gain are controlled directly through dedicated knobs and buttons and, where necessary, menus are accessed using soft-keys.

When negotiating the menu tree, **soft-keys** make the selection and control of menu items more intuitive. When using soft-keys, the display itself prompts the operator to press the correct button. By an intelligent mix of soft-keys, menus, and special function controls, some manufacturers have been able to create radars that are easy to use and require very little reference to the owner's manual—a notable feat!

Tip—Reducing Glare

If you cannot dim your display adequately to reduce glare in the wheelhouse at night (either because you do not have a tinted screen or because the night is so dark), you can use a dark green plastic garbage bag. Simply tape a piece of the garbage bag over the display and stretch it tight. If the plastic is thin enough, you'll be able to see the display through the plastic, without losing much resolution. Keep one edge of the plastic loose, so you can easily flip it out of the way to inspect your radar display more closely.

Day and Night Displays

As daylight wanes, your eyes adjust by becoming more sensitive to light and your radar appears brighter. As a result you must reduce the brilliance of your radar display, or it will act like a light bulb in the wheelhouse, seriously compromising your ability to maintain a lookout. Radar sets are equipped with controls to reduce the brilliance of the display and the illumination behind the keys and knobs on the control panel. LCD radars are also equipped with controls to reduce back-lighting of the display.

You may find that no matter how much you reduce the brilliance of your display you are unable to reduce it enough to stop light contamination of the wheelhouse. Most radars are equipped with a removable viewing shade, which is designed for use in daylight, but which can also be fitted with a tinted plexiglas cover for night use. With the addition of this tinted cover, the display should be dim enough.

Modern colour radars permit you to select different colours for night viewing. This too, can greatly reduce light pollution.

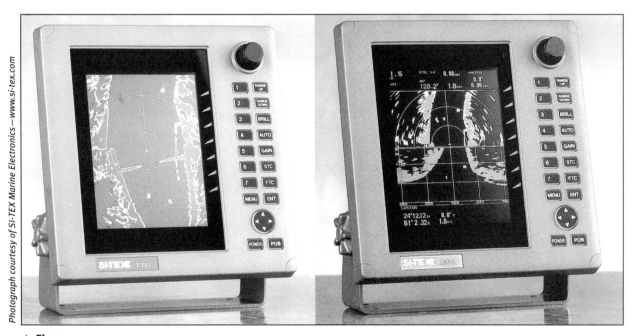

Photograph courtesy of Si-TEX Marine Electronics—www.si-tex.com

▲ **Fig. 3-15**
Day and Night Colours
A Si-Tex T 721 Colour LCD radar in day (left) and night (right) colour modes.

Reverse Colours

An LCD display may be capable of showing reverse colour—light echoes on a dark background for night operations, and dark on light for daytime. (Most CRT displays do not provide this option.) My preference is for light echoes on a dark background—even during the daytime. I believe that this intuitively reinforces the mental image of a searchlight illuminating targets. Thus the light on dark display shows the areas illuminated as lighted targets against a dark background.

Chapter Four

Why Radar Works

In this chapter we will introduce you to some of the basic concepts necessary to understand why your radar works in the way that it does. It is not necessary to have a complete understanding of "HOW" radar works. The whole point of owning a radar set is to simplify your life when operating your boat in challenging conditions. You do not need to be overburdened with technical detail—so this chapter provides the minimum technical detail you will need. If you are interested in understanding more about "HOW" your radar works, please refer to the appendices.

BASIC PRINCIPLES OF RADAR

Principles of Reflectivity

Any object that is struck by a microwave radar pulse may:

1. reflect the pulse

2. absorb the pulse

3. or be transparent to microwave energy, in which case the pulse will pass through the object.

There is no such thing as a perfect reflector. Even the most highly polished mirrors absorb some light—and as it is with light, so it is also true with microwave radiation. Some materials are highly reflective and some (such as the skin of a stealth bomber) reflect very little energy at all. It is the amount of reflected energy that concerns us, because only the reflected energy will return to the antenna and produce an image on the display.

The amount of microwave energy that an object will reflect back in the direction of the scanner is determined by:

- Materials—Whereas wood and fiberglass are poor reflectors, most metals reflect microwaves very well.

- Shape—Round objects tend to scatter radar energy, so even a highly reflective round object will reflect just a small amount of the incoming radiation back in its direction of origin.

- Surface texture—A smooth surface reflects microwaves very well, but if it is oriented at an angle to the incoming energy, much of the energy will be deflected away from its direction of origin. Rough surfaces scatter the reflected energy in all directions, so at least some of the reflected energy returns to its origin. However, no surface is perfectly smooth, so scattering almost always occurs and sends some of the energy in the right direction.

◆ Orientation—Even a highly reflective flat surface will reflect the energy in its direction of origin, only when it is oriented perpendicularly to the incoming energy.

◆ Size—Obviously a large target will reflect more energy back than a small one. At long range, some small, poorly reflective targets are not visible on radar at all.

From the principles above, you can make the following assumptions:

1. Landforms that present a flat face toward the radar antenna reflect radar energy very efficiently.

2. Sloping foreshore, especially mud or hard sand with no boulders, is very difficult to observe on radar because it deflects the radar energy away from its source. The shoreline of a mudflat usually reflects at least a little energy, but it may be so weak as to be masked by clutter.

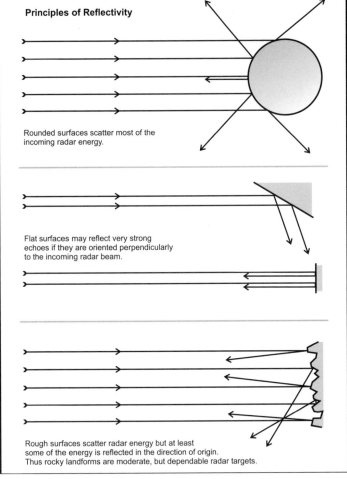

Principles of Reflectivity

Rounded surfaces scatter most of the incoming radar energy.

Flat surfaces may reflect very strong echoes if they are oriented perpendicularly to the incoming radar beam.

Rough surfaces scatter radar energy but at least some of the energy is reflected in the direction of origin. Thus rocky landforms are moderate, but dependable radar targets.

▲ **Fig. 4-1**
Principles of Reflectivity
Rounded surfaces scatter most incoming radar energy.

Smooth surfaces may reflect very strongly if they are oriented perpendicularly to the incoming radar beam.

Rough surfaces scatter radar energy, but at least some of the energy is reflected in the direction of origin. Thus rocky landforms are moderate, but dependable, radar reflectors.

◀ **Fig. 4-2**
Rip-Rap Breakwater at Port Sidney
Because of the multiple surfaces of the rocks that form numerous interior corners, this breakwater returns a very strong radar echo.

Fig. 4-3 ▶
Pebble Beach at Sidney, British Columbia
This beach will return a strong echo because it is composed of pebbles, each of which presents a tiny vertical reflecting surface. Also, the isolated boulders should return strong individual echoes. However, if this beach were composed of mud, the only efficient reflectors would be the boulders.

3. Buildings, and bridges, especially those of metal, reflect radar energy very efficiently—partly because they have so many square corners.

4. A small fiberglass or wooden boat reflects poorly—unless it has a large flat superstructure and is viewed from directly abeam—which is why such boats are advised to carry radar reflectors.

5. Trees and bushes reflect radar less efficiently than rock; however, because they are composed of many different surfaces, they reflect better than very smooth rock that is angled away from the antenna.

6. The strongest echoes are received from highly reflective materials or surfaces such as large slab-sided ships that are oriented perpendicular to the radar beam at short range.

Fig. 4-4 ▶
A Large Slab-Sided Ship Viewed at Close Range
The ship creates such a strong return that it overwhelms the display. The ship has been detected 90° to starboard but, with the exception of the landmass at approximately 225°R, all the echoes on the display are caused by the ship.

Imagine that your radar beam is a very powerful searchlight illuminating a white stucco house on the shore. As you travel along the shore, the rough stucco surfaces of the building will be clear in the beam, but the windows will appear dark. This condition continues until you are perpendicular to the windows, when the windows suddenly and momentarily return a brilliant reflection of the

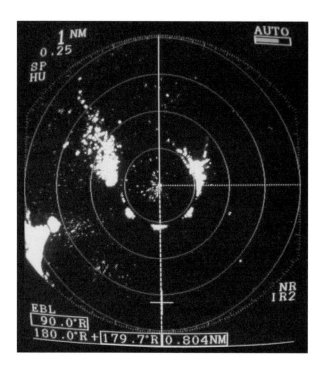

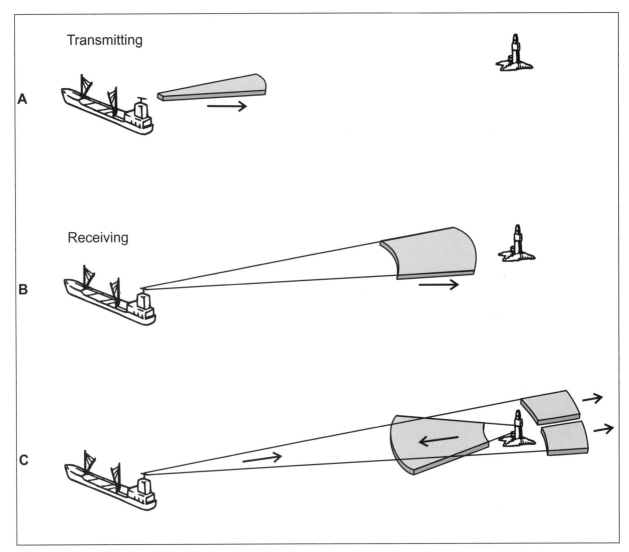

▲ **Fig. 4-5**
Radar Pulses
A—The ship-borne radar emits a directional pulse.
B—The radar immediately switches to "receive" mode and begins to "listen." The microwave pulse spreads out, covering a larger area the farther it travels from the antenna (attenuation).
C—A very small part of the pulse strikes a lighthouse and is reflected. The rest of the pulse continues to travel away from the ship. Due to the cylindrical shape of the lighthouse, only a small portion of the reflected pulse returns toward the ship. The returning pulse is highly attenuated; *the strongest echo is probably less than one hundred thousandth of the strength of the broadcast energy.*

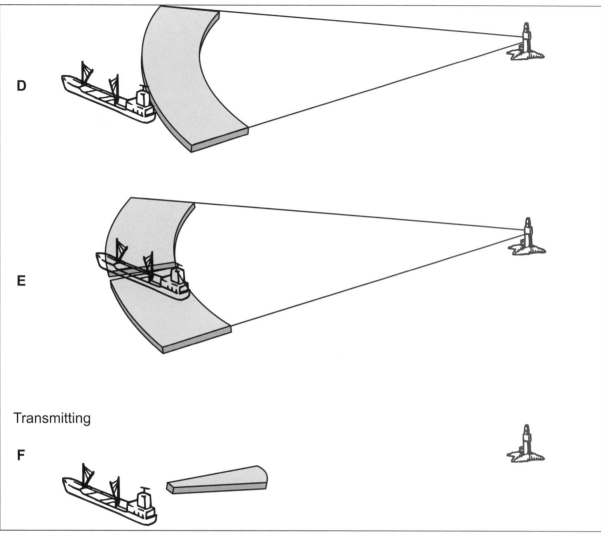

▲ **Fig. 4-6**
Radar Pulses (continued)

D—The radar antenna starts to detect the returning pulse. Since the returning pulse is so attenuated, the radar must amplify the returning signal. By calculating the time it took for the signal to travel to the target and back, it now knows the distance to the closest part of the target.

E—After a time, the transceiver can no longer detect the returning pulse.

F—After a period of time (proportional to the range scale used), the radar stops "listening" and broadcasts another pulse of microwave energy. During this time, the antenna has turned an exceedingly small amount. The total time elapsed—called the Pulse Repetition Interval—is generally less than 1 millisecond. From this single cycle, the radar obtains a picture of a tiny "pie-slice", including the range and bearing to every target in that slice, and the radial thickness of each target. The radial thickness is based on the length of the echo. The bearing is determined by the direction of the antenna. With this data, the radar builds an image of a single "pie-slice", and then proceeds to build an image of the next.

When the radar is set to long-range, the listening phase is much longer, because it takes much longer for the echoes to return from extreme distances.

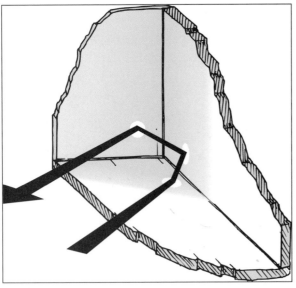

◄ **Fig. 4-7**
Radar Reflectors [See Chapter 11]
If you orient three surfaces at exactly 90° to each other to form an inside corner, any beam that enters the corner will be reflected in its direction of origin. The "inside corner" is the principle used in most radar reflectors; highly reflective, smooth materials are oriented in such a way as to reflect the maximum amount of energy in the direction of your scanner.

◄ **Fig. 4-8**
Killer Whale Dorsal Fin
Because of its large flat surface, the dorsal fin of a bull killer whale should be visible to even a small radar at 2 Nm range or greater.

◄ **Fig. 4-9**
Radar Reflector on a Navigation Buoy
The light and tower from a navigation buoy at the Canadian Coast Guard Base in Victoria, BC. Note the "inside corner" radar reflector mounted just above the solar panel.

searchlight beam. Then the windows become dark again as soon as the searchlight beam is no longer perpendicular to the windows. In the same way, a very smooth surface is less "visible" to radar than a rough surface, except when viewed perpendicularly.

Microwave Pulses

Radar is an acronym for **RA**dio **D**etection **A**nd **R**anging. In other words, radar works by detecting objects at a distance and finding the "range" or distance to the object. To do this, radar simply sends out microwave (radio) energy packets along a tight beam and then listens for the echo. By calculating the amount of time it takes for a particular pulse to be reflected as an echo from an object, the radar can determine the distance to the object. And since it already knows the direction in which it broadcast the energy beam, it can display the direction of the object.

This is the same principle used in sonar, except that sonar uses sound to detect objects underwater. But sound travels significantly slower than radar energy which travels at the speed of light. So rapid is the speed of light, that a radar can send out a pulse and detect the echo of an object ten miles away, within 0.062 millisecond. (A millisecond is one thousandth of a second.)

Every pulse has a specific length, normally expressed in units of time. The Furuno FR-70 series radar uses pulse lengths of 0.08 microsecond (0.08 millionths of a second) at short range scales to 0.8 microsecond (0.8 millionths of a second) at long range scales.

At this point, you may ask, "Why should I be concerned with all the technical detail?"

The answer is simple. If you can understand how the microwave pulse travels out from the antenna, reflects off an object and returns, you will have no trouble interpreting and controlling your radar.

Since the length of the pulse is directly related to the *thickness* of the smallest **echo, or "pip,"** clearly there is a minimum "pip" thickness, and that minimum thickness will represent a specific distance in the real world. If the pulse length is 0.8 microsecond, the minimum thickness of the "pip" represents a distance of 120 meters.

Analog Radars

Older analog sets actually paint the returning pulse directly on the display using a spot of light that moves along the time base. When the pulse is transmitted, the spot begins moving away from the time base origin; and when the radar receives an echo, as long as it continues to receive it, the moving spot "paints" the image directly on the display. Each time the radar transmits a pulse, the time base moves a fraction of a degree in a slightly different direction, synchronized with the direction the antenna is facing at the time. In this way, an image is built up on the display. Persistence of the painted spots allows the image to remain on the screen, dimming slightly, until it is repainted by the moving time base.

Modern raster-scan displays however, actually process the received signals and show a new image on the display several times per second—similar to the operation of a television or computer monitor.

It is doubtful that you'll ever see an analog radar on a small pleasure craft, but you may see one on larger commercial vessels or fishing vessels. These sets were just as sensitive as the newer raster-scan units. Though they do not have all the same features as a modern software-driven raster-scan set, they possess the same basic features as any radar, and they are amazingly sophisticated.

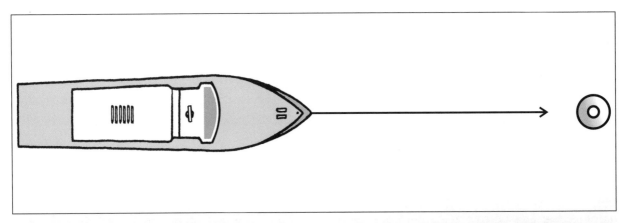

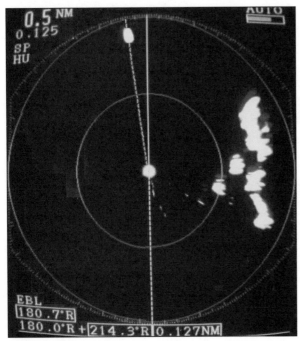 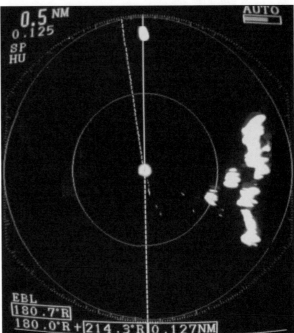

▲ **Fig. 4-10**

Heading Flash Error

When a buoy is sighted directly ahead, its echo appears on the display 9° to port. You must adjust the synchronization between the heading flash and the scanner to bring the image of the buoy directly under the heading flash.

Each radar is different, but in most cases, you will have to access the set-up software menus to make the adjustment; but for some radars you will need the help of a technician.

First, make sure that you have a target dead ahead and that you select a range scale that places the echo of the buoy at the outer edge of the display.

When you adjust the synchronization, make sure the entire image rotates to starboard, bringing the echo of the buoy under the heading flash.

Right: Notice that the entire image has rotated 9° to starboard.

Synchronization of the Heading Flash

As a scanner rotates, so does the time base. In fact, synchronization of time base and scanner direction is essential to generating a PPI. When the time base points directly ahead, it generates the heading flash. But if the time base and the scanner are not synchronized, the heading will not line up with the echoes of objects that are dead ahead.

If the display shows something to port or starboard that is actually dead ahead, it will also show objects dead ahead that are actually a few degrees to port or starboard. This condition greatly increases the risk of collision with the object, especially if it is a buoy that you intend to pass close to starboard. If you know the error exists, you may be able to do something about it, but if you're unaware, you might make bad decisions based on the radar information.

When you notice this type of error, correct it as soon as possible. If you are unable to correct it immediately, set your Electronic Bearing Line to indicate the direction that is actually dead ahead and try to ignore the heading flash until you have your set adjusted. [See **Chapter 11**.]

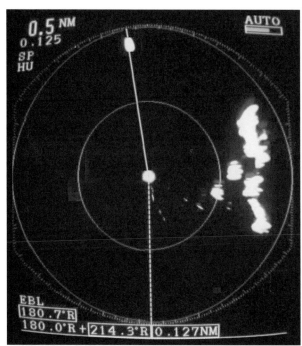

▲ Fig. 4-11
Incorrect Heading Flash Correction
If, instead, you rotate the position of the heading flash 9° to port, the display will not be truly head-up.

Radar Horizon

The radar horizon is a little farther away than the visible horizon—about 15% farther—because microwaves are subject to less atmospheric bending than light. However, the same principles apply to the radar horizon as to the visible horizon.

♦ The higher you locate your radar scanner, the farther the radar will be able to see objects at sea level.

Echo Strength

Most radars show echoes in different shades of the same colour, depending on the strength of the received echo. For instance, the echo from a small boat will be relatively weak unless the boat is fitted with a good radar reflector. As a result the radar will paint it in a shade indicating its weakness. Once a target has been painted, its image will begin to fade; if the same target isn't repainted it will disappear after a single revolution of the time base. But if you have echo trails active, the weaker images will persist for a number of minutes.

New colour-radars display echo strength according to a scale of specific colours. In these sets, red usually represents the strongest echoes, and blue the weakest. Some models permit you to choose the colours to represent different echo strengths.

◆ Your radar may be able to detect objects that are beyond the horizon because some portion may project above the horizon. Sailboats with radar reflectors in their rigging may be visible to your radar even when the hull is not. Also, your radar will be able to see the tops of mountains at considerable distances, even though the shoreline is over the horizon.

When choosing a radar, it does not make sense to purchase a high power radar with a long-range antenna if you mount the radar so low it cannot detect vessels more than a few miles away.

Transponders

So far, we have discussed a transceiver, which is a combined transmitter / receiver. A radar transponder, though, is equipment which, on being stimulated by the beam of an operating radar, **trans**mits in res**pon**se (transponds) with a non-directional series of microwave pulses at the same frequency. When your scanner intercepts this pulse of microwave energy it plots it on the display.

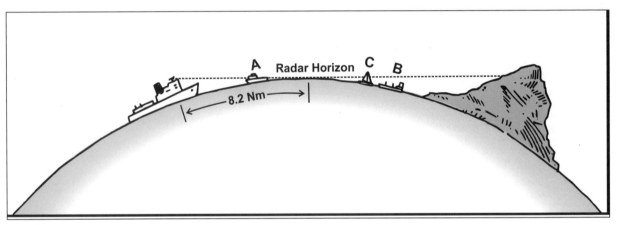

▲ **Fig. 4-12**
Radar Horizon
From the height of the scanner on our vessel, we know that the radar horizon is 8.2 Nm away.
Vessel A is above the radar horizon.
Vessel B is below the radar horizon.
Vessel C is below the radar horizon, but it is equipped with a radar reflector in the rigging that allows it to be detected by our radar.
The tops of the mountains in the distance show up on our radar, but the shoreline is invisible.
Small boats and low-lying land may not be visible until within a few miles.

RACON

A RACON is a specific type of transponder, designed to assist mariners in identifying certain buoys or fixed structures.

When a buoy-mounted RACON is triggered by a radar pulse, it transmits a series of coded pulses which, when received by your radar, appear as a thick dotted or dashed streak, extending outwards from the echo of the buoy. By emitting combinations of short and long pulses, any RACON-equipped buoy is identifiable by its unique Morse-code signature on your display.

A RACON does not respond to every pulse of your radar. Instead it responds once in a given period of time, so your antenna (and time base) may go through several revolutions before you see the Morse code signature again. However, once you have seen one RACON, you cannot possibly mistake it for any other type of target; it will provide you with instant identification of the buoy or structure on which it is located.

Unlike radar reflectors, a RACON is not just a passive radar reflector. A RACON actively responds to any received radar pulses; but since it is an active radar transmitter, it **can** fail to operate. RACON-equipped buoys and structures are identified on charts. So if you observe a buoy or fixed structure that is RACON-equipped, but which fails to appear on your radar, you should report the malfunction to the local Coast Guard.

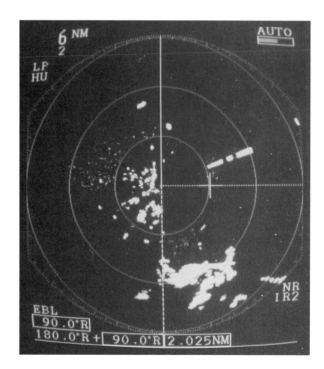

Fig. 4-13 ▶
RACON (RAdar Transponder BeaCON)
The position of the RACON buoy is at the innermost end of the long dash—approximately 2 Nm distant at 070°R.

Chapter Five

Controlling and Interpreting the Display

To obtain the best information from your radar, you will need to understand how to control and interpret the image.

Radar detects the reflections of its own microwave beam from distant objects so the images you view on your radar display are actually visual representations of microwave echoes reflected by *real objects* in the *real world*. Any force or factor that interferes with the simple reflection or refraction of the beam will affect the radar's performance.

In many cases you can infer the characteristics of an object by manipulating and interpreting the image of its echo. But in order to do so, you must have a basic understanding of how the different controls work; whether they affect the outgoing pulse or the incoming echoes, or whether they simply alter some feature of the display.

Gain

Simply put, "Gain" is the radar's sensitivity control. By increasing the gain, you increase the radar's ability to detect and display weak echoes. At high levels of gain, the radar will begin to display "noise" or "speckling." This noise is caused by internal interference from other electrical circuits on board, by transient reflectors such as raindrops, birds and spray, and by interference from outside sources. If the gain is turned too high, this noise will clutter the entire display and may make it impossible to view real targets. [See **Fig. 2-3.**]

Standard Control Icons

After the Second World War, when radar made its appearance in civilian shipping, the International Maritime Organization wasted no time setting standards for radar equipment used in international shipping. One of the standards was for common icons to represent specific control functions. Over time these icons began to appear in small boat radars as well.

Since that time, many radar control functions have moved from the front panel of the display box to an entry in a software menu and, as a result, these universally understood icons have started to disappear again. At this time, few small radars use the international icons which is unfortunate, because the standard icons made it possible for operators to use the radar without understanding a single word of the instruction manual.

On the other hand, there are dangers in reducing the gain too much. If the gain is set too low, only the strongest echoes will be visible on the display. Weak targets may not be visible at all. It is very important to set the gain to the right level [See **Fig. 2-3.**], when you consider that those weak targets may include:

- rocks that are barely awash
- small wooden or fiberglass boats
- sandbars and mud banks.

To set the gain properly for the range scale you are using, turn it up slowly until you can detect speckling (some people call it **grass**) on the display. If you turn the control higher, this speckling (grass) will begin to cover the entire display. Reduce the gain until there is just a little speckling showing; this will be the most appropriate gain setting for the range scale.

When adjusting the gain, you should ensure that the "anti-Sea Clutter" and "anti-Rain Clutter" controls are turned off. *These controls affect the gain and must be adjusted to their correct levels only after you have set the gain.* (See the setting up procedure in **Chapter 2**.)

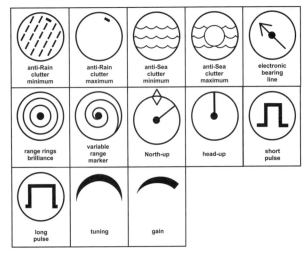

▲ **Fig. 5-1**
International Standard Control Icons

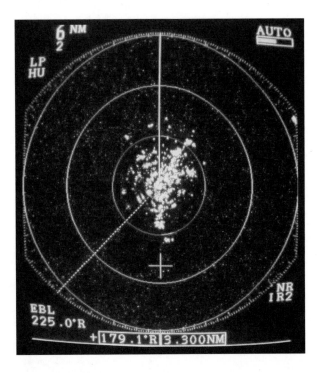

◄ **Fig. 5-2**
A Properly Tuned Radar
A properly tuned radar showing light speckling across the entire display. This radar is set to the maximum sensitivity levels at which it will display a useful picture. Any higher gain setting will produce so much speckling that it will overwhelm the display and drown out the echoes of small targets. Using the "anti-Sea Clutter" control will help reduce sensitivity at the center of the display. Note that the speckling (or grass) appears even in radar shadows because it is a function of electronic "noise", not a reflection from any true target.

Auto-Gain

Some radars are equipped with automatic gain settings. My experience is that the auto-gain function is not very satisfactory at setting the optimum gain level. In general, I always turn off the auto-gain, and control the gain manually instead.

To get the most out of your radar you must regularly adjust the gain and clutter settings [see below]. Engaging the auto-gain function makes this impossible.

Some lower-priced radars however, do not have a specific control knob or key for gain settings. Instead, they may have an auto-gain on/off toggle somewhere in a software menu. Since mechanical knobs and switches are more expensive to manufacture than software controls, reducing the numbers of knobs and switches helps to keep the price of the radar down. However, if there is no physical gain control knob or key, it means that the optional manual gain control must also be contained in a menu, which is a problem, because it is such a commonly used function.

If your radar is equipped with auto-gain only, its utility will be limited. You must decide for yourself whether the low price of the radar compensates for this limitation.

"Anti-Sea Clutter" Control (STC)

One of the best reflectors of radar energy is the surface of the water. The interface between air and water reflects sunlight admirably, as you will notice when you are heading into the setting (or rising) sun. When the sea is calm, however, the radar energy simply reflects off the surface of the water and continues in its original direction.

But when the radar beam encounters waves on the surface, especially their steep, concave downwind surfaces, the radar energy is efficiently reflected back to its source—your own vessel. Since each wave returns a separate echo, this "Sea Clutter" can overwhelm your radar display with small rapidly changing echoes, especially at short ranges.

Typically, Sea Clutter appears only at short range. Consequently it will be clustered around

---

The "anti-Sea Clutter" control function is also known as "Sensitivity Time Control" (STC) or "Swept-gain". You will often see the acronym "STC" used instead of "anti-Sea Clutter". The full term "Sensitivity Time Control" is simply a technician's way of stating that the sensitivity is suppressed more near the center of the display than at the edges.

While conducting research for this book, I invited myself aboard a number of pleasure boats at a local marina. On one vessel, I found one of the earliest Furuno daylight radars; I had used this exact model in the past and found it to be a wonderful little set.

However, when I powered it up, the image on the display was remarkably sparse, considering that we were in a crowded marina. "I always like to set up the radar, so that the display isn't filled with extraneous stuff," the owner told me.

As I turned off the "anti-Sea Clutter" control and slowly turned up the gain, I remarked that while it was a good idea to reduce clutter, he should be careful not to eliminate small target echoes at the same time. When a little speckling appeared, numerous targets also appeared. In his attempt to clean up the radar image, the owner had actually hidden the echoes of a stone breakwater and of hundreds of boats in the immediate vicinity. With the gain (sensitivity) turned down and the "anti-Sea Clutter" control turned up, the only echoes strong enough to show on the display were the mountains to the east and west.

▲ **Fig. 5-3**
Sea Clutter

"Sea Clutter" is usually greatest in the upwind direction. The steep downwind faces of waves reflect radar pulses back in the direction of the radar scanner, causing "Sea Clutter" to appear on the display. However, downwind of the vessel, the shallower slope of the backs of the waves deflects the radar pulses away.

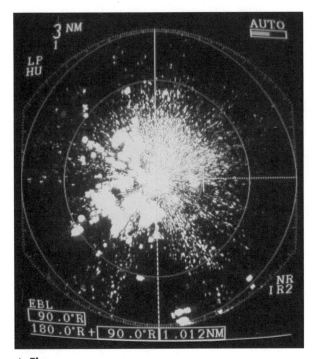
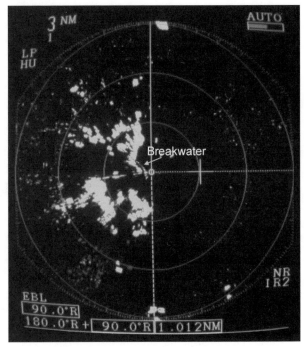

▲ **Fig. 5-4**
Effect of Sea Clutter on the Display

Left Even though the gain has been set properly to control the "grass" at long range, serious sea clutter is present in the first 1.5 Nm. This sea clutter obscures even the shoreline, so it is almost impossible to discriminate the echoes of small boats and rocks from the general interference. This image was taken just after leaving Victoria Harbour. The Ogden Point breakwater is close abeam to port.

Right After turning up the "anti-Sea Clutter" control (thereby reducing sensitivity at close range) several nearby targets are now visible, including the Ogden Point breakwater.

the center of the display and will extend further in the upwind direction.

In order to control this clutter, the "anti-Sea Clutter" control actually decreases the gain (sensitivity) of the radar for a few microseconds after each pulse is transmitted, effectively reducing gain at very close range. As you increase the "anti-Sea Clutter" control, the gain (sensitivity) is reduced for a longer time, the result being that the gain is suppressed farther and farther away from the center of the screen.

Since sea clutter is a problem only at short range, the suppression of gain is limited to short-range targets. At long ranges, where sea clutter is not a problem, the "anti-Sea Clutter" control has no effect.

As a result, you should:

- *Never use the gain control to reduce Sea Clutter because, by doing so, you will affect the sensitivity of your set at long ranges as well and may eliminate weak- to medium-strength targets at a distance.*

- *Adjust the "anti-Sea Clutter" control to its minimum effective level. If you turn it too high you will eliminate not only sea clutter, but also you may eliminate weak- or medium-strength targets that you need to see—such as other vessels.*

- *Regularly check the "anti-Sea Clutter" level by turning it down. If you can turn it down (thus raising short-range sensitivity) without overwhelming the display with sea returns, you should do so—always keeping the "anti-Sea Clutter" control at its minimum effective level.*

If a small vessel is visible out your wheelhouse windows at close range, check to see if you can detect it on your radar. If you have to, turn down the "anti-Sea Clutter" control until the vessel appears on your display. This will provide visual confirmation to help you set the "anti-Sea Clutter" control to the correct level.

When you change range scales, the radar may automatically change the length of the transmitted pulse. As a result, the incoming echoes may have very different characteristics than they had in a higher or lower range scale. Consequently, *whenever you change range scales, verify that you have set the gain and "anti-Sea Clutter" controls to the optimum levels for that particular range scale.*

During very heavy weather, storm waves may return such strong echoes, that other vessels may

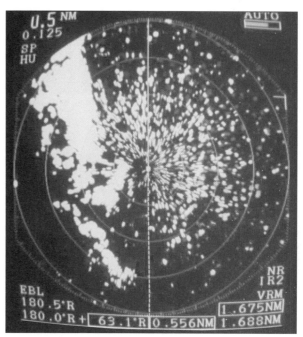

▲ **Fig. 5-5**
Sea Clutter
The display after rounding Cadboro Point into Haro Strait and encountering 2 to 3 foot seas (0.8 to 1.0 meter) from the northeast. Notice that the clutter is most significant forward and to starboard (northeast). In Sea Clutter conditions this severe, it is difficult to eliminate all the sea returns without also hiding nearby targets. If a small vessel comes in sight at short range adjust the "anti-Sea Clutter" until you can see the vessel on your radar.

be masked by the Sea Clutter, no matter how high you set the "anti-Sea Clutter" control.

"Anti-Rain Clutter" Control (FTC)

If water/air interfaces are such good reflectors of radar energy, it stands to reason that rain, fog, and spray droplets will also return echoes that can clutter the display. Each droplet however, is such a tiny and intermittent reflector that the cumulative return from a rainstorm is a weak echo, covering a large area. The resulting "Rain Clutter" can appear anywhere on the display (unlike "Sea Clutter" which always appears around the center of the screen.)

Just like the "Sea Clutter" effect, "Rain Clutter" can mask weak- and moderate-strength

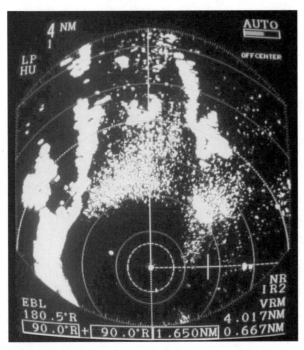 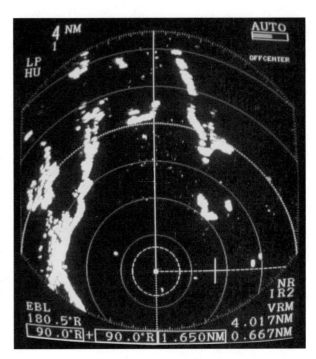

▲ **Fig. 5-6**

Rain Clutter

Left Rain clutter often shows as discrete patches. Sometimes, in heavy driving rain or snow, the clutter can become so extreme as to completely overwhelm the display.

Right By turning up the "anti-Rain Clutter" control, the unwanted rain echoes can be eliminated, exposing the strong echoes of other boats (and even small islands) within the rain cloud.

Note also that the remaining echoes are more distinct and lack the depth of the echoes in the left panel, but they are also easier to interpret and show more detail about the image areas.

Persistence of Sea Clutter

As you have seen above, correct setting of the "anti-Sea Clutter" control may still leave some "sea returns" on the display. So how do you tell if an image on the display is a true target or simply a wave? Waves are transient in nature. Their images flicker into and out of existence with each rotation of the time base. So if you want to differentiate between true targets and waves, simply watch the image. If it is a true target it will persist beyond a single revolution of the time base. If it is a wave it will not.

The "anti-Rain Clutter" control function is also known as "Fast Time Constant" (FTC). You will often see the acronym—almost never the full expression. It is simply technical jargon, which means that suppression of the back end of an echo takes place uniformly across the display.

targets. The solution is based on the unique properties of the rain-clutter return, which is actually composed of millions of small weak echoes. When the "anti-Rain Clutter" control is engaged, the radar circuitry actually suppresses the "back end" of every incoming echo, leaving just the leading edge to provide an image on your display. This has very little effect on large, strong echoes from land and ships, because the returns from these objects have significant depth; removing the "back end" of the echo still leaves lots for the radar to work with. The "anti-Rain Clutter" control however, effectively reduces or eliminates the clutter caused by rain, snow and hail.

Your radar may be fitted with a variable "anti-Rain Clutter" control, or a fixed on/off toggle that has only one level of suppression. Either is useful.

A variable "anti-Rain Clutter" control will suppress more or less of the "back end" of each individual echo to the point of actually eliminating the entire echo if the control is turned too high. Unlike the "anti-Sea Clutter" control, the "anti-Rain Clutter" suppression effect applies over the entire screen. As a result, you should turn up the "anti-Rain Clutter" control *only to the point where it reveals the strong echoes hidden within the rain.*

Pulse-length Control

If you study the owner's manual specifications for your particular radar, you may notice that the radar transmits pulses of differing lengths depending on the range scale. In some simple radars there is just a single pulse for short-ranges

and another for longer-range scales. High-end radars may even use a different pulse length for each range scale.

Many radars automatically select the appropriate pulse length for each range scale, but some radars offer a choice. If your radar is equipped with this feature, it will be included as a toggle switch physically mounted on the control panel, or a software toggle in the radar's menu tree. Somewhere on the display there will also be an indication of pulse length; either LP for "long pulse," MP for "medium pulse," or SP, for "short pulse."

"Radial thickness" means the thickness of a "pip" or other image on the display measured from the center of the display to the

Long pulses are used for longer range scales, because the longer pulse is more reliably reflected by distant targets and the returning, highly attenuated echoes are more easily detected by the scanner.

If two targets are grouped closely together so that one target is just slightly beyond the other, the "pips" of the two targets may merge and appear to be a single target. However, if you reduce the length of the transmitted pulse, the

Long pulse means better target detection. **Short** pulse means better range discrimination.

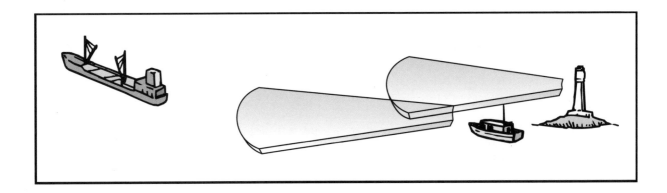

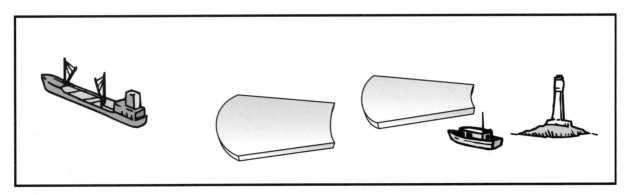

▲ **Fig. 5-7**
Range Resolution
Above—Radar set on "long pulse;" the two returning pulses overlap resulting in a single target visible on the display.
Below—With the radar switched to "short pulse," the returning pulses are now separated, resulting in two targets being visible on the display.

radial thickness of the "pip" may also be reduced, and consequently the two targets will appear as separate "pips" on the display.

So, at shorter ranges, when detection of distant targets is not an issue, it pays to use shorter pulse lengths to obtain better "range resolution" (discrimination). This is why specific pulse lengths are used for each range scale the radar is equipped with.

If your radar is equipped with a manual pulse-length control, you can manually select shorter pulses at any particular range scale to obtain better range resolution (and thus a clearer picture) or you can use long pulses to more easily detect weak targets at a distance.

Using the "Anti-Rain Clutter" Control to Enhance Range Resolution

As you turn up the control, you will notice that each echo on the display becomes thinner as more of its trailing edge is removed by the circuitry. This is because each returning pulse is effectively compressed by the "anti-Rain Clutter" function. *The effect on strong, solid target echoes is exactly the same as using a shorter pulse length—affording better range resolution at any particular range scale.*

When it is especially important to obtain the clearest picture and the best range resolution, you can select the shortest range possible, the shortest pulse possible, and engage the "anti-Rain Clutter" control. This effect is useful for precise navigation or position fixing; for instance, when

the chart shows two exposed rocks close together, you may not be able to recognize the particular rocks unless you can resolve them into separate images on your display.

Using the short pulse and "anti-Rain Clutter" controls may be critical in identifying these dangerous rocks, but remember, this combination reduces your ability to detect weak or moderate echoes at a distance; *use the "anti-*

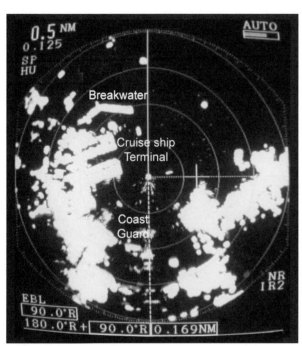 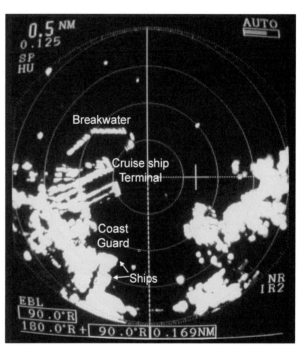

▲ **Fig. 5-8**
Using the "anti-Rain Clutter" Control to Enhance Range Resolution

Left
On exiting Victoria Harbour, the Ogden Point Cruise Ship Terminal is abeam to port. Note that even though the radar is operating on short pulse, the images of the docks and warehouses lack definition and "side-lobe echoes" and other interference have cluttered the view of the channel astern.

Right
The same location viewed with "anti-Rain Clutter" control applied. In this image, Ogden Point Terminal can be seen much more clearly. The radar shows each dock as a discrete target. In addition, two ships can be seen alongside the Coast Guard base at the lower left. Targets on the display are clearer and more easily identified. By using the "anti-Rain Clutter" control, the operator has simulated the effect of using a short pulse length.

Also, application of the "anti-Rain Clutter" control has eliminated unwanted "side-lobe" echoes. [See page 92.]

Rain Clutter" control sparingly, and turn it off when you no longer need it.

If your radar does not have a pulse-length control, you can still obtain the best resolution by using the shortest range possible and obtain-

ing the benefit of the short pulse length associated with that range scale. This is one more reason why you should always adjust the range scale to place a target of interest in the outer 1/3 of the display.

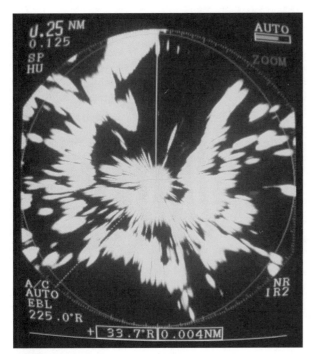 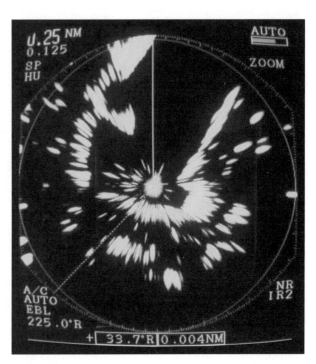

▲ **Fig. 5-9**
Effect of "anti-Sea Clutter" Control
Image centered on the City Docks in Victoria Harbour, British Columbia.
At short ranges, the radar's sensitivity can be reduced by using the "anti-Sea Clutter" and "anti-Rain Clutter" controls in order to obtain a clear picture of close up targets.

Left
Note that the center of the display is cluttered by the returns from targets at extremely close range.

Right
By applying both the "anti-Sea Clutter" and "anti-Rain Clutter" controls, targets to the immediate left of the sweep origin resolve into a number of discrete targets. These are the masts and rigging of other boats at the same marina. [See **Fig. 5-10**.]
Clearly, for extremely close range navigation, it is essential to suppress the radar's sensitivity. But be careful— when you switch back to a higher range scale, you must readjust the "anti-Sea Clutter" and "anti-Rain Clutter" controls. Otherwise you won't be able to detect targets at longer range.

◄ **Fig. 5-10**
Photograph of the City Docks in Victoria Harbour
Baidarka is the middle of three boats. To the left are the masts and rigging of other vessels that appear in **Fig. 5-9.** When adjusting your radar for navigating at very short ranges, it's a good idea to adjust the sensitivity (using the "anti-Sea Clutter" and "anti-Rain Clutter" controls) to ensure that close targets such as pilings and other vessels still show without overwhelming the display with clutter.

Offset and Zoom

If you want to view an area that is just offscreen, you can do so by increasing the range scale. For instance, suppose you want to take a close look at the entrance to a small bay about 1.75 Nm ahead of you, and your radar is presently set to 1.5 Nm range scale. You could simply increase the range scale to 3.0 Nm.

However, when you do so, the area you are interested in is brought within the middle third of the display, and reduced in scale. In addition, as we have seen previously, the range resolution is also diminished because the higher range scale requires the use of a longer pulse.

The solution is to use the "offset" or "shift"

Fig. 5-11 ►
Offset Mode
By shifting the sweep origin (representing your own vessel) to the lower 1/3 of the display, you can "peek" further ahead, while still maintaining the advantages of the shorter pulse length associated with the lower range scale.

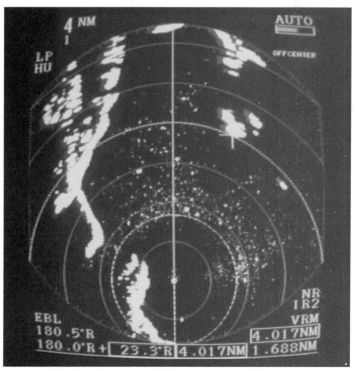

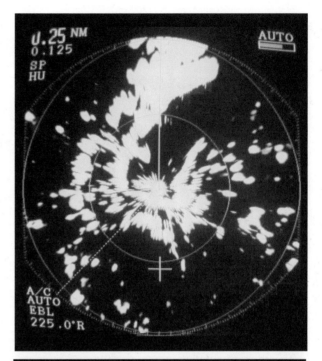

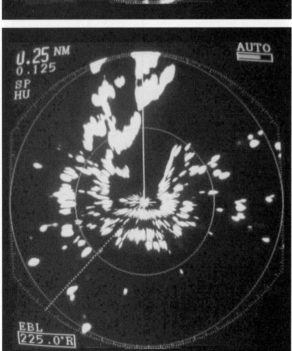

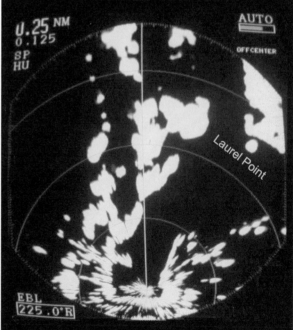

▲ **Fig. 5-12**

Alternatives to "Zoom"

Upper Left: The Inner Harbour at Victoria, British Columbia. Because the Zoom function merely enlarges the image on the display and does not provide any additional detail, simply zooming in on the image may not be adequate. If you want to view the narrows at

Laurel Point in greater detail, you should

Upper Right: reduce the range scale, and

Lower Left: increase the "anti-Rain Clutter" setting.

Lower Right: If the area of interest is now off-screen, use the offset function to bring it back onscreen. You may also have to increase the "anti-Sea Clutter" to control overly strong echoes at short range.

feature of your radar. (These days virtually all radars are equipped with this feature.) By engaging the "offset" feature you can move the point representing your own vessel to any place on the display. As you do so, offscreen areas are brought within the display while the opposite side disappears offscreen. Many boaters move the center of the Plan Position Indicator (PPI) to the lower third of the display, thus extending their view ahead. The advantage of using the offset function is that you can extend your view forward (or to the side) without compromising the enhanced range resolution provided by the lower range scale.

Using the offset feature, you can obtain a longer range view ahead while still retaining the better resolution of a lower range scale. The disadvantage is that you must accept a severely reduced view astern. When operating at high speed, there is very little risk of other vessels overtaking you—and if they do, they will approach your stern slowly, so you have lots of opportunity to observe them as they approach. But, if you are operating at displacement speed or sailing, you should use this feature with caution because it will reduce your ability to observe a high-speed vessel overtaking from astern.

"Zoom" mode permits you to enlarge the image of any part of the display (usually 2X magnification). To engage, usually all that is required is to place the cursor over the area of interest on the display and engage the "zoom" switch. Most radars do not permit you to enlarge to such a degree that the sweep origin disappears off the display.

Dual Pulse Radar

In 2002, Si-Tex introduced an LCD radar with a unique capability; not only can it display two radar windows, but it can actually display different range scales in each window. Where it is necessary to use a different pulse length for each window, it does so. This is as good as having two separate radars, set to different range scales.

The Si-Tex T-1040 and T-1140 series do this by alternating pulse lengths each revolution of the scanner. The only drawback is that this means each displayed image must wait for two revolutions of the scanner to be updated. However, Si-Tex has solved that problem by speeding up the rotation of the scanner in certain circumstances.

How Beam Width Affects Bearing Resolution

The slotted-waveguide antenna used in most marine radars is highly effective in generating a tight directional beam. The rotation of the antenna spreads this beam through 360° in order to illuminate the world around you.

Most X-band (3-centimetre) radar scanners rotate at approximately 20 to 30 rpm and trans-

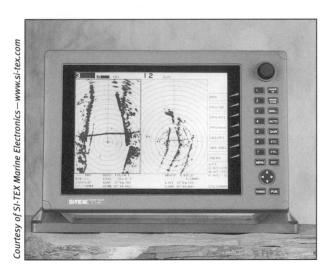

Courtesy of SI-TEX Marine Electronics—www.si-tex.com

◄ **Fig. 5-13**
Si-Tex Dual Pulse Radar
A Si-Tex dual pulse radar. The two images are actually completely separate images, derived from different pulse lengths.

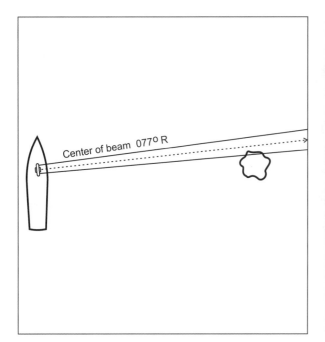

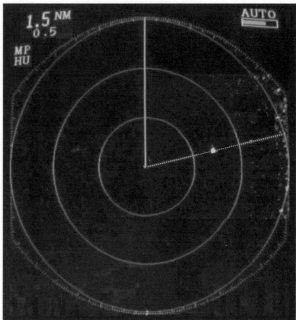

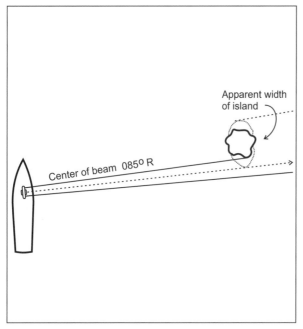

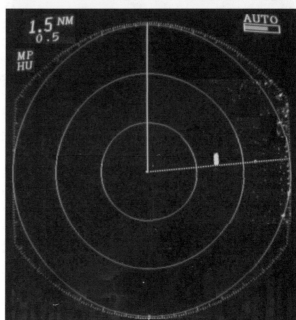

▲ Fig. 5-14
Beam-width Distortion
Upper   As soon as the leading edge of the beam touches the island, it returns an echo. At this point the scanner is pointing 077°R (relative to the vessel's heading).
Lower   The island continues to return an echo as long as any portion of the radar beam illuminates it. In this case, the beam must rotate to 085°R before it ceases to contact the island.

As long as any portion of the beam illuminates any portion of the target, it will return an echo, and that echo will be painted on the display. In this case, the beam is 2° wide, and the island is 6° wide. The result is a distorted image 8° wide. This characteristic of the radar is known as **beam-width distortion**. The only way you can reduce the effects of beam-width distortion is to buy a new, wider antenna.

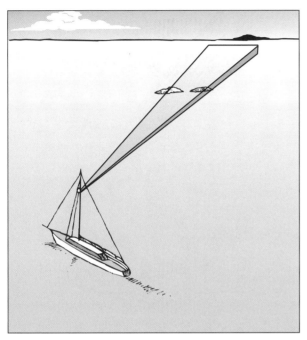

▲ Fig. 5-15
Bearing Discrimination
Approaching two closely grouped islets on 3.0 Nm range scale, the 2° wide beam contacts both islets at

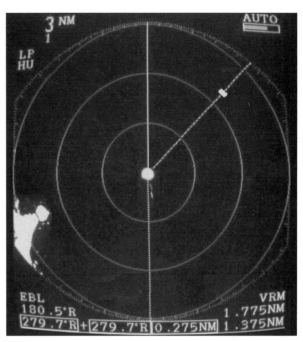

the same time. The result is that the images of the two islets merge. The radar is unable to resolve the echoes of targets that are less than or equal to 2° apart.

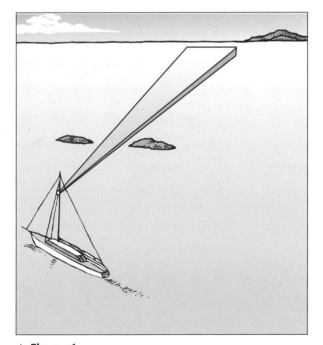

▲ Fig. 5-16
Bearing Discrimination (continued)
As you approach the two islets (and reduce range

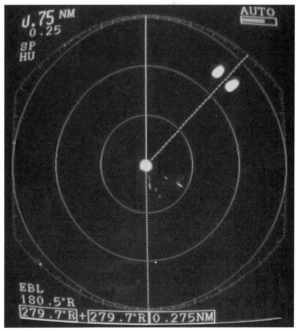

scale), their angular separation is now significantly wider than the beam, and therefore, the radar shows the two islets as separate echoes.

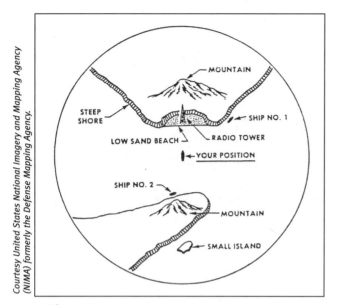
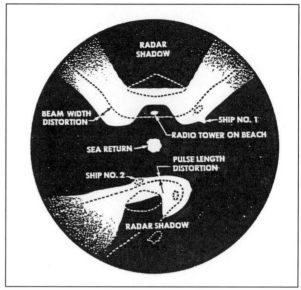

▲ **Fig. 5-17**
Combined Effect of Beam-width and Pulse-length Distortion
The combined effects of radar shadow, pulse-length distortion and beam-width distortion.

mit approximately 500 to 2000 pulses per second. This means that, depending on the width of the beam, a small target will be struck by 15 to 30 pulses per rotation.

The horizontal width of the radar beam is dependent on the size of the rotating antenna. A 48-inch antenna will generally have a beam-width of slightly less than 2°, whereas the beam-width of an 18-inch antenna may be as much as 5° or more.

This horizontal beam-width is an inherent characteristic of the antenna and, as shown in **Fig. 5-15**, the beam width directly affects the ability of your radar to show closely grouped targets as separate echoes. The result is that, in many cases, *groups of islands may appear as a single echo, and entrances to narrow passages may not be visible until they are quite close.*

As shown in **Fig. 5-14**, when illuminating an island that is 5° wide with a 48-inch (2° beam-width) antenna, the resulting image on the dis-

play will be 7° wide. Thus the total width of an echo will be the true angular width of the target, plus the beam-width. *In other words every target will be distorted in bearing (not range) by an amount equal to the beam-width, and the minimum bearing resolution will be the same as the beam-width.*

If your radar antenna is only 18-inches, you can expect to have a minimum bearing resolution of 5° or 6°, and a target 5° wide will be 10° wide on the display!

Obviously, it makes no sense to purchase a high-powered radar display unit unless you

---

Because of beam-width distortion, you can measure a range (distance) to an object much more accurately than you can measure the bearing to that object. This is why experienced mariners usually use radar ranges to fix their position, rather than radar bearings.

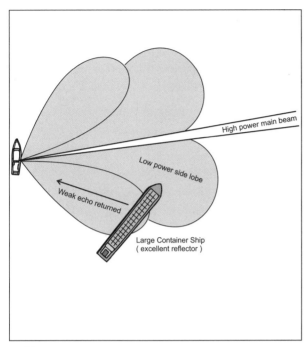

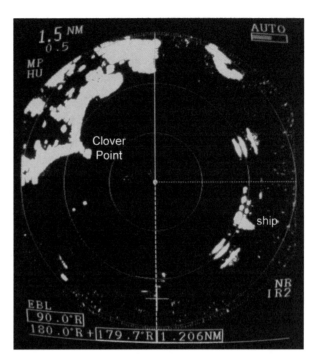

▲ **Fig. 5-18**
Side Lobe Echoes

- The radar beam rotates clockwise, so the side lobe in advance of the main beam strikes the ship first. Since the container ship is such an excellent reflector of radar energy, an echo is returned that is strong enough to be painted on the display. Even though the echo comes from the container ship, the echo is painted in the direction the antenna is pointing at the time—not necessarily the direction of the ship.
- The main beam then strikes the container ship, and the side lobe moves away from the ship. A very strong echo is returned to the antenna.
- When the main beam passes the ship, side lobes on the trailing side of the main beam return echoes which are also painted in the direction the antenna is pointing at the time, thus significantly stretching out the image of the ship on the display.

match it to an antenna of appropriate size. Buy as large an antenna as you can afford, consistent with the other characteristics of your radar.

Side Lobe Echoes

No radar beam is perfectly formed; instead it spills over into areas to either side of the beam. The effect is similar to a flashlight beam (not a laser) which is surrounded by a "halo" of less intense light. When we say a beam is 2° or 5° wide, we mean that any energy outside the margins of the beam is less than 50% of the strength of the energy in the middle of the beam.

The low power areas of radar energy on either side of the main beam are known as **side lobes**. These **side lobes** can have a significant effect on the appearance of the display, and consequently you must manage these **side lobes** to reduce their effect.

Since the side lobes contain relatively little broadcast energy they return an echo only when they encounter an excellent reflector such as a large slab-sided ship, or a cliff face at close range which is perpendicular to the radar beam. The

Fig. 5-19 ▶

Extreme Side Lobe Effects

Side lobe echoes smear the image of the ship around the display. When the target is close enough, the side lobe effect may be strong enough to smear the echo around 360°.

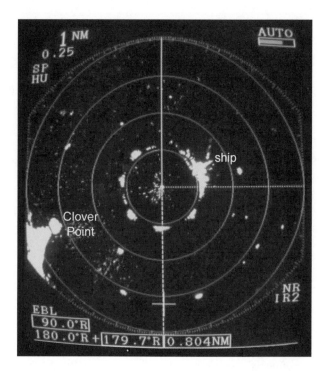

effect of side lobe echoes is to smear the image of the ship or cliff face around the display. If the target is close enough, it can even return a reasonably strong signal from lobes directly behind the antenna, thus smearing the image around almost 360°.

◆ Side lobe echoes appear as "ghostly" echoes, not nearly as strong as the echo from the main beam itself. In **Fig. 5-8** echoes from buildings and ships at the Victoria Coast Guard Base have generated weak side lobe echoes that obscure the channel astern of the vessel.

◆ Side lobe echoes can obscure other target images, so you may wish to eliminate or reduce the false echo.

◆ Simply increasing the "anti-Sea Clutter" setting will, in most cases, filter out these false echoes. However, by doing so, you will also weaken (or eliminate) the echoes of small poorly-reflective boats in the area.

◆ You must be very careful about cancelling out the side lobe echoes in this way. Do so only when necessary, and return to your normal gain or "anti-Sea Clutter" settings as soon as possible.

Vertical Beam Width

When your boat pitches and rolls under the influence of weather and waves, the radar beam does not describe a smooth circle around the horizon; instead, it rolls up and down as it rotates. If the beam were as narrow vertically as it is horizontally, it would be purely a matter of chance for it to illuminate any particular object, so for maximum effectiveness, it must be at least 20° vertically so that it sweeps broad swaths around the horizon.

A radar beam has vertical side-lobes as well as horizontal side lobes. As a result, you will find that you can often observe an overhead cable or an aircraft even when the sea is calm and your vessel is not rolling at all.

Since the beam rotates at approximately 24 rpm, it is unlikely to miss an important target for more than one or two sweeps of the scanner. However, when the beam dips toward the water's surface on a roll—especially if it strikes the advancing face of a wave—it will return a strong echo. This is one of the reasons Sea Clutter is so much more prominent at close range.

◄ Fig. 5-20
Vertical Beam Width
As the radar beam tilts toward the sky, it completely misses the ship in the distance; on the next sweep, the beam strikes the ship squarely, returning a very strong echo.

Finally, as the beam tilts downward, it illuminates the sea surface, missing the ship again. Portions of the wave fronts are oriented perpendicularly to the radar beam and thus return a strong echo, forming part of the close-range sea clutter prominent during heavy weather.

This example takes place during very rough weather. Under more moderate circumstances, due to the vertical width of the beam, objects such as ships and shorelines are illuminated by every sweep of the scanner.

Blind Sectors and Ghosts

If a portion of your ship's structure interferes with the radar beam, it creates a blind sector on the display—a sector in which no targets can normally be seen.

The radar beam may also reflect off the portion of the ship's structure responsible for the blind sector, or it may reflect off other structures or other ships, thus causing one or more of the many different types of ghosts.

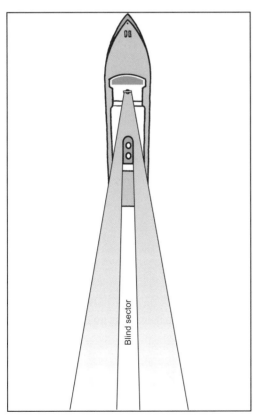

◄ Fig. 5-21
Blind Sector
In order for an image to appear on the display, a microwave pulse must be broadcast, and some portion of that pulse must return as an echo. Obstructions, such as a ship's funnel close to the antenna, can block the beam. Any return from the funnel itself will be so close to the antenna, that its image will merge with the sweep origin on the display.

Fig. 5-22 ▶
Blind Sector on the Display
The radar beam is blocked and cannot illuminate anything in the direction of the
blockage, not even the choppy surface of
the sea. When any waves are present, you
can turn off the "anti-Sea Clutter" control
and see the blind sector clearly defined by
the lack of Sea Clutter in the direction of the
obstruction.

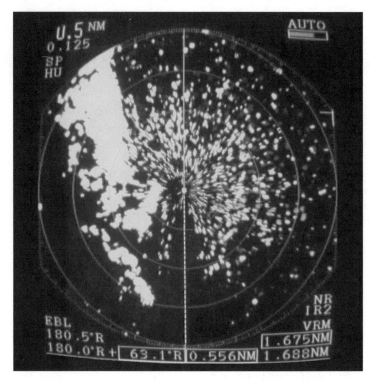

Ghosts are images of targets that are not
where they appear to be. You must be
careful to identify ghosts, otherwise you
might be fooled into thinking they are
real contacts, when they aren't. However, if you understand the causes of
ghosts, you may be able to identify them
when they occur, as well as being able to
infer something about the conditions that caused
them in the first place, which is especially important. If you understand the conditions that cause
the ghosts, you will be able to anticipate them in
the future.

◀ **Fig. 5-23**
A Supply Ship in Quebec City
Note that both radar scanners are located
on the centerline directly forward of the
lattice mast. The lattice mast may permit
enough radar energy to pass so that it does
not cause a true blind sector. However, the
installation is almost guaranteed to produce
ghost images astern on both radars.

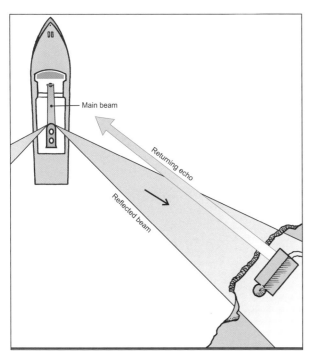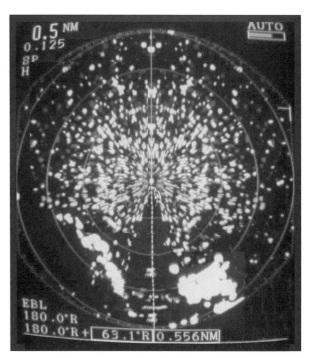

▲ **Fig. 5-24**

Ghosts Appear in Blind Sectors

Under certain circumstances, a ghost image may appear in the blind sector. ***In fact, a ghost that always appears at a certain range and bearing is a strong indication of a blind (or partially blind) sector.***

In the illustration above, the funnel blocks the radar beam, but some of the radar energy is reflected in different directions. The reflected beam strikes the outer walls of the lighthouse and returns as a weak echo.

The result is similar to the effect produced by side lobes. The echo is strong enough to generate an image, but because the radar antenna faces directly astern at the time the echo is received, the image appears directly astern, in the blind sector.

Ghost images are caused by side lobes of the main radar beam, or by reflections that act like side lobe echoes.

In some cases the obstruction responsible for a blind sector may also cause a ghost by reflecting the main beam in a different direction. This type of ghost will appear in the blind sector. In fact, ***a ghost that appears to follow your vessel at a constant range and bearing is a sure indication of a blind sector***. In that case ***do not try to eliminate the ghost by reducing the gain or increasing the "anti-Sea Clutter" control;*** ***there will be nothing to see in the blind sector anyway***.

Remember: *The ghost, or blind sector, may not always be found astern.* A permanent ghost aft and to port of the sweep origin is probably the result of an antenna/scanner that is mounted forward and to starboard of the mast or some other reflecting surface, such as a funnel or stack.

The best way to identify a ghost is to keep the gain properly adjusted, and to manipulate the "anti-Sea Clutter" control regularly. When you reduce the sensitivity by increasing the "anti-

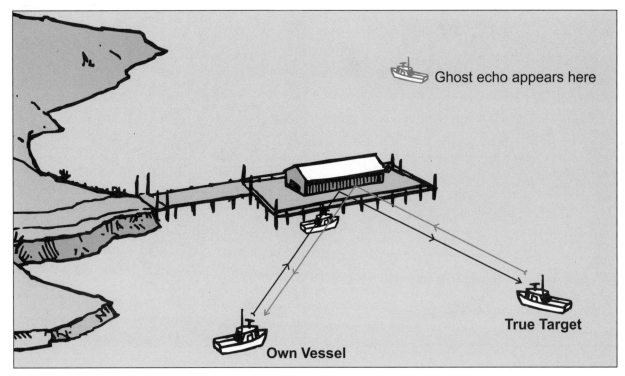

▲ Fig. 5-25
Ghost Images

A strong reflector such as the side of a metal warehouse can reflect the radar beam very efficiently. If the radar beam reflected by the side of the warehouse illuminates a small vessel, the echo may return to your scanner directly, or it may bounce off the warehouse again. In either case, it will fool the radar into thinking that there is a target beyond the warehouse, when in fact the target is in a distinctly different direction.

◄ Fig. 5-26
In this photograph it is clear that there are no permanent targets beyond the breakwater that would account for the "ghost" images in **Fig. 5-27**. Even the lighted structure at Brotchie Ledge was outside the range of the radar at the time.

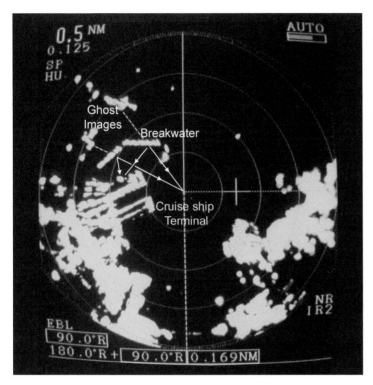

◄ Fig. 5-27
Ghost Images Created by a Stone Breakwater

The Ogden Point Docks are clearly visible abeam to port. Several ships are secured alongside. Beyond the breakwater lie the ghost images of those ships. The main radar beam has reflected off the stone breakwater, struck the sides of ships at the docks, and returned to the antenna by bouncing off the breakwater a second time.

Sea Clutter" control, you will be able to distinguish ghosts by their low echo strength, and their irregular and poorly-defined margins. Whenever you suspect ghosts may be present, you should increase the "anti-Sea Clutter" control to verify the ghost and to ensure that no weak targets are hidden by the ghost image.

Do not be too concerned about blind sector ghosts; they are very common. The most sensible thing you can do is to ignore them. Just increase the "anti-Sea Clutter" every so often to see if there is another target hiding under the ghost. If not, resume your previous "anti-Sea Clutter" levels.

Ghosts tend to be more apparent when there are strong reflective surfaces in the area (very much like side lobe echoes). In **Fig. 5-27** the ghost image is so strong because the Ogden Point breakwater is constructed of smooth stone blocks that reflect microwaves like a mirror.

Fig. 5-28 ▶

Multiple Echoes

Multiple echoes occur when the radar beam bounces back and forth between two large, and highly-reflective ships.

A—The radar beam bounces off a nearby ship.

B—The beam bounces back to and off our own ship. The antenna receives this reflection as the first and closest target image.

C—The beam again bounces off the nearby ship.

D—The beam strikes our own antenna again. The antenna receives this reflection as a target echo as well, but since the beam has travelled twice as far, the radar interprets this to mean that there is a second target, twice as distant.

Sometimes third echoes show up as well, though they're usually very faint.

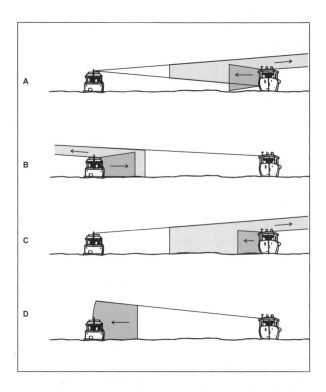

Interference

When you are in the vicinity of another vessel with operating radar, your antenna will detect the side lobes and main beam of that radar. Because most radars are tuned to a slightly different frequency, the interference from other radars may not impact upon your own. However, in many cases, the other radar *will* interfere with your radar's operation.

When a number of radars are operating in the vicinity, the chances of your radar experiencing interference increase. Consequently, manufacturers have incorporated interference-rejection circuits in most radars.

Interference appears as a spiral series of dots or dashes radiating outward from the center of the PPI. Radar interference patterns appear throughout the display (even in radar shadow areas), which distinguishes interference from clutter. Interference patterns also change with each revolution of the time base.

When you engage your radar's interference-rejection (IR) circuitry, it simply removes the interference from the display.

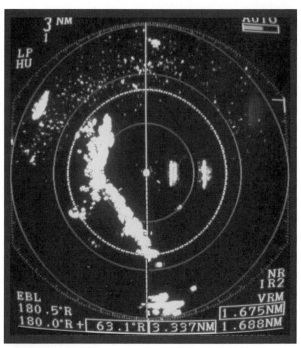

▲ **Fig. 5-29**

Multiple Echoes

In this screen capture, there is only one actual target ship, approximately 0.5 Nm to starboard. The second echo to the right is a multiple of the first.

Fig. 5-30 ▶

Overhead Power Line Effect

Overhead power lines can return a surprisingly strong echo. Often, an overhead cable will not be visible itself, but will produce a very strong echo from the point where your radar beam strikes it perpendicularly. Vertical side lobes of your radar beam continue to produce a strong echo until shortly before you pass under the cable. If you move across the channel, the echo will move across the channel as well, which can lead you to believe the echo is a ship approaching on a steady bearing. Avoiding action will do you no good; the target follows you and brightens until finally, when the target approaches very closely, it suddenly disappears.

You may also get a conventional echo from the cable, but it is normally a poor reflector, and produces a faint image.

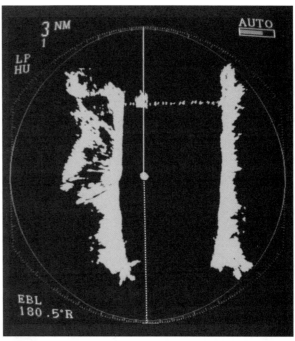

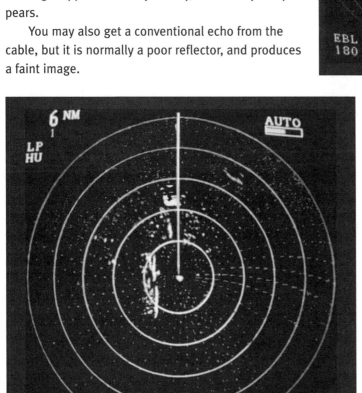

◀ Fig. 5-31

Interference

The classic spiral interference pattern is clearly visible on this radar's PPI. This is a mild case of interference. When your radar experiences interference from a number of radars, the interference pattern may obscure small targets.

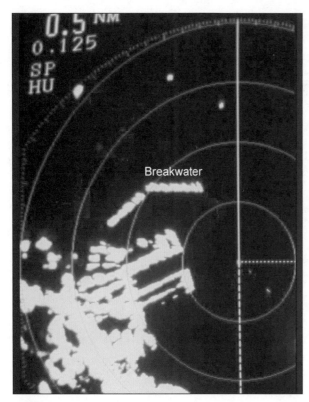 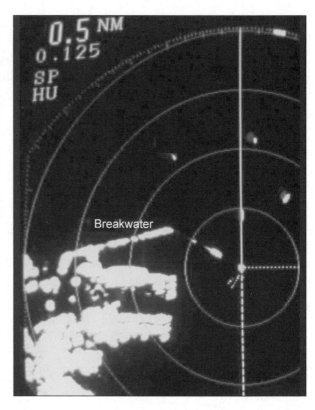

▲ **Fig. 5-32**

Target Aspect

Left When the radar beam strikes the Ogden Point breakwater at an angle, the seaward leg of the breakwater returns a very strong echo.

Right When the vessel is directly off the end of the breakwater, the radar beam strikes the structure end-on. Most of the seaward leg of the breakwater is hidden by the navigation light structure at its end. Thus the navigation light returns an echo, but the seaward leg of the breakwater does not.

This situation shows that you cannot always identify a target by a single static image; instead you must observe how the radar image changes over time.

Chapter Six

Interfacing Equipment and the Integrated Bridge

Head-Up vs. North-Up Displays

In previous chapters we have considered only Head-up displays in which the direction of the ship's head is at the top of the radar display, but this is not necessarily the only way to display radar information.

Newcomers to radar often experience difficulty understanding the radar images or relating the displayed images to a chart, because the orientation of the radar display (Head-up) is different from the chart orientation. In a printed chart the orientation is almost always North-up, so new

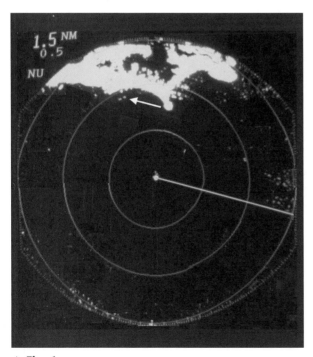
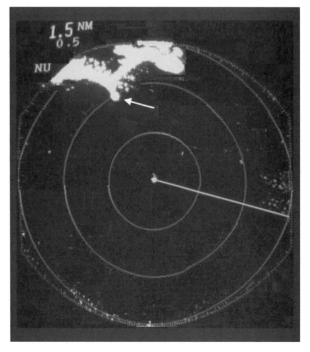

▲ Fig. 6-1
North-Up Mode
In North-up mode, north remains at the top of the display no matter what direction the vessel is heading.
When on a steady heading, targets move in a direction opposite to the direction of the heading marker.

navigators often rotate their charts until their direction of travel is upwards. This allows them to reconcile the radar image and the chart with their visual point of view.

In rough weather, a vessel's bow inevitably yaws back and forth under the influence of waves, no matter how closely the helmsman attempts to steer a specific compass course. As a result, the Head-up image rotates one way and then the other. At best, you will find this behaviour to be an inconvenience; at worst you will be unable to measure bearings or track targets.

Early in the development of radar, manufacturers found that if they could synchronize the radar display with the vessel's heading, they could provide a stable display that did not react to the yawing of the vessel. An added advantage was that they could orient the top of the display to coincide with any point of the compass, (generally true north, but sometimes magnetic north, or even the course the vessel was steering).

North-up (stabilized) radar displays are now available from most manufacturers. This mode of display presents the radar image in exactly the same orientation as a paper chart and, as a result, some users may feel more comfortable using radar in a North-up mode because it matches the orientation of the chart.

Since North-up displays are actually stabilized by the heading data from an electronic compass, in rough weather you will notice that your heading marker yaws back and forth, but the displayed images of land and other targets remains stable, making it far easier to measure ranges and bearings to targets.

Another useful mode of stabilized presentation

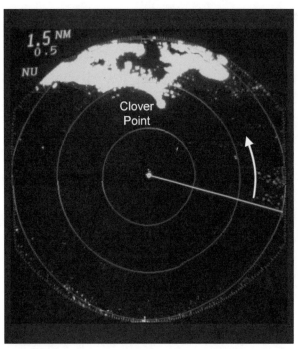
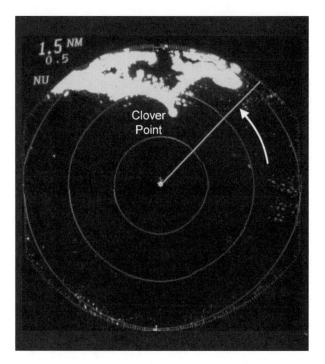

▲ **Fig. 6-2**
North-Up Mode (continued)
When altering heading, the heading marker rotates around the display—the land features retain the same orientation.

is "Course-up" mode. In Course-up mode, the vessel's planned course is at the top of the screen. Once again, the display remains stable while the vessel's heading flash yaws back and forth but, in this case, the heading flash will yaw back and forth centered on the top of the display. When you alter your course, you must enter the new course into the radar to ensure the new course is "up."

Use Course-up display mode only when you are going to be on your current course for a significant time. If you are navigating through an intricate channel with numerous course changes, you will have to reset the course setting on your radar every time you alter course. In this situation you are much better off using either North-up or Head-up modes. Course-up mode is especially useful when you overlay the radar image on an electronic chart.

Not all radars are capable of displaying North-up or Course-up mode. Your instruction manual should tell you if your radar is capable of this mode of display, and the display should provide an indication of mode—either Head up (HU), North-up (NU), or Course-up (CU). If there is no mode indication on the display, chances are your radar is not capable of North-up mode. *Be aware of this indication and of the radar display mode.*

For your radar to display North-up mode it must be North-up capable, and it must be set up to display in that mode. You must ensure that it is supplied with reliable heading data from either a Flux-gate compass, a gyrocompass, or one of the new generation of GPS compasses. If you use an autopilot, you already have one of these instruments.

GPS Heading Data

When setting up your radar for North-up display, the need for accurate heading information makes things a little more complex, because there are only certain types of useful heading data. You can obtain heading data from a flux-gate compass or gyrocompass, or even from one of the new generation GPS compasses, but *you should never try to use the course data from a standard GPS, DGPS or WAAS receiver as the heading input for your North-up radar.*

As you may have noticed, a GPS does not actually provide heading data. Instead, it provides Course Over the Ground (COG), which is quite different. [See **Fig. 1-21**]

A GPS does not measure COG directly, instead it calculates it from a series of positions. If, due to small fluctuations of the GPS signal, it believes that you have moved from one position to another, it will calculate a course and speed even if your vessel is stationary. Since the GPS calculates the COG from the apparent random movement of the GPS position, it will generate COG data that varies randomly. As a result the COG of a stationary vessel can "wander around the clock".

Once your vessel begins to move, its true motion overwhelms the apparent motion and, as you increase speed, the COG data becomes more accurate. The faster the speed of travel, the more accurate is the course information provided by the GPS. But even at high speed, there may be times when rolling error causes the GPS to display unreliable course data.

As a result, most GPS manufacturers have designed the software in their equipment to blank out the "Course" data when the speed of travel drops below 2 or 3 Knots. Other GPS equipment just displays a rapidly changing "Course" which, when the vessel is fully stopped, may "wander" completely around the compass. *Consequently you should never use a GPS to provide heading information to another electronic device.*

North-up or Course-up stabilized radars eliminate the single most significant cause of radar bearing error: errors in arithmetic when converting relative bearings to true or magnetic bearings.

In North-up mode, north is at the top of the display, eliminating the need to rotate your chart to reconcile it with your radar. However, the heading marker now points in the direction of travel, which could be toward any point of the

North-up, Course-up and Head-up Modes

It is a matter of choice which presentation mode you should use in various circumstances. Each has its pros and cons.

In North-up mode:

◆ Echo trails work well—when you alter course, it is the heading marker that rotates, not the target images, so echo trails will not "smear."

◆ It is far easier to take ranges and bearings in rough weather because the display is stabilized.

◆ Bearings give an accurate indication of direction (whether true or magnetic); they are not relative to the ship's head.

◆ It is easier to understand your relationship to land masses and other fixed targets, so it is an ideal presentation mode for long range navigation and piloting.

◆ When you alter course in a collision avoidance situation, the target does not rotate around the screen; instead it simply begins its new relative motion line from that point. You do not need to reset the EBL.

In Head-up mode:

◆ Echo trails operate well, but yawing of the vessel will cause the images to smear

◆ What you see ahead of you (and to port and starboard) corresponds to what you see on the radar.

◆ It is easier to understand the actions of other moving targets in relation to your own vessel, so it's an ideal presentation mode for practicing collision avoidance, especially at short range.

◆ When you alter course in a collision avoidance situation, the target will rotate around the display in a direction opposite to the direction you have turned and will begin a new relative motion line from that point. You must reset your EBL to track the new relative motion line.

In Course-up mode:

◆ Course-up mode is stabilized like North-up mode, so echo trails work well, and it is easy to measure bearings and ranges.

◆ Like Head-up mode, you can relate your point of view to the radar display, so it is very useful for collision avoidance.

◆ Course-up mode requires resetting each time you alter course (unless your autopilot is interfaced to the radar).

◆ When you alter course in a collision avoidance situation, the target rotates around the display. You must reset the EBL in order to track the new relative motion line of the target.

◆ Course-up mode is not very useful in short range collision avoidance situations because it requires that you remember to reset the course when the situation may be changing very rapidly.

◆ Course-up mode is useful in conjunction with radar overlay.

compass. It is unlikely that the heading marker will point toward north for very long when you are in North-up mode.

Because the heading marker may now point toward the bottom or the side of the display, it may actually be more difficult for a novice to intuitively understand the radar image and especially whether a target lies to port or starboard. In general, novices prefer Head-up displays, because all information is presented relative to one's own vessel and one's own *point of view*.

Once you have gained some experience with your radar, you should practice using North-up mode for navigation whenever possible because it does provide a more easily understood display when navigating and piloting at medium to long ranges.

Connecting Equipment Together

Almost all modern marine electronic equipment is capable of interfacing with other devices, which means that an individual boat owner has the ability to create a truly "integrated" instrumentation package for his vessel. The result is an almost bewildering number of possibilities for interconnecting navigational devices.

The cornerstone of these integrated systems is a universal marine electronic language that allows various electronic instruments to communicate with each other.

Using this electronic language, it's now possible to interconnect virtually every instrument on the bridge of any vessel and display the resulting information on just one or two computer-type monitors according to the skipper's requirements.

A new terminology is developing to describe this new way of interconnecting navigation equipment; this terminology is very similar to that used in computer networks—and for good reason. At the time of going to press, Furuno has developed a Local Area Network (LAN) technology known as "NavNet," and Raytheon uses "hsb²" or "SeaTalk" systems.

Thus a sounder transducer, a GPS antenna, and a Radar scanner are all just "sensors" for various types of navigational information. You can

---

National Marine Electronics Association (NMEA) 0183

NMEA0183 is the standard set by the National Marine Electronics Association for interfacing marine electronics of different types.

Using the universal "language" of NMEA0183, almost all modern marine electronics can now be interfaced, allowing information to be supplied to virtually any other electronic equipment. The various "dialects" of NMEA0183 consist of a series of similar "sentences," each relating to one aspect of navigation. For instance, one sentence may refer to *range*, the next to *bearing*, etc.

The navigational message output by a GPS Navigator (the "talker") is composed of numerous sentences that instruct the receiving equipment (the "listener") to display certain information on-screen or to use the data generated from the talker's calculations. The NMEA0183 standard requires that the listener know what sort of data is being spoken, so a "talker ID" sentence tells the "listener" whether the message comes from a sounder, GPS, or radar.

A new NMEA2000 standard is now available that allows multiple "talkers" and "listeners" to share data bi-directionally—that is, in both directions down a single wire. Using NMEA2000, electronic navigation devices, engine monitors and even entertainment systems can share the same signalling channel.

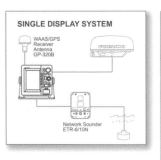

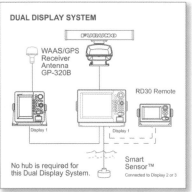

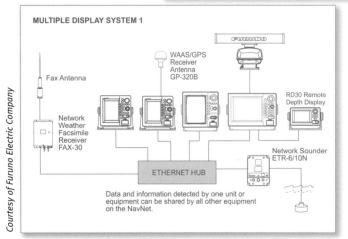

◄ **Fig. 6-3**
Furuno NavNet Variations.
Every sensor can talk to any display unit. As a result, you can display any information on any display.

capture the data with a "sensor" or "black box" and direct it to any monitor or display unit. Marine electronics salesmen agree—it won't be long before almost all marine electronics are available as separate "sensor" and "display" units. And if you add a computer loaded with an electronic charting program, extraordinary navigational power becomes available.

Currently, most equipment is manufactured with both a "sensor" and a "display" component. Radars are manufactured as an antenna/scanner and a display unit. Sounders have transducers and display units. A GPS has an antenna head and a navigation/display module. However, in recent years, manufacturers have also begun to produce display units that are intended to operate with two or three sensor inputs, such as radars that can also display sounder and GPS plotter information. There are also computer programs designed to receive input from a series of sensors, such as GPS and radar, and to display them on a common display, either in the same window or superimposed, one upon the other, as in **Fig. I-4.**

Once you have integrated your electronics package, you can custom-design the display units. Sometimes you may wish to display the chart-plotter in a window on the same display as the radar image, or you may dedicate one display to radar and another to display both chart-plotter functions and sounder displays. The possibilities are virtually endless.

▲ **Fig. 6-4**
A Furuno Sounder "Sensor"

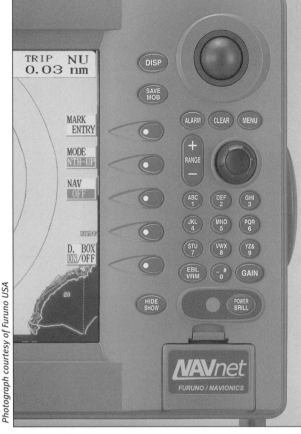

▲ **Fig. 6-5**
A Furuno GPS Antenna/Receiver "Sensor"
This unit provides raw GPS data to any display unit or waypoint navigator.

▲ **Fig. 6-6**
Standard Furuno NavNet Controls
Certain controls are common to every Furuno NavNet display which makes it possible to display any type of "sensor" data on any display unit. Note the use of soft-keys that change their function depending on the displayed page.

Managing Multiple Windows

There are numerous ways to interface your equipment and, as a result, there are numerous ways to display the resulting data. You can display all the data on a single display unit or on more than one; but unless you install as many display units as sensors, you will inevitably have to share one display with two or more data sources.

Ideally you should dedicate a separate display to each type of sensor, but this is not always possible. Both budgetary constraints and space limitations will cause you to compromise when setting up your pilothouse. Consequently, you must manage the use of multiple data sources on one display unit by:

◆ switching back and forth between two or more full screen displays

◆ using separate windows for each data source.

Clearly there are no longer any technical difficulties in integrating the display equipment on your bridge. It is the management of the information displays that may cause trouble.

If you apply Murphy's law to the management of multiple data windows, just when you

Fig. 6-7 ▶

An Integrated Furuno NavNet Display

In this model both the radar and chart displays can appear full-screen or as a window superimposed on the other display. Here the chart and sounder windows are reduced in size, and the radar display fills half the screen.

Photograph courtesy of Furuno USA

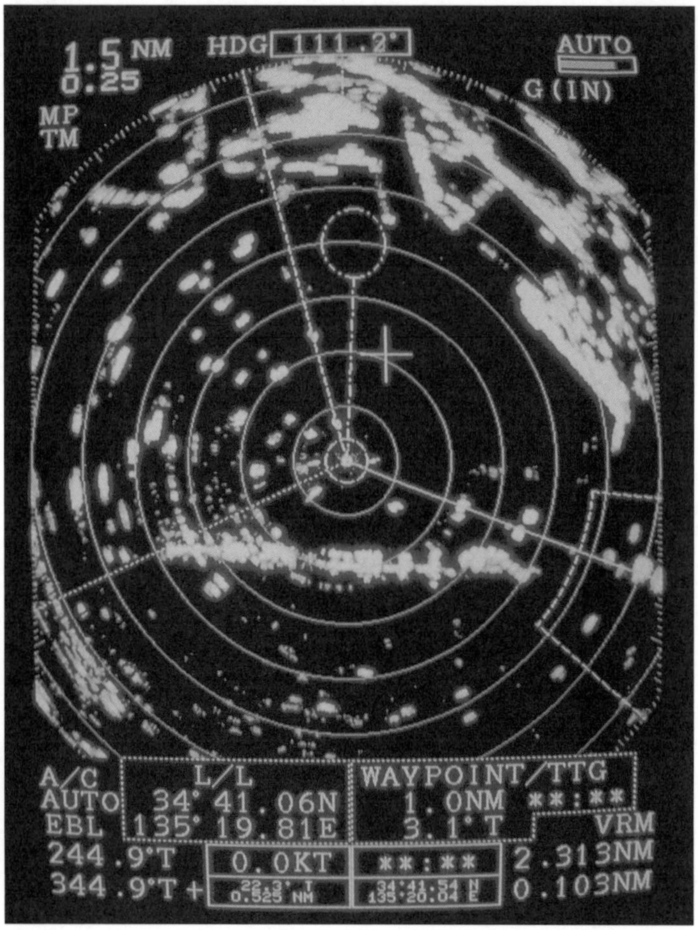

Screencapture courtesy of Furuno USA

◀ Fig. 6-8

On-Screen Waypoint "Lollipop" Display

A Furuno radar display accessing navigation data. The radar is in "stabilized" Course-up mode. The "active" waypoint appears as a "lollipop"—a circle connected to the center of the display by a straight line representing the bearing to the destination waypoint. Since the radar is in "Course-up" mode, the images of fixed targets, such as land and the "active" waypoint, do not rotate around the display with the yawing of the vessel.

In Course-up mode, the "lollipop" appears at the top of the display, and the heading flash wanders back and forth with the yawing of the vessel. By ensuring that the heading flash crosses the waypoint circle, you can navigate toward the destination waypoint with ease.

In Head-up mode, however, the "lollipop" will wander back and forth with the yawing of the vessel, and the heading flash will remain fixed.

Note that the ship's latitude and longitude, as supplied by the GPS, are displayed on-screen, as are the range and bearing to the waypoint.

need a specific window display, it won't be visible or, when you make it visible, it won't be configured properly. You must keep all your windows relevant to the situation you are in. ***If you must hide a radar window, be sure that it is configured correctly in case you need it in a hurry.***

Certain situations will require that you display certain information. For instance, in shallow water you may need to have your sounder constantly available, or in close quarters situations, keep your radar window visible.

Real-time environmental sensors such as radar and sounder windows must be immediately available. Practice calling up or enlarging the radar and/or sounder windows in a hurry. Also be sure that you remember the settings used on the radar display, such as range and display mode (Head-up, North-up), and the gain and anti-clutter settings.

On-screen Waypoint Displays

Using the "international language"—NMEA0183—most modern radars can read data supplied by a GPS Navigator. This capability provides the radar's brain with the data it needs to display a graphic representation of the destination waypoint, as well as other information such as vessel position, waypoint position, and waypoint range and bearing—all of which it displays in the margins of the radar image.

The ease with which any helmsman can steer to an "active" waypoint is the greatest advantage of this type of interface. Either of the stabilized display modes gives satisfactory results, but you can also use a waypoint "lollipop" in unstabilized, "Head-up" mode.

You must remember that the heading information provided by a GPS is not reliable. Instead, connect the radar to an alternative source of heading data, such as a flux-gate or gyro-compass. If you use GPS heading data, it will cause the "lollipop" to wander back and forth in an arc around the center of the display whenever the vessel is proceeding at low speed. When your vessel stops, the waypoint will rotate completely "around the clock" (along with the entire image).

Caution: *This method of navigating to a waypoint "lollipop" may produce a Hooked Course Line.* [See **Fig. 7-15**]

Interfacing Radar with Electronic Chart Systems (ECS)

Perhaps the most useful integration of navigation technologies is the combination of Electronic Chart Systems (ECS) with a radar display. Imagine being able to view, at a glance, not only your own position on an electronic chart display, but also a transparent radar image overlaid on the chart at the same scale. The result is a single seamless display that shows the permanent, charted features, as well as the transient features—such as other vessels the radar has detected—but it does

Radar Waypoint Display

My experience has shown that radar waypoint displays can be extremely useful. Imagine yourself in a narrow channel or under restricted visibility when you can become confused about the correct direction to follow on the next leg of a route. When properly set up, your radar will display the direction to steer and automatically switch to the next waypoint at the same time as the GPS Navigator. Since many vessels are now equipped with flux-gate compasses in order to run an autopilot, all it takes to set up the interface is a small amount of a technician's time and some wire!

not obscure any of the chart data. (Rain and snow squalls, birds, and other transients will show on the display as well, so you must interpret the picture and determine which is which.)

Once properly installed, a radar overlay significantly increases the usefulness of the electronic chart and aids situational awareness.

At times you may notice a difference between the position of a permanent charted feature and its radar image. This is probably due to one of the following:

◆ An error in the GPS positioning input

◆ A chart error

◆ A horizontal datum problem (your GPS may be set to NAD27 instead of WGS84).

[See **Chapter 11**]

In any case, discrepancies between the chart and the radar image will alert you to the possibility of error, and the need for caution. [See **Chapter 11**]

If you notice that the radar image of a buoy appears elsewhere than at its charted position, and if the permanent charted features coincide with their radar images, you can assume the buoy is out of position and take that fact into consideration when approaching the buoy. You will instantly be able to discriminate between isolated targets such as rocks

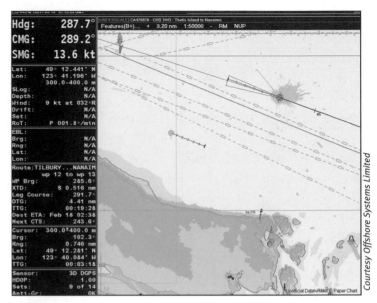

Courtesy Offshore Systems Limited

▲ **Fig. 6-9**

An Offshore Systems Ltd. ECPINS (Electronic Chart Precise Integrated Navigation System) with radar overlay. This is one of the ECDIS systems used on large commercial ships. [See below.] With vector charts, intelligent voyage planning and chart overlay, these "big ship" systems led the way for the development of small vessel electronic chart systems. Here the ship is at the upper right of the display, heading northwest. The echo of each target is clearly visible, superimposed on the charted image. Land echoes coincide with the charted landforms, meaning that the electronic chart and GPS positioning input is working properly. Note that the radar image is transparent, not solid.

or buoys. If another radar target appears in the vicinity of a buoy—which is also visible on the radar—the overlay allows you to distinguish between the buoy and the other vessel.

In order to align the chart with the radar

Active Waypoints and "Course-up" Display Mode

An additional advantage of this type of interface is that the radar can read the direction to the "active waypoint" and use it as the "course" for a "Course-up" presentation. In this case, so long as you are on an active course line to a waypoint, you can utilize a Course-up display on your radar without worrying about manually inputting the course settings. When the GPS automatically switches to the next waypoint, the display automatically rotates to present the new course in the Course-up mode.

> **Just because you can put all your navigational eggs in one basket does not necessarily mean you should do so. Consider the implications; should the central display fail, you may find yourself without any navigation instruments.**

image, either the radar must be capable of North-up stabilized mode or the chart display must be capable of displaying the vessel's heading. Both of these options require input from a flux-gate or gyro-compass.

The great advantage of the radar overlay is that it adds one more type of graphic information in one place, thus allowing you to get on with the most important aspect of navigation—safely guiding your vessel along its route. *The radar image enhances the electronic chart—allowing for increased situational awareness,* and it also permits you to concentrate all your navigational electronics into one display package.

Radar Overlay Equipment

Although most modern radar sets are capable of passing radar data to an ECS, not all ECS hardware and/or software can process and display radar information.

When you are ready to choose a system you will be faced with a number of different types. You must ask yourself if you want a dedicated unit that was designed and manufactured for a specific task, or a multi-taskable unit that will do many things well, but not perfectly. In other words, do you want an expert instrument, or a Jack-of-all-trades?

Remember that there are two basic elements in any electronic instrument; the sensor unit (radar scanner, sounder transducer, GPS sensor) and the display unit. Display units can be combined into one to reduce costs and space or they can be separate units, dedicated to particular functions. Most marine manufacturers offer both

types, or they will put together the type of equipment you desire from components.

At the heart of an Electronic Chart System is a powerful computer. It draws chart information from CDs, cartridges or other sources and position information from a GPS, and displays your vessel against the chart or map of the area. Some of the more sophisticated systems show charts in three dimensions, weather systems, and other information such as tides and currents.

If you intend to install one of these systems interfaced to a personal computer, be sure to meet or exceed the system requirements recommended for the software. If your computer is under-powered for the task, you will face slow response, inability to access charts, crashing software and a host of other problems. These systems require high levels of computing power—they perform extraordinarily complex tasks.

Radar Sensor and Computer

You can feed data directly from a radar scanner to many types of electronic chart displays. Probably the most common type of interface involves a radar scanner feeding data to an electronic chart system on a personal computer using a standard Windows environment.

Advantages:

◆ You can hook up a number of sensors to the same computer and then select the appropriate window to view the data you need at the time.

◆ Versatility. Normally you can view either the electronic chart or the radar image, or you can display them in separate windows, or you can overlay the radar image over the electronic chart.

◆ Low cost. You need not purchase a separate display for the radar data, so you avoid duplicating display functions.

Disadvantages:

- *All your eggs are in one basket. If your computer crashes, you have no radar and no electronic chart (and maybe no sounder either).*

- You can never view a full screen well without hiding another display. There are times when you need to view the radar image alone. When you do so you will not be able to view your charts.

- You must resist the temptation to use the navigation computer for other purposes. The more programs you run on a computer, the more prone it is to crashes, especially when you least expect it. This can be embarrassing at best, and disastrous at worst.

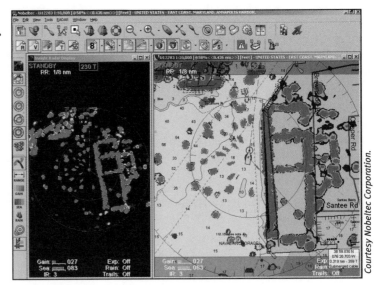

Courtesy Nobeltec Corporation.

▲ **Fig. 6-10**

Nobeltec Insight Radar Overlay

A Nobeltec radar overlay on electronic charts. Pure radar data is shown to the left. On the right, the same image is overlaid on the electronic chart. Note that the two windows are at different scales, yet on the right the chart and radar image appear at the same scale.

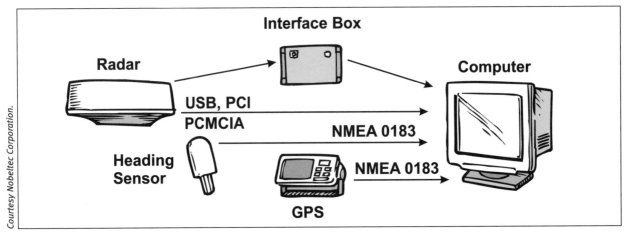

Courtesy Nobeltec Corporation.

▲ **Fig. 6-11**

A Nobeltec Radar Sensor / Personal Computer Combination.

Stand-Alone Radar and Computer

You may choose to install a dedicated radar scanner and display, then feed raw radar data from the radar to the electronic chart computer. This is one step away from the system described above, but it allows the use of a dependable, dedicated, stand-alone radar display in addition to the PC.

Advantages:

◆ Security. With this type of system you still have the capability of feeding raw sounder data to the computer and can open various windows dedicated to different sensors, but you have a dedicated stand-alone radar unit that is not subject to the vagaries of the computer's operating system.

◆ Versatility. You can still view the radar image on the computer in a window dedicated to the radar or as an overlay on the electronic chart.

◆ Dependability. The radar image is always available, uncluttered by chart images which may be crucial at times when you are engaged in short-range collision avoidance.

◆ Duplication. You may find it useful at times to run your dedicated radar in short range, head-up mode for collision avoidance and, at the same time, set the computer to a radar-only window, in North-up long range mode for navigation.

Disadvantages:

◆ Cost. You must purchase a separate dedicated display for the radar data.

◆ Space. You may have trouble finding a good location for two separate displays.

Proprietary Systems

Many manufacturers now sell radar/electronic chart plotter equipment that will display either the radar image alone or an electronic chart or both at the same time—in separate windows or as a radar overlay.

Photograph courtesy of Furuno USA

▲ **Fig. 6-12**
A Furuno NavNet Radar / Chart Plotter
This radar incorporates Navionics vector chart technology. The radar image (light grey) is superimposed over the vector chart to produce a truly integrated display.

Advantages:

◆ Security. This kind of system is designed for the job and does not incorporate a personal computer or a Windows operating system; the preliminary indications are that they are reliable and dependable.

I have used numerous stand-alone radar sets and most have been ultra-reliable, running for years with just an annual servicing. Manufacturers have intentionally made their sets durable for long service. Many radars sold in the 1970s and early 1980s are still in use. No personal computer can claim the same.

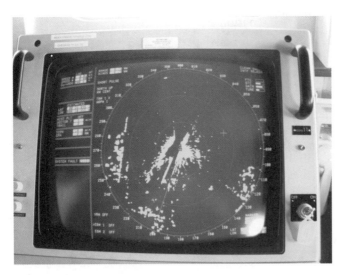 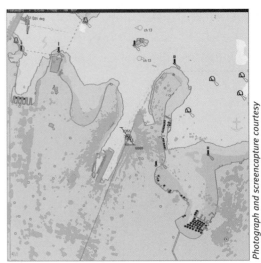

Photograph and screencapture courtesy of Offshore Systems Limited

▲ **Fig. 6-13**

Stand–alone Radar and ECDIS (Electronic Chart Display and Information System)

Left:A stand-alone radar which is the source of radar data for an Offshore Systems ECDIS.

Right: The ECDIS applies the radar image as an overlay to the electronic chart. Clearly, with the radar overlay, ECDIS provides a level of situational awareness that is impossible to obtain from either radar or ECDIS independently.

♦ Versatile, but not as versatile as a separate personal computer, which may actually be a good thing because these systems are designed specifically for the job they do. You cannot load them down with software.

Disadvantages:

♦ All your eggs are in one basket; though it is much less likely that you will have a problem.

♦ You can never view a full screen well without hiding another display. There are times when you need to view the radar image alone. When you do so you may not be able to view your charts.

Electronic Chart Display and Information Systems (ECDIS)

Small-vessel Electronic Charting Systems (ECS) are a perfect example of the trickle down of technology from "big ship" professional ECDIS systems. In the late 1980s, **Electronic Chart Display and Information Systems (ECDIS)** were first conceived and realized. From inauspicious beginnings as an initiative of private companies and hydrographic services, ECDIS has grown into a modern system with international standards, and national authorities are now committed to implementing it as a primary aid to navigation system for commercial shipping.

ECDIS is a "big ship" professional system, yet the inevitable trickle-down of this technology has propelled the development of the small-vessel electronics of today and foreshadows the technology of the future.

ECDIS utilizes Differential GPS, *powerful* processing capability, inputs from on-board sensors and instrumentation, highly sophisticated vector electronic charts, and radar overlay. ECDIS is also available with an ARPA option, thus truly integrating all navigation and collision avoidance technologies in one place.

Most professional mariners agree that ECDIS provides the ability to intuitively understand a wealth of information that, in a non-ECDIS environment, they must gather from a variety of sources. A mariner must make real-time decisions but, if he has to spend too much time collating information from different sources, his decisions are then based on old data that reflect his vessel's past history. While history is important, the present moment contains all the forces he must take into account. For the first time, ECDIS makes possible complex navigation decisions based on real-time information.

However, as the processing power of personal computers increases exponentially, ECDIS's lead on small vessel systems is decreasing all the time. Already there are small vessel EC systems that rival ECDIS for complexity and sophistication; some actually exceed the performance of ECDIS. While small-vessel navigation technologies have developed independently of international standards, ECDIS has been regulated internationally and thus has developed in a more deliberate manner.

Chapter Seven

Further Adventures in Navigation

The use of radar for navigation depends on radar-conspicuous targets—or any other fixed object that can return an echo. Without targets to range on, a radar will present an essentially blank display. In other words, radar is useful as a navigation tool only in the presence of land.

When approaching landfall, you must navigate by ranging on the highest coastal mountains, with correspondingly reduced accuracy. But as you approach the coast and more shoreline detail emerges, radar navigation becomes increasingly accurate and thus more useful. Radar achieves its greatest accuracy when targets are closest—precisely the time when you need it the most. Close to land, you will find that, with practice, you can resolve a position to within a few tens of meters.

All of the techniques in this chapter may be used in good as well as in poor visibility. If you want to become proficient in navigating with radar, you must practice and be willing to make mistakes. Obviously if you make mistakes, you must be able to fall back on visual navigation backups. *So, practice these techniques during good daylight visibility until you feel comfortable using them in more challenging circumstances.*

Fixing Position Using the Variable Range Marker (VRM)

The inherent accuracy of a range measurement made by the Variable Range Marker (VRM) far exceeds the accuracy of an Electronic Bearing Line (EBL) measurement. Therefore it makes far more sense to use radar ranges for position fixing whenever possible.

Range Scale	VRM accuracy *	EBL accuracy **
3.0 Nm	55 meters	200 to 400 meters
	(180 feet)	(650-1300 feet)
0.5 Nm	10 meters	30 to 60 meters
	(33 feet)	(100-200 feet)

*   A careful VRM measurement has an inherent error of less than 1% of the overall range scale.

**   The inherent accuracy of the EBL measurement is dictated by the beam-width distortion of your scanner (3° to 5°).

You can obtain a highly accurate position using just two VRM measurements of radar-conspicuous objects—but only under the following conditions:

♦ The reference points must be conspicuous, with very little foreshore.

• You must be able to identify the reference point precisely on the chart.

• The reference points must be as close to 90° apart as possible.

At times you may be forced to take a third range measurement from a less-than-ideal feature in order to reconcile the ambiguity of the intersection of two radar ranges. [**Fig. 2-14**] For example, from a relatively featureless shoreline without clear points or headlands, or one that has an extensive rocky foreshore. It can be difficult to figure out exactly where to set the point of your compass on the chart, resulting in a degree of uncertainty in the circle of position. The quality of a position fix is only as good as that of the poorest circle of position used. If you are dubious about one of the circles, use it only to resolve the ambiguity in the other two circles, and plot your position at the exact point where the other two circles intersect, instead of the middle of the "cocked hat". [See **Chapter 2**]

▲ **Fig. 7-1**
Review—Obtaining a Position by VRM

Fixing Position Using the EBL

Because of beam-width error, which shows up as a circumferential distortion, targets are "smeared" around the circumference of the display. Most small targets on the display appear to be wider than they are deep. Also, because they are distorted in width, but maintain the same distance from the center of the display, they appear slightly curved. This is a characteristic of all small targets, such as ships and small isolated rocks, especially on the outer third of the display.

Taking VRM Measurements

Often it is not possible to find three well-placed geographic features, in which case it is acceptable to measure from two; but a position derived from three radar-conspicuous targets situated approximately 60° apart will give you the most accurate results. If you lay out your task ahead of time, you can complete three VRM observations in very little time.

1. Identify the three points you intend to measure with the VRM.

2. Using a pencil, make a visible dot on the chart at the exact point you intend to measure with the VRM.

3. Quickly measure to each reference point; read the VRM, and write down the value beside the dot on the chart.

4. If you have crew available, ask them to write down the numbers as you read them off. With practice, you will be able to read and record three VRM measurements within 15 seconds.

5. Plot each range circle, using a compass centered on the dot.

Checking the accuracy of the VRM

Since your positioning is based on VRM measurements, it is important to know how accurate the VRM is. Any measurement includes a certain amount of inherent error. A VRM measurement is no different. You can easily find the exact amount of error and then apply a correction to any future VRM measurements you make.

Fig. 7-2 ▶
Measuring VRM Error Against a Known Distance

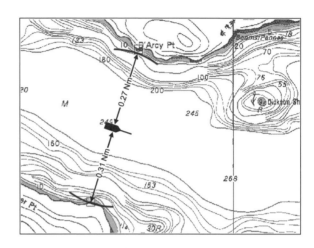

1. Find two points in a channel that are clearly defined and have very little foreshore.
2. Measure the charted distance using dividers. (*0.62 Nm*)
3. Place your vessel directly between the two points and select a range scale at which you can see the two points, toward the outer third of the display, if possible.(*0.5 Nm*)
4. Measure the distance to the two points using VRM.

    D' Arcy Pt.   0.27 Nm
    Opposite Pt. 0.31 Nm
    Total   **0.58 Nm**

5. Add the two VRM measurements and compare the total to the distance you have measured from the chart. The difference equals twice the VRM error.
6. In this case the difference is 0.04 Nm, so the radar VRM error is 0.02 Nm and the correction factor is +0.02 Nm at this range scale. **Note:** *If the VRM error is this low, you will not experience any problems.*
7. You must repeat the process on other range scales to obtain the correction factor for those range scales.

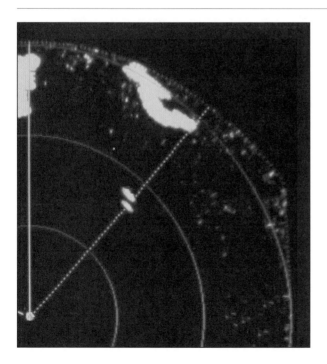

◀**Fig. 7-3**
Small Isolated Target
When taking a bearing from a small isolated target, place the EBL directly through the center of the target. In this case, it is likely that the target is a point target, and that the apparent width of the target is caused by beam-width distortion.

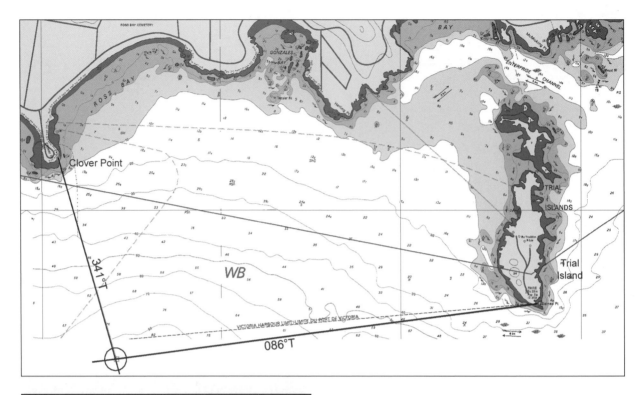

◄ ▲ Fig. 7-4
Obtaining a Position by EBL
Left
Heading of the vessel is 026°M
Magnetic Variation is 20°E
Relative bearing of Clover Point (east side) 295°T
Relative bearing of south tip of Trial Island 040°T

Above
Magnetic bearing to south end of Trial Island
    = Relative Bearing plus Magnetic Heading
    = 040°R + 026°M
    = 066°M
True Bearing to south end of Trial Island
    = Magnetic Bearing plus Easterly Variation
    = 066°M + 020°
    = 086°T
If you repeat the process for the bearing taken on Clover Point it will read 341°T.
When you plot these bearings on the chart, you will see the true position at "A".

Small isolated rocks and buoys and small boats will appear to be 2° to 5° wide, and larger targets will appear to be 2° to 5° wider than they actually are. The amount of distortion is directly related to the size of your antenna—larger antenna equals less distortion.

In order to obtain the best accuracy, you must take bearings only from clearly identifiable types of objects:

◆ When taking bearings of a small isolated object, such as a rock or a buoy, **set the EBL on the exact center of the target.**

◆ When taking a bearing off a larger target, take the bearing from just inside the edge of the tar-get (tangent bearing), do not just "kiss" the edge of the target; this will account for some of the error in the derived bearing.

◆ Avoid taking bearings of targets so far away that parts of them are below the horizon.

◆ Some objects might make good visual bearing targets (such as towers or flagpoles), but these will not appear conspicuously on the radar display.

◆ Decrease the gain or increase the "anti-Sea Clutter" control to reduce bearing distortion as much as possible.

When selecting objects from which to take bearings, you should also follow the same criteria you would use when choosing objects for visual bearings:

Radar Bearing Errors

Unstabilized Radar

In Head-up mode, beam-width distortion isn't the only cause of error in taking bearings. In addition you may find that the following conditions add to the inaccuracy of radar bearings:

◆ Yawing of the vessel while reading the bearing

◆ When you take the bearing from the radar, you must then read the compass heading. In that short moment, when you turn your attention from the radar to the compass, the compass heading may change by a signifi-cant number of degrees. This is especially true in rough weather. If you must take a radar bearing, have a crew member ready to read the compass heading at the same moment you read the radar bearing.

◆ Mistakes in arithmetic

When you read a "relative" bearing, you must still calculate the "magnetic" or "true" bearing by adding head-ing, variation and deviation. Even the most mathematically-inclined make mistakes, especially if the vessel is yawing due to the influence of weather.

Stabilized and Unstabilized Radars

In North-up mode you may not have to add the compass heading to the radar bearing yourself; the radar takes care of that and displays the bearings in degrees "Magnetic" or "True." However, there are other sources of error inherent to any radar bearing; do not let a North-up radar fool you into believing that its bearing read-outs are accurate just because they are automatic.

◆ Magnetic Variation

◆ If you have not entered the variation correctly, or if the radar's software does not accurately represent the variation, the final bearing read-out will be in error.

◆ Local magnetic disturbances

This is a problem for both stabilized or unstabilized radar.

◆ Unknown amounts of compass error will inevitably result in unknown amounts of bearing error.

• *Select targets that are as close to 90° apart as possible.*

• Avoid targets that are close to 180° apart.

• If you must select more than two targets, select three targets that are as close to 120° apart as possible.

Remember that unless your radar is in North-up or stabilized mode, the bearings shown are relative to your own vessel's heading. On your display, the bearings are identified by an "R" (for relative) after the readout. If your display is in North-up mode, the bearings will be either "M" for magnetic, or "T" for True. (You can set "T" or "M" bearings through one of the radar's setup menus.)

To reconcile "Relative" bearings to your compass:

• Add the current heading to the bearing.

• If the total is over 360°, subtract 360°.

• The bearing will now be referenced to your compass. If you have a magnetic compass, you must still compensate for magnetic variation before you plot the bearing on the chart.

When you plot the bearings on a chart, you will most likely end up with a "cocked hat". Since each bearing is likely to be in error about the same amount, you can assume the true position is in the center of the "cocked hat".

Fixing Position Using a Mixture of Ranges and Bearings
One range and one bearing

• The simplest description of location using the range and bearing of a single geographic feature (ie: Clover Point bearing 340°T at 0.68 Nm). In its simplest form, you might say "0.7 Nm SSE of Clover Point."

• Because it is based at least in part on a radar bearing, this form of position lacks accuracy.

• The true position is most likely on the range circle, but not necessarily on the bearing.

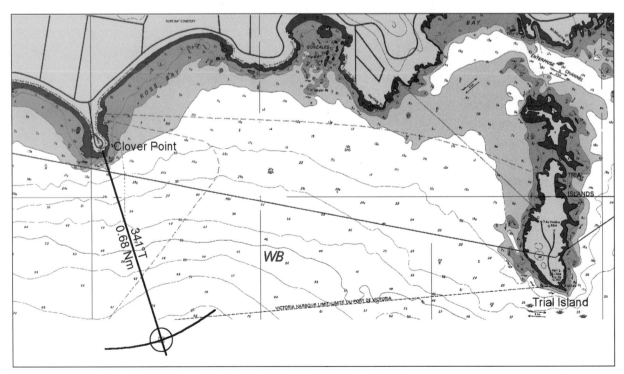

▲ **Fig. 7-5—One Range and One Bearing**

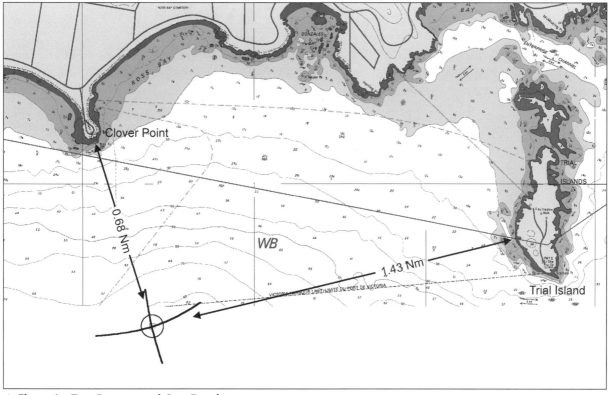

▲ **Fig. 7-6—Two Ranges and One Bearing**
Position derived from a range and bearing from Clover Point, and a range from the closest point of Trial Island.

Two ranges and one bearing

♦ Two ranges are adequate by themselves for fixing a position if they are between 60° and 120° apart.

♦ If the objects to which you have measured the range are more than 120° or less than 60° apart, a third range will provide greater accuracy than an additional bearing. In most cases, the bearing will be less accurate than either of the ranges.

♦ Sometimes an object is suitable for taking a bearing, but not a range, and vice versa. In **Fig. 7-7**, the south tip of Trial Island makes a suitable target for a bearing but not for measuring a range (distance). The closest point of Trial Island is suitable for taking a range, but not a bearing.

Radar Waypoint Display

My experience has shown that radar waypoint displays can be extremely useful. Imagine yourself in a narrow channel or under restricted visibility when you can become confused about the correct direction to follow on the next leg of a route. When properly set up, your radar will display the direction to steer and automatically switch to the next waypoint at the same time as the GPS Navigator. Since many vessels are now equipped with flux-gate compasses in order to run an autopilot, all it takes to set up the interface is a small amount of a technician's time and some wire!

One range and two bearings

Because the range is probably much more accurate than the bearings, you must assume that your true position is on the arc of the range circle, midway between the two bearing lines.

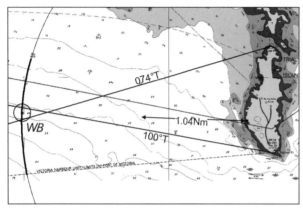

▲ **Fig. 7-7—One Range and Two Bearings**
When your radar targets are closely grouped, you can obtain a position from a single geographic feature, in this case, Trial Island. This position is derived from tangent bearings of the north and south ends and a range to the closest point of the island. You can depend on the range measured to the closest point of the island, but the bearings are likely to be in error. However, you can average the error of the two bearings by assuming your position is on the arc of the range measurement midway between the bearings.

Visual Bearings

Visual bearings mixed with radar ranges can add great value to a position. Especially if you are short of radar-conspicuous targets and the visual bearing is of a non-radar-conspicuous target such as a building ashore.

You can observe a transit any time two geographic features line up with your eye. When you observe two radar-conspicuous objects lining up, you have a "radar transit".

Mixing Sounder and Sonar Information

When you take a range or a bearing of an object you are actually establishing a line of position (LOP) or a circle of position (COP). In general, all you need to determine a position is the crossing of two lines (or circles) of position, provided they do not cross at too acute an angle.

You can use a regular depth contour as a line of position too, provided that it is fairly straight, and the bottom slopes regularly.

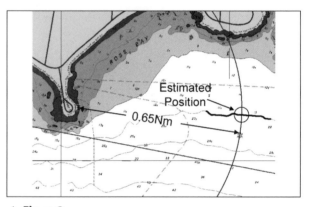

▲ **Fig. 7-8**
Using a Depth Contour as a Line of Position.
Before plotting the depth as a line of position, remember to compensate for the height of the tide. In this case, the actual sounder reading was 22 meters, but the tide level was a little more than 2 meters, so you must compensate for the height of the tide by subtracting 2 meters from the reading.

The range to Clover Point is 0.65 Nm and the corrected depth is 20 meters. Since the depth contours are regular, indicating a smooth slope to the south, the 20-meter depth contour makes an excellent line of position.

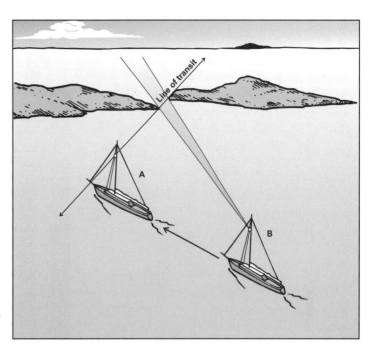

Fig. 7-9 ▶
The Moment of Transit
If you steer across a line of transit, beginning with the two objects "open" (Position B) and continuing until they are closed (Position A), you will observe the precise moment of transit. Learn to identify the moment of transit on the radar by recognizing the appearance of the display at the same time as you visually confirm the transit.

▲ Fig. 7-10 ▶
Two Islands in Transit
These two islands are in transit. Note that the EBL is "cut into the shore" on both islands.

Using the EBL to Observe Transits

There will always be a residual, unknown amount of error in any radar bearing. However, you can also use your EBL to observe transits of fixed geographic features. A transit occurs any time two recognizable geographic features line up with your radar or your eye. On a chart, only one line can connect two specific features. So if you observe a transit by radar, you must be on the line of transit—or at least reasonably near it

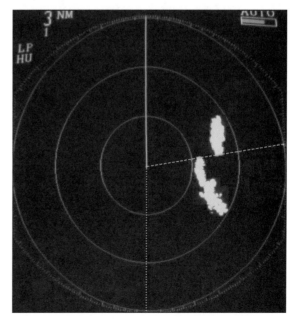

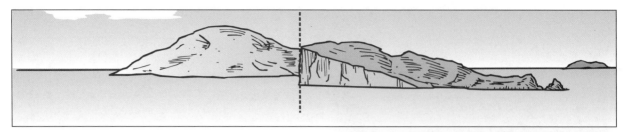

▲ **Fig. 7-11** ▶

Two Islands not in Transit

These two islands may appear to be in transit on the radar, but they are not. The island in the background is partly in the radar shadow of the nearer island.

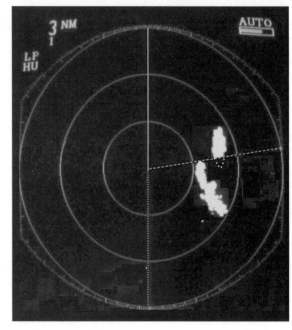

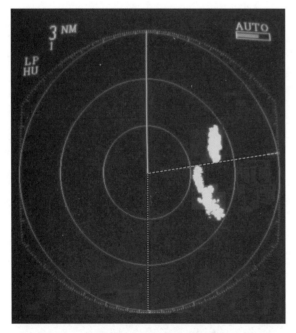

◀ **Fig. 7-12**

Two Islands in Pseudo-Transit

These two islands are not in transit—they are "open." However, on radar, beam-width distortion makes them appear to be in transit. When using transits on radar you must take into account the "pseudo-transit" effect.

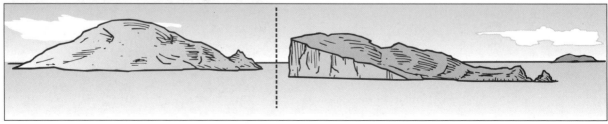

Fig. 7-13 ▶

Transits—Checking Your Compass

Because a transit is a line of position derived without reference to a compass, you can easily check your vessel's compass error by comparing it to the direction of the line of transit by:

- Measuring the direction of the transit line off the chart.
- Steering directly towards the transit, ensuring that the two points stay in line, or
- Observing the compass bearing of the transit. (This is possible only if you have a pelorus or an accurate azimuth ring on the compass.)
- Comparing the compass reading to the direction of transit. The difference is your compass error for that heading.

Direction of transit = 045°T less variation 22° E = 023°M

Compass reads 020°

Therefore the compass reads 3° too low on this heading. (Deviation = 3° East)

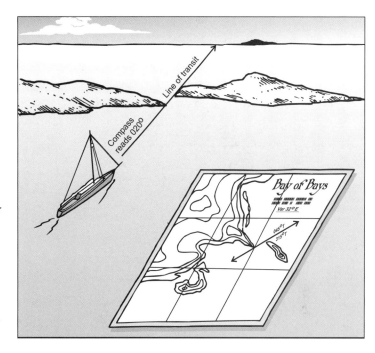

(given the inherent beam-width error). You can use your EBL to observe these radar transits.

- In practice, a radar transit has less accuracy than a visual transit—in other words you can identify the moment of transit more accurately with your naked eye than you can with a radar's EBL. At night or in fog, though, you will find radar transits to be extremely useful.

- A radar transit is likely to be far more accurate than a bearing taken from the same radar, because the compass does not enter into the calculation.

- A transit taken from two small isolated rocks is

Consider all piloting to be "Blind Piloting"— night or day—and verify every landmark by eye.

likely to be more accurate than one taken from two tangent shorelines—for the same reason isolated rocks make better targets for taking radar bearings.

- You can compensate for the error inherent in tangent bearings of a shoreline, by "cutting into the shore" with the EBL. You must practice, comparing visual transits to radar transits to learn how much to "cut into the shore." This practice with transits will help you take more accurate radar bearings as well.

- When two points are on opposite sides of the EBL, beam-width distortion may produce the appearance of a transit where there is none, or two shorelines may appear to be in transit even though one point obscures the other.

Navigation and Piloting

Navigation is the art of finding out where you are and how to get to where you are going. **Piloting** is the art of staying on course and monitoring your progress along your intended track in situations where it is impractical to fix your position every few minutes by traditional means.

Blind Piloting is the art of staying on your intended track, relying only on your instruments. The track you choose to follow when blind pilot-ing may be significantly different from the track you would follow in good visibility. If you want to learn the art of blind piloting, you should always follow the "blind pilotage" track— restricted visibility or not. In this way you will be

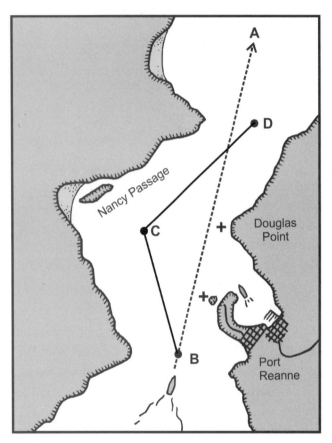

◄ **Fig. 7-14**
Mid-Channel Fever
When the skipper says "Steer a mid-channel course", the natural tendency for an inexperienced helmsman is to steer for point A, which appears to be correct. A glance at the chart, however, shows that this heading will place the vessel perilously close to the rock off Douglass Point. Also, the helmsman may suddenly encounter another vessel at close range departing Port Reanne.

Using the radar, the helmsman can steer a course from B to C to D—a truly mid-channel course.

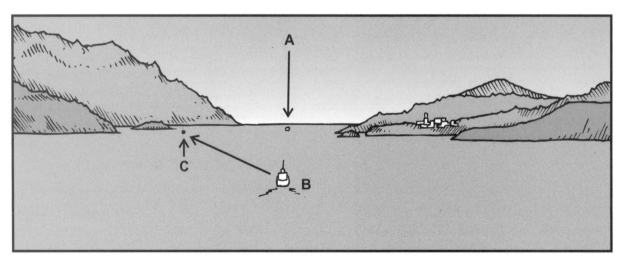

Fig. 7-15 ▶

The Hooked Course Line

At 1200 hrs you depart Chest Island, in Smith Sound, British Columbia, headed for the channel between False Egg Island and Tie Island. By 1206 your vessel has already been set off course by a 3-Knot current ebbing out of Smith Sound. Even though you continuously compensate by steering for the channel, by 1212 hrs you are the wrong side of Wood Rock, and in just a couple more minutes, you will run aground on Edward Rock. Obviously just steering for the channel is not good enough. You must monitor your progress along the intended track and, as soon as you notice that you are being set to the west, you must overcompensate for the current and recover the intended track. Otherwise, you risk running aground on Wood Rock or Edward Rock.

If you steer using a GPS, the cross track error (XTE) function should alert you to this kind of danger.

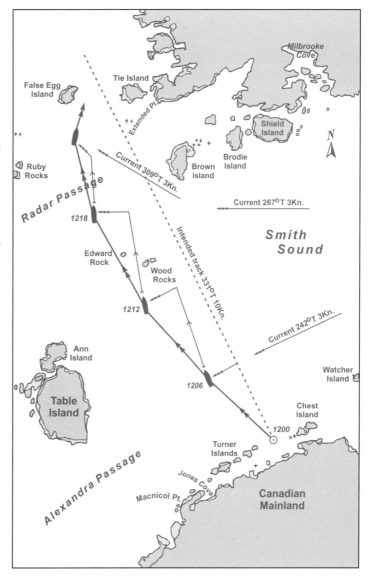

Practice and Consistency

Practice is a very powerful tool for building your skills. But if you behave differently while practicing than you would during the real event, you may build some dangerous habits.

There is an apocryphal story about a police officer who learned to take a firearm away from an assailant faster than the assailant could react and fire. This officer spent countless hours practicing disarming his wife until, indeed, he could actually wrest the gun from her grip faster than she could pull the trigger. He would then return the weapon to her and practice again.

One day, while on the job, he was confronted by an armed robber, so he put his new skill to work. In a blur of action, he grabbed the gun and removed it from the assailant's grasp, long before the robber had time to react. But the officer's training didn't stop here. He had practiced grabbing the gun from his wife and returning it to her so many times, that now he was responding automatically, he did the same, and returned the gun to the robber—who promptly shot him dead.

Moral: If you practice blind pilotage only occasionally and revert to navigating by eye at all other times, when you are under stress you will revert to the principles of eyeball navigation, even if it isn't appropriate to do so.

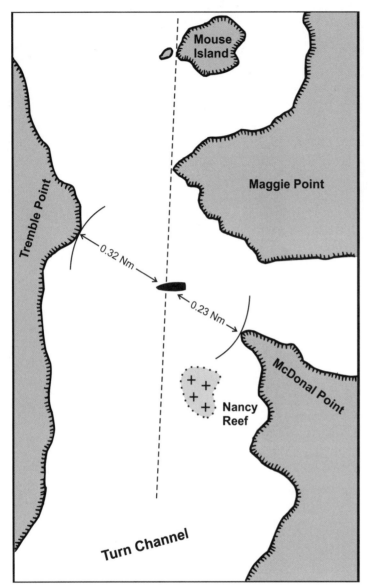

◄ Fig. 7-16
To Determine When to Turn
Using a Transit
As soon as Mouse Island appears beyond Maggie Point, it is safe to turn south into Turn Channel. Do not attempt to turn earlier—you may run aground on Nancy Reef. You will have some warning of Maggie Point's appearance because you will first see the small rock to the west of the island. In this case, you can identify the moment of transit by the appearance of Mouse Island beyond Maggie Point.

Using VRM
You may also use the VRM to determine when it is safe to turn. The distance from the transit to Tremble Point is 0.32 Nm. Set your VRM to 0.32 Nm and do not turn south until the image of Tremble Point on your radar display moves within the VRM circle. Or, alternatively, set your VRM to 0.23 Nm and do not turn south until McDonal Point emerges from the VRM circle.

Fig. 7-18 ►
Maximum Safe Distance Off
Left: You can also use a clearing range to define a *maximum* safe distance offshore. Here, you should not pass more than 0.27 Nm off the point.
Right: On the head-up radar display, you can tell that on the present heading, you will pass less than 0.25 Nm off the point. Imagine a line drawn forward from the outer edge of the 0.25 Nm range ring extending forward. If the image of the point tracks down the display along the imaginary line parallel to the heading marker, you are maintaining the correct track.

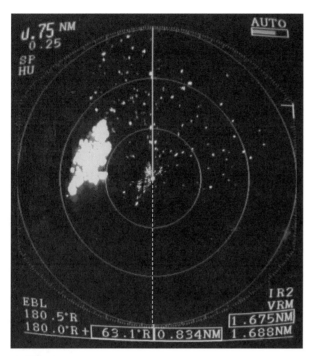 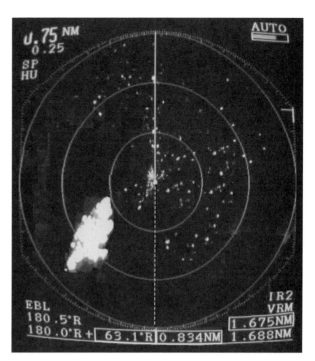

▲ **Fig. 7-17**
Maintaining Distance Off

If you can draw an arc around an identifiable point on the chart, you can define a ***clearing range***—within which distance it is not safe to approach the shoreline. Here, numerous submerged rocks and kelp patches require you to pass at least 0.25 Nm offshore. Since 0.25 Nm is one of the fixed range rings, you do not even need to use the VRM. Simply steer so as to ensure that the image of the land does not enter the 0.25 Nm range circle.

You can use this same technique to safely round a point where there is an offlying danger.

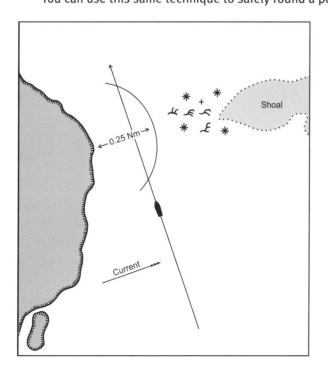 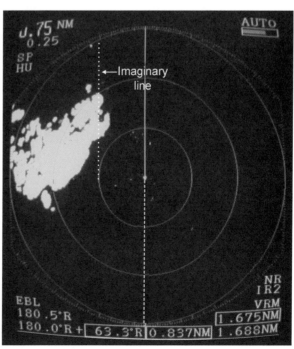

ready at any time for sudden fog, or the onset of night.

Using radar you can ensure that not only are you on the right heading, but also that you are following your intended track. In open water, or in wide channels with no dangers, this is not normally a problem, but when you must follow an unmarked channel, or when you must stay away from shoal areas, this becomes very important.

You may be tempted to steer toward an object ahead, but if you fail to account for tidal currents, wind and waves, or if your steering is just plain sloppy, you may find that these forces move your vessel bodily off its intended track. Even though you may still be headed toward the chosen object, you may actually be straying into danger. [See **Fig. 7-15**]

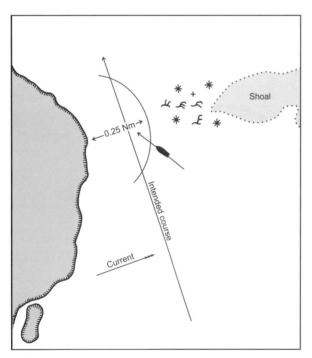 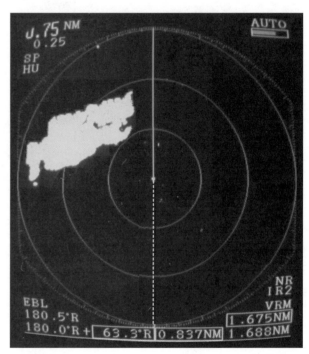

▲ **Fig. 7-19**
The Effect of Current
Left: However, if there is a current setting you to the east, you may end up in this situation.
Right: On the head-up radar display, things do not look much different than they did previously, but you are perilously close to the rocks and shoals. The problem is that you have only one reference point to work with.

Chapter Eight

Further Adventures in Blind Piloting

Parallel Indexing

If you are not subject to any lateral drift at all, simply steering to a specific compass course is all you need to do to follow your intended track. But when an outside force such as tidal current, wind, or waves, forces your vessel off its intended track, simply steering to a compass heading is not good enough.

As shown in Chapter 7, you can very closely estimate a compass direction by the use of transits. If you steer along a transit, you can stay on course without even referring to your compass. You can also follow a transit that is offset from your intended track—a technique known as parallel indexing.

However you establish the parallel index line, its purpose is to help you steer so that the images of selected geographic features move astern along

---

Using an Offset EBL

If you look back to **Fig. 7-18,** you will see that instead of just imagining a line drawn forward on the display, it would be useful if you could actually draw a line on the display, parallel to the heading mark, but offset by an appropriate distance.

Indeed it is possible to do so. Most modern raster scan radars are equipped with an "offset EBL"—that is an EBL whose origin can be offset to any point on the display by manipulating a cursor. When parallel indexing, set the cursor directly to port or starboard the exact distance the reference point (or transit) is offset from your safe course-line. Then all you have to do is rotate the EBL until it faces directly forward (or aft).

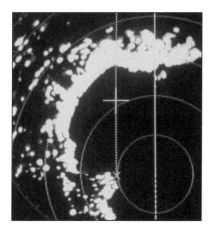

◄ **Fig. 8-1**
Using an Offset EBL
Most radars allow you to move the origin of at least one of the EBLs to any location on the display. This means you can set a line parallel to the heading marker, and then steer so the reference point appears to move along the EBL, until it is past and clear.

a track that is exactly parallel to the heading marker but offset by a specific distance.

Setting up an Offset Transit [Fig. 8-3]

When setting up an offset transit, you must first establish the reference lines on your chart.

♦ Establish a preliminary course line on your chart. Verify that it is clear of dangers.

♦ Find a transit of two radar-conspicuous points that is roughly parallel to this line.

♦ Draw a line connecting the two reference points and extend it a distance beyond.

You may feel that you do not need to learn blind pilotage because you have an Electronic Chart System (and possibly an autopilot) which should ensure you follow your intended track. But when your computer crashes, freezes, or commits an "illegal operation" you will be glad you learned how to parallel index by radar.

Parallel Index Cursor

Some radars are equipped with a *parallel index cursor*—a series of parallel lines on the display; you can rotate the lines through 360° and can move them closer together or farther apart. Other radars are equipped with an offset EBL which can serve the same purpose. [See **Sidebar** on the previous page.] In older radar equipment, you may instead find a series of parallel lines printed on a clear, rotating cover over the display.

If your radar is not equipped with a parallel index cursor or an offset EBL, you can create the same effect by taping a sheet of clear acetate film over the display and using a dry-erase marker to establish a series of lines parallel to the heading marker.

Screencapture Courtesy of Furuno Electric Company

◄ **Fig. 8-2**
Parallel Index Cursor
In this radar display, the parallel index cursor is set at 191.4°M and 0.175 Nm. Once the parallel index cursor is engaged, it is controlled by the secondary EBL and VRM controls. Note that the secondary EBL and VRM readouts now indicate the parallel index cursor bearing and range/distance apart.

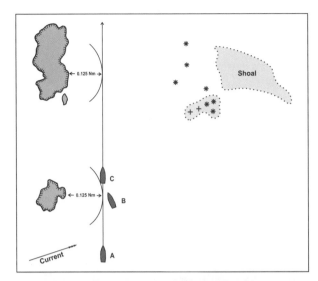

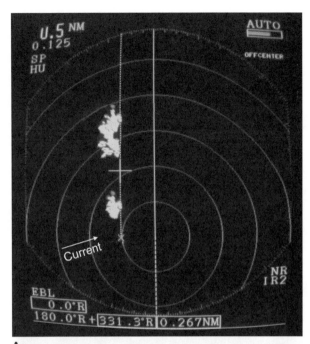

A

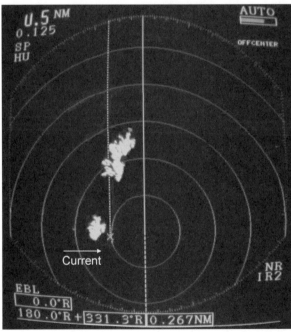

B

▲ Fig. 8-3
Offset Transits

Set your intended track parallel to a transit of two geographic features on the chart. Here you have chosen a track that is displaced 0.125 Nm from the transit formed by the two islands. As long as you steer so that both points remain on the offset EBL, you will inevitably be on the intended track. (A)

If a strong current takes you off course and you have to alter course to counteract the current, the two islands will rotate off the EBL. However, you will

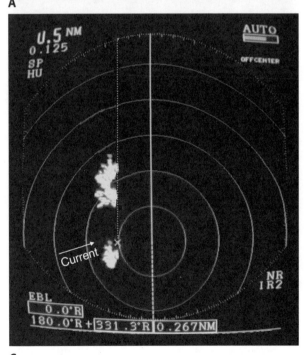

C

instantly recognize what has happened, because the transit of the two islands will no longer be parallel to the offset EBL. (B) All you have to do is bring your vessel back onto the offset transit and continue along your intended track. On the radar display the two islands will rotate back onto the offset EBL. (C) This process is known as **Parallel Indexing.**

- Measure the distance from one of the reference points to the course line, then using a compass draw a range circle around the reference point with a radius equal to the distance from the reference point to the course line.

- Draw another range circle (the same radius) around the second reference point.

- Draw a line on the chart tangent to the two range circles. This is your new course line.

- Double check to ensure the course line is clear of dangers.

- Set-up a parallel index line on your radar that is offset from the center of the display by a distance precisely equal to the radius of the range circles you have plotted on the chart. If you are using an offset EBL, make sure it is pointing to 0° or 180° depending on whether the reference point is ahead or astern.

▲ **Fig. 8-4**
Using an Offset Transit Astern
As long as you stay on the same heading, you can parallel index on a single point. However, it is always safer to track two points in transit. In this case, the vessel is Parallel Indexing on a single feature at a lateral displacement slightly less than 1/8 Nm. [See **Fig. 8-3**]

Using a Manual Parallel Index

When you are using a mechanical parallel index, either the manual cursor that is supplied with an older analog set, or even a dry erase marker on acetate film, the marks you have made will be valid only if you do not change range scales. When you switch to a lower range scale, the mechanical parallel index remains the same physical distance from the center of the display but, on the lower scale, this distance represents a shorter range than it did originally. Never change range scales when parallel indexing with a mechanical or manual cursor, unless you have prepared a new parallel index cursor at the correct distance from the center of the display for the new range scale.

Parallel Indexing—North-Up

To ensure that you remain on track you must track the movement of two reference points tangent to a parallel index line. As shown in **Fig. 7-19**, using a single reference point will still allow you to drift off course and into danger, unless you also maintain the compass heading. This is virtually impossible when you are trying to counteract a current.

However if your radar is in North-up mode, Parallel Indexing becomes much simpler.

In fact, in North-up mode it isn't necessary to use two reference points. Since the radar continues to be oriented toward North, you won't require a second reference point to form a transit. All you will need is a single point of reference. ***Whenever possible use North-up when parallel indexing!***

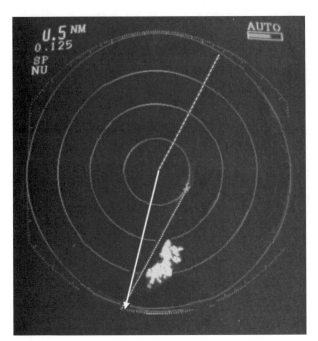

▲ **Fig. 8-5**
Parallel Indexing on a Single Point with an Offset EBL—North-Up
In North-up mode, you need only a single reference point to establish a parallel index. Here the reference point has drifted off the parallel index, and you have turned to port to bring your vessel back on track.

Setting up a Parallel Index

When setting up a parallel index, you must first establish the reference lines on your chart.
In North-up mode:

♦ Establish the safe course-line on your chart. Ensure it is clear of dangers. Using parallel rules, identify the heading you must follow when on the course line.

♦ Identify a radar-conspicuous reference point in the area. Do not use a buoy for this purpose unless you have verified its position.

♦ Measure the distance from the reference point to the course line.

♦ Set your VRM to this distance.

♦ Set the cursor to a point that is on the VRM, perpendicular to the intended heading.

♦ Offset the EBL to this point. Then rotate the EBL until it is pointing in the direction of the heading you must follow.

Note: *You can plot a number of Parallel Indices on your chart in advance, so that all you have to do is set the offset EBL to the correct position prior to starting a new course line. This will permit you to set up most of your work in advance for a track with numerous legs.*

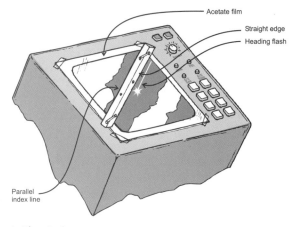

▲ **Fig. 8-6**
Setting up a Manual Parallel Index

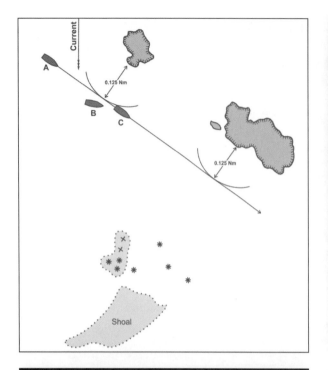

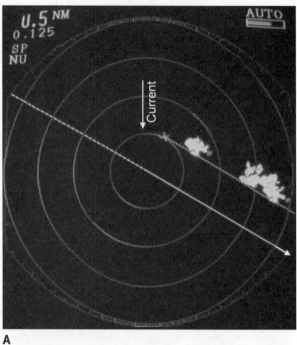

A

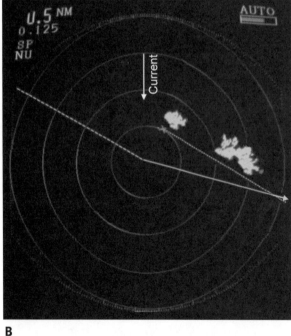

B

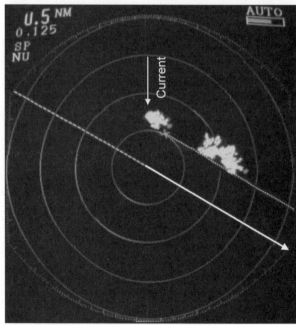

C

▲ **Fig. 8-7**
Parallel Indexing — North-Up
In a North-up display of the same situation as Fig. 8-3, the radar image is referenced to compass directions, not to your ship's heading. As a result the display does not rotate as you change course; your heading marker does. (B) And therefore you can see instantly that the features chosen as parallel index reference points have drifted laterally away from the index line. By altering course and heading back toward the islands you can bring them back onto the parallel index, thus easily maintaining your intended track. (C)

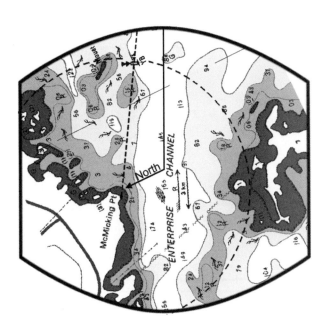

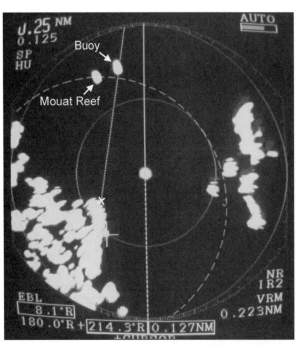

▲ Fig. 8-8
Verifying the Position of a Buoy—With Offset EBL and VRM
On the chart, the distance from McMicking Point to the South Cardinal buoy at Mouat Reef is 0.23 Nm at 123°T.

By radar the buoy bears 008°R at 0.223 Nm. Your vessel's heading is 095°M, plus 20° for variation equals 115°T. Thus the bearing is 123°. Since the range and bearing from the chart and the radar agree, the buoy must be in its charted position.

Verifying the Position of a Buoy

When you offset the origin of the EBL, the associated VRM is also offset. This means that you can take a range and bearing from any point on the display to any other point. Normally only one of the EBL/VRM pairs can be offset. But this is plenty to allow you to verify the position of a buoy, for instance. On your chart, simply measure the range and bearing from a radar-conspicuous point to the buoy and compare that range and bearing to the corresponding distance on your radar display.

If you are in Head-up mode you must correct the radar bearing to account for the your vessel's heading at the time.

Verifying the Position of a Buoy— Without Offset EBL

Without an offset EBL, you can still obtain a rough idea whether a buoy is in position by simply measuring the distance on the display between a point of land and the buoy using a pair of dividers. Then set one point of the dividers on the sweep origin and measure the distance to the other point of the dividers using the VRM.

It is not quite so easy to measure the bearing, so for all practical purposes you should depend on the VRM measurement. If the two distances are a reasonable match, you can assume the buoy is probably in position.

If your vessel is equipped with ECS and radar overlay, it is immediately apparent when a buoy is out of position. [See **Fig. 8-19**]

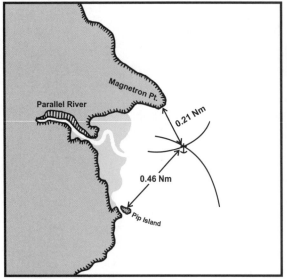
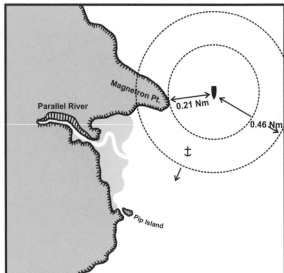
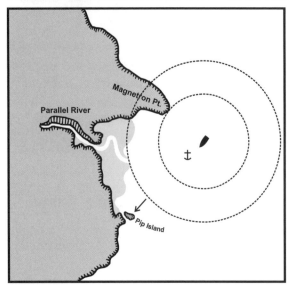
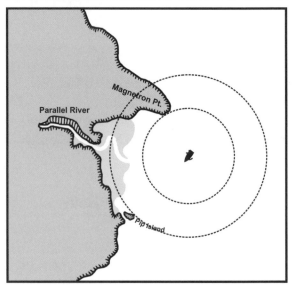

▲ Fig. 8-9
Using Ranges to Indicate When to Anchor

Just off the mouth of the Parallel River there is a small anchorage, surrounded by steep drop-offs and shoal water. You must anchor in exactly the right place, which you have marked with an anchor symbol on the chart.

◆ First, measure the distance from the anchorage to two radar-conspicuous points on the chart. These points should be as close to 90° apart as possible.

> Magnetron Point - 0.21 Nm
> Pip Islet   - 0.46 Nm

◆ Set your VRMs to these distances, then approach Magnetron Point.

◆ Once the 0.21 Nm VRM touches Magnetron Point, turn toward Parallel River, maintaining your distance off by keeping the image of Magnetron Point at exactly 0.21 Nm.

◆ As the 0.46 Nm VRM approaches the image of Pip Islet on the display, slow down and prepare to anchor.

◆ When the 0.46 Nm VRM touches Pip Islet, stop your vessel. Verify that you are still 0.21 Nm away from Magnetron Point and, if so, drop your anchor. You will be in exactly the correct location.

You can use this technique to bring your vessel to any specific location, such as a pinnacle well known for fishing, or to recover a lost anchor, etc.

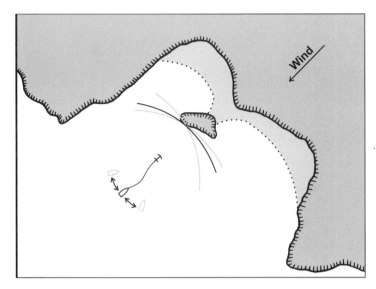

Anchoring

You can use your VRM to identify when to anchor. [See **Fig. 8-9**] The VRM can also help you perform an anchor watch [See **Fig. 8-10**] or help you anchor in a busy anchorage without fouling other vessels or their ground tackle. [See **Fig. 8-11**]

◄ **Fig. 8-10**
Anchor Watch

With the wind out of the northeast, your vessel lies to the southwest of its anchor. Ahead is a radar-conspicuous target—a small islet; so set the VRM to just touch the islet.

Under the influence of the wind, your vessel "horses" back and forth and, as the anchor rode lifts off the bottom and stretches, your vessel falls back and springs forward again. The VRM will also move in relation to the image of the islet on the display, but your vessel will always swing back to the same position, and the VRM will always return to the image of the islet.

If the VRM moves away from the image of the islet and does not return, you will know that the anchor has dragged.

You must reset the VRM if the wind shifts, or if the current turns, and your vessel lies at a different angle to the wind.

Fig. 8-11 ▶
Anchoring

Set your VRM to the distance of anchor rode you expect to use in this anchorage, taking into account the expected weather and the depth of water. Then find a "hole" in the mass of anchored vessels large enough for your VRM. By ensuring that the VRM circle is clear of other vessels and that you have adequate room to leeward, you can anchor with ease and yet be certain you do not collide with other vessels during the night. When the wind changes direction, all vessels should have room to swing.

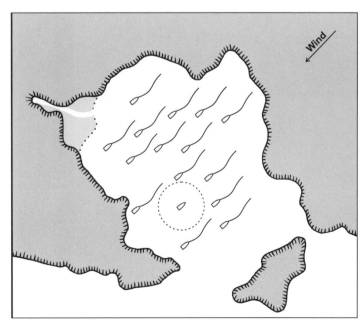

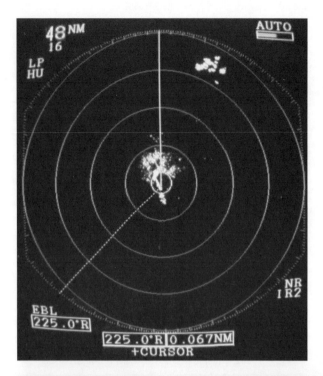

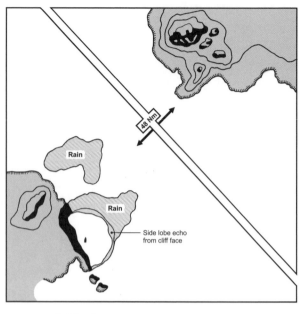

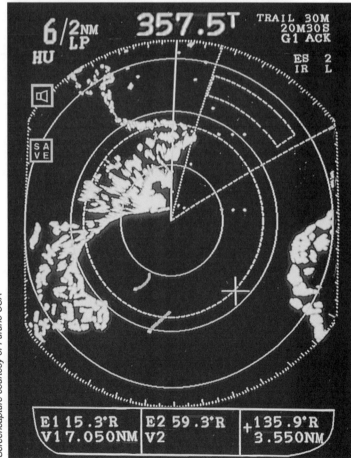

▲ **Fig. 8-12**
Long Range Detection
On 48 Nm range scale, only the tops of the hills on a distant island are visible to a scanner mounted 12 feet above the water. At this range scale, the radar utilizes a long pulse and boosts the power. Since the "anti-Sea Clutter" control is turned up, sea returns in the first three nautical miles are suppressed. But a nearby cliff stimulates a ring of side lobe echo, and local rain clutter appears beyond.

When you make a landfall, you will see the tops of the highest mountains first. Yet it is difficult to determine the precise location of the mountain peak on radar. As you approach the coastline, more detail emerges until, within a few miles of the coast, most shoreline features are visible.

◄ **Fig. 8-13**
Guard Zone
A guard zone has been defined ahead and to starboard of the heading flash. Any echo that appears within the guard zone will set off an alarm.

Approaching a Narrow Entrance

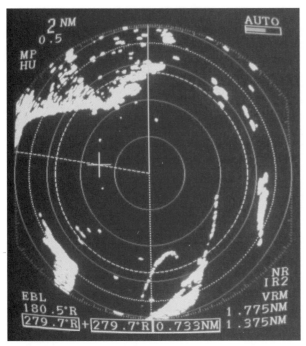 

▲ **Fig. 8-14**

Approaching a Narrow Entrance

On 2 Nm range scale, the breakwater entrance at Port Sidney is virtually invisible due to beam-width distortion. You must continue ahead, knowing only that you are headed in approximately the right direction. As you get closer and reduce the range scale, the breakwater entrance becomes visible. At 0.5 Nm range scale you can see the buoy off the breakwater, just off the starboard bow. You can also see a small vessel exiting the marina.

If you are not sure where the entrance is as you look at the display, you should intentionally steer to one side of the marina or the other. In this case you must steer to the left (south) of the marina entrance because of a rock just east of the buoy. When you approach the shore, you will know that the breakwater entrance is to the north. Then simply run parallel to the shore until you can clearly identify the breakwater entrance.

Guard Zones

Most modern radars have the capability to establish a Guard Zone. Using the EBL and VRM, you can define the limits of a Guard Zone; any target that enters the zone will set off an alarm. This may be useful when tracking other targets in a collision avoidance situation, or when making a landfall.

For the purpose of maintaining an automated anchor watch, you can even set up a zone that completely circles your own vessel. When *any* target (including land echoes) enters the Guard Zone, the alarm will sound. The theory is that the land image will enter the Guard Zone only when the anchor actually drags.

Any reasonably reflective target entering the Guard Zone will set off the alarm (whether it is a seagull, or simple sea clutter) and, consequently, you may be tempted to increase the "anti-Sea Clutter" control. But be aware that if you set it too high, you may mask the echoes of other ves-

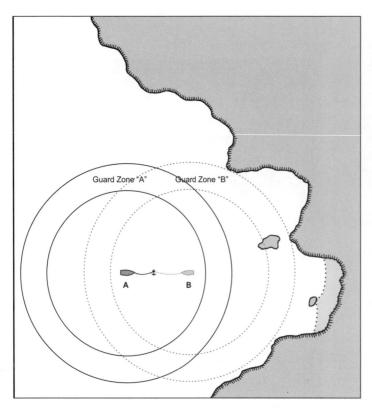

◀ **Fig. 8-15**
Using a Guard Zone for Anchor Watch
Unlike a GPS Guard Zone, which is based on a geographic position, a radar guard zone remains centered on the position of your vessel at the time. With the wind out of the east, a vessel has established a circular guard zone centered on position A. However, when the wind veers to the west, the vessel swings to the opposite side of the anchor and settles down at position B. When it does so, the land echoes now enter the guard zone, setting off the alarm.

When establishing a radar guard zone, be sure to take into account the distance the vessel will swing on the anchor.

sels and small isolated rocks. If you set the "anti-Sea Clutter" control too low when using the Guard Zone for anchor watch, you may find yourself suffering from a lack of sleep.

The Use of Radar Overlay in Navigation and Piloting

If you are considering a radar overlay system, keep one thing in mind: *the combination of radar imagery and electronic chart systems (ECS) enhances the electronic chart, but the electronic chart may not enhance the radar image.* Adding the radar image to the chart allows a more intuitive assessment of the navigational issues and helps to identify other vessels and transient targets. But adding the chart imagery to a radar display may simply obscure some of the very targets you most need to be able to see, such as weak echoes from small boats buried in the sea clutter at close range.

You will *always* have a need for an unobstructed radar image—especially in collision avoidance situations. So, if you do not have a dedicated radar display, be sure that you can

One of the greatest benefits of combining radar imagery with electronic charts in confined waters is a significantly increased confidence level in ownship position. Since radar information and ship's position come from different sources, it is difficult to imagine a close correlation of the two sets of information unless they truly represent the actual position of ownship.
Helmut Lanziner,
Xenex Navigation Inc.

quickly switch back to a window that shows only radar imagery. If you must, set up a special window for precisely that purpose.

If your vessel is equipped with this technology, you won't need to use some of the other techniques in this book, such as parallel indexing, because you will be able to track the movements of your vessel directly on the chart. However, if your computer crashes, freezes, or simply throws a tantrum, you will need to revert to basic navigational skills again; *so do not throw out your paper charts and parallel rules yet.*

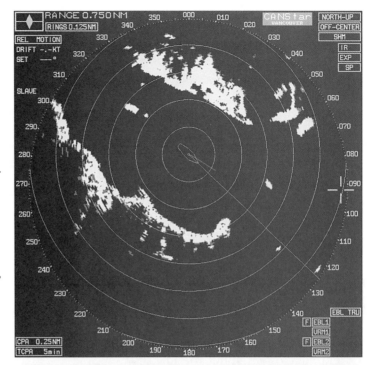

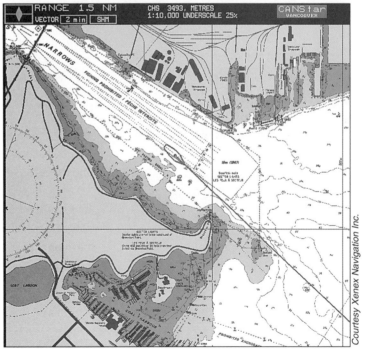

Fig. 8-16 ▶
Radar and Charted Shorelines
Top
In Vancouver Harbour, the radar image shows a well-defined shoreline and three unidentified targets ahead. The radar also shows what is probably a tug towing a barge astern.

Bottom
The ECS shows the vessel's position in relation to shoal waters that should be avoided and provides an understanding of the position of the vessel in relation to other geographic features, but it does not show other traffic.

Situational Awareness

You will find that a radar overlay on electronic charts is an excellent tool for helping you develop "situational awareness"—the ability to see the "big picture"—instead of a small part of the situation revealed by each individual electronic sensor. It simplifies your task when navigating, especially in difficult conditions, by presenting all the information you need in the same place, so you do not have to move your attention continuously back and forth between the radar to the chart.

When operating with radar only, you are forced to rely on your ability to interpret the radar picture and to come to rapid conclusions about the identity of various target echoes. The radar/ECS integrated display helps you navigate by relieving you of the need to interpret the radar image; it also helps you to differentiate between fixed nav-aids and buoys and other vessels.

The integrated radar/ECS thus gives a great advantage to less-experienced boaters; but you shouldn't let the radar overlay lull you into a state of complacency. Even though the computer relieves you of a large amount of the

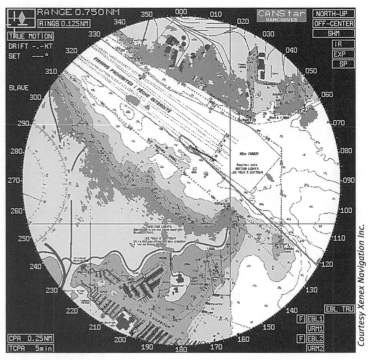

▲ **Fig. 8-17**
Xenex Radar Overlay

When the two displays are combined, you can find all the relevant information in one location, adding to your understanding of the "big picture":

◆ You can tell at a glance that the GPS positioning on the chart is accurate. If it were not, radar images would be offset from the targets they represent.

◆ You can identify radar targets and immediately understand their relationship to the chart.

◆ You can immediately differentiate between charted objects and transient targets such as other vessels. In this case the target just to starboard of the heading flash is a fixed aid to navigation, while the other two small targets are probably small craft. The large target ahead and to port is a ship coming alongside or departing the Fibreco Wharf.

Officers who routinely operate ECDIS (the "big ship" standard for electronic charting) without a radar overlay in reduced visibility conditions have expressed serious concerns about the fact that the ship's radar sometimes does not get the attention it should, due to the fact that they are concentrating on the ECDIS display during difficult maneuvers in shoal waters.

Helmut Lanziner, Xenex Navigation Inc

work of navigation, you must still manage the navigation system to ensure safety. For instance, you will still need to:

- Regularly switch to long range to scan for approaching vessels.

- Manage sea clutter and rain clutter levels to ensure you are aware of all small targets in the area.

- Systematically observe the behaviour of other vessels for collision avoidance purposes.

- Ensure you are following the safest track.

- Monitor the match of the radar image to the charted shorelines to ensure that the integrated system is behaving properly.

Remember: *These systems can fail. And being new and innovative systems, they will fail in new and innovative ways.* Use the integrated radar/ECS to increase your situational awareness of the "big picture," but never forget that it is an "aid" to navigation and should not be treated as a sole source of navigation information.

Offset Radar Images

It may happen from time to time that the radar imagery and the chart image do not line up properly. This may be caused by:

◆ The characteristics of the actual shoreline

For example, changes in the height of tide, mud beaches that do not reflect radar energy, shore ice that creates a false shoreline on the display, etc.

[See **Sidebar**]

◆ An error in the GPS positioning

If this is the case, it is most likely a transient phenomenon. Simply observe the display for several minutes and the images should coincide again. However, if the problem persists, it may be due to a faulty GPS antenna connection or interference from metallic objects or radio sources in the vicinity. [See **Chapter 11**]

◆ A chart error

The chart may simply have been drawn incorrectly, or the land forms may have changed since the chart was drawn. It isn't unusual to find errors in charts, especially those charts based on surveys dated before 1983.

◆ A horizontal datum problem

Your GPS may be set to NAD27 instead of WGS84. However the problem may also be in the electronic chart itself. All electronic charts should be geo-referenced to the appropriate datum (NAD83 or WGS84) but sometimes the datum shift is not applied or is incorrectly applied at the factory. The result is a chart that does not coincide with the real world. You will probably find your own vessel icon actually tracking over land portions of the chart. If this is the case, you should contact the distributor of the electronic charts for an upgrade kit.

◆ A buoy may be out of position

◆ A radar error. [See **Chapter 11**]

If I had to choose between radar and GPS/electronic charts, I would choose radar without any hesitation. Radar gives you an actual real-time image based on real events in the real world. When referenced to a chart (either electronic or paper-based), GPS merely tells you where you are, as long as everything else is in the right place. But it has no relevance to actual events as they occur.

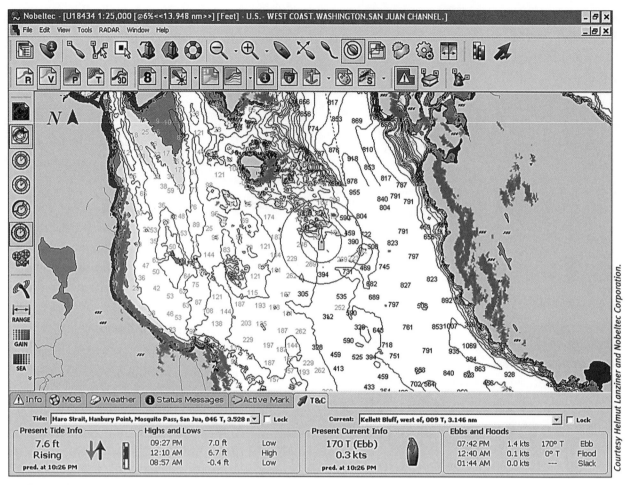

▲ **Fig. 8-18**
Offset Radar Image
In this radar/ECS image, the radar input does not coincide with the charted image. Since this area is well charted and travelled area (San Juan Islands, Washington), it is doubtful that the chart is this much in error. Instead the GPS input may be faulty.

When you encounter a mismatch between the radar image and the charted shoreline, first establish whether the mismatch is a result of the radar characteristics of the shoreline itself. You can look for clues in the electronic chart itself.

♦ Low sloping upland areas may not reflect radar efficiently. As a result, the radar shoreline may be at the inland extent of the marsh area. [See the upper right portion of **Fig. 8-21**]

♦ At low water, the radar shoreline should lie between the upper and lower extent of the charted foreshore. At extremely low water, the radar shoreline should coincide with the most seaward extent of the charted foreshore. ***In the case of a very gently sloping foreshore, this could represent a significant distance***.

♦ Sloping mud or sand beaches are poor reflectors, and thus may not appear on the display at any height of tide. In this case, the most seaward radar image may come from a berm above high water or from sea cliffs.

Fig. 8-19 ▶
Buoy out of Position
Note that the buoy ahead and to port does not coincide with its radar image. Since the rest of the radar overlay matches up to the chart, it is virtually certain that the buoy is out of position.

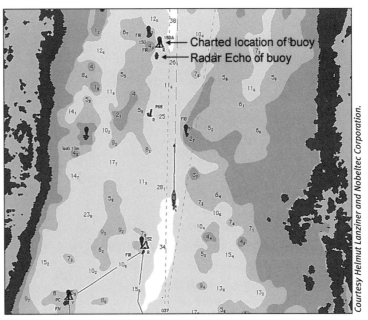

Courtesy Helmut Lanziner and Nobeltec Corporation.

◆ Shore ice may create a false shoreline that is seaward of the actual shoreline. This false shoreline may be narrow or extensive.

Attempt to visually verify the presence of shore ice; in most cases the width of the false shoreline will be variable.

If the entire radar image is shifted in one direction relative to the chart, it is an indication that the problem is a result of a chart problem, a datum problem or a GPS positioning error. [See **Chapter 11**.]

Some radar/ECS packages permit you to apply an offset to the chart to match the radar image to the charted shoreline. However, if you do not understand the cause for the mismatch, you should not try to adjust for it. After all, over time, the magnitude of the error may change. In order to get the radar image and the charts lined up again, you may have to fix a fundamental

Fig. 8-20 ▶
Electronic Chart Error
Canadian Hydrographic Service (CHS) raster chart 3858—Flamingo Inlet, Queen Charlotte Islands, British Columbia. This chart is drawn to an unknown datum. The electronic latitude and longitude grid overlaid on the chart to enable it to be used with the navigation software is in the wrong place. The result is that the vessel track appears to cross over the land portion of the chart. It is impossible to reconcile a radar image with this chart.

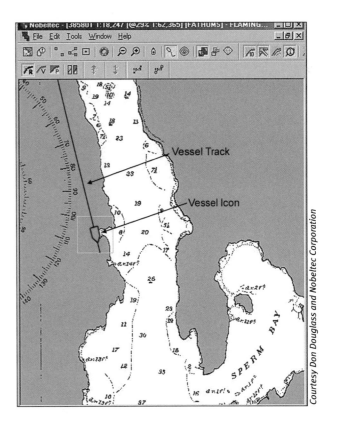

Courtesy Don Douglass and Nobeltec Corporation

Fig. 8-21 ►

A Xenex Navigation Radar Overlay

In this image the radar overlay permits you to
identify exactly which portion of the shoreline
is intertidal. Without radar overlay you must
estimate the position of the high-water line.

▼ Fig. 8-22

Nobeltec Insight Radar Overlay

In this image of the entrance to Victoria
Harbour, the radar overlay matches the chart
well, except for the echo showing between the
two docks behind the breakwater. This echo is
probably the image of a cruise ship alongside
the docks; you can assume the overlay is
working properly. Other uncharted targets are
vessels entering and exiting the harbour.

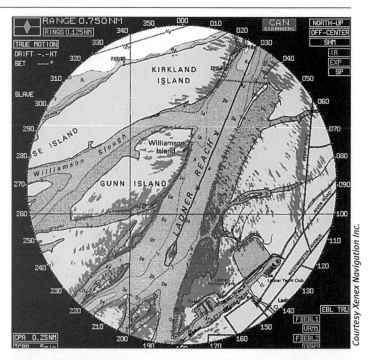

Courtesy Xenex Navigation Inc.

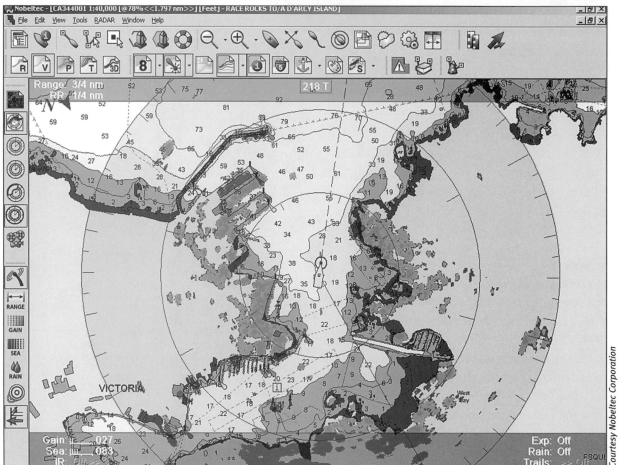

Courtesy Nobeltec Corporation

problem with the equipment first, such as an intermittently faulty antenna connection or a software or hardware problem.

In many radar/ECS packages, adjusting for the error may not be possible. Your best course of action is to continue using the electronic chart/radar interface, making allowances for the error, or to remove the radar overlay entirely. If you do not have another radar display, be sure that the radar window on your interfaced unit is set to radar only.

North-Up or Course-Up?

In the same way that you can display your radar image North-up, Course-up, or Head-up, you can also choose to display your ECS North-up or Course-up.

In an integrated radar/ECS display, the two image sets must obviously be displayed in the same orientation. And since most navigation software is capable of displaying charts in either North-up or Course-up mode, you can do the same with the interfaced radar/ECS display. You should display the integrated image in whichever presentation mode makes you the most comfortable.

Some people find that the radar makes immediate sense to them in Head-up mode, and they have no trouble reconciling a paper chart with the image. Others find they must rotate the paper chart to match the radar display in order to feel comfortable with the "Head-up" display mode. In the same way, you may be perfectly happy using the radar/ECS interface in North-up mode whereas others find it useful to view the integrated radar/chart image in "Course-up".

Before you purchase a radar/ECS display system you should seriously consider which type of chart and which type of system will work best with your preferred method of viewing the radar.

There are two basic types of chart available— raster and vector.

Raster or Vector Charts?

Raster Charts

A **raster chart** is an image of a paper chart that has been scanned into a computer and stored in digital form. As anyone who has worked with computer graphics knows, these images take up a lot of disk space (some raster charts are 6 megabytes or more.) But because they are exact copies of nautical charts, the appearance of raster charts is familiar to all mariners.

Raster charts are normally oriented North-up. Should you wish to display the chart in a "Course-up" mode (for instance in an interfaced radar/ECS display), the soundings and names on the chart will be displayed at an angle, or even worse—upside down. This is an inherent property of raster charts, since they are merely images of a paper chart.

Vector Charts

A **vector chart** however, is a completely different beast from a raster chart. It is not a scanned image at all but a highly complex collection of information stored in a database format. This format requires far less storage space than a raster image format (and less processing power). Vector charts are derived from the same authorized hydrographic data as their raster cousins.

Since a vector chart is actually a collection of information, it cannot just be scanned into electronic format. Instead, the data that forms the original paper chart must be extracted and separated into separate groupings or "layers." These "layers" are then stored separately in the database.

Each time you call up a vector chart, the computer extracts data from the database and then draws the chart anew. When you increase the scale, the computer not only recognizes that certain features—such as landmasses—should be enlarged, but also that certain features (such as depth soundings and navigation marks) require different treatment. As you zoom in on a portion of the chart, additional depth soundings and other data appear, and geographic features appear in greater detail, though the depth soundings and navigation marks are not enlarged. You do not need to switch to a larger scale chart; the computer just draws a larger scale image based on the information in the database.

In a vector chart, the soundings and names retain their proper orientation even when you choose to rotate the display to "Course-up" mode.

In a raster chart, all the features of the chart rotate together.

Another advantage of using vector charts is that you can select which chart information to display and which to hide. The result is that you will have greater flexibility in setting up your display and, consequently, greater comfort in working with it. For instance, you may wish to remove the charted contour lines which may interfere with your ability to see weak or moderate strength targets. Be careful, though, to hide chart

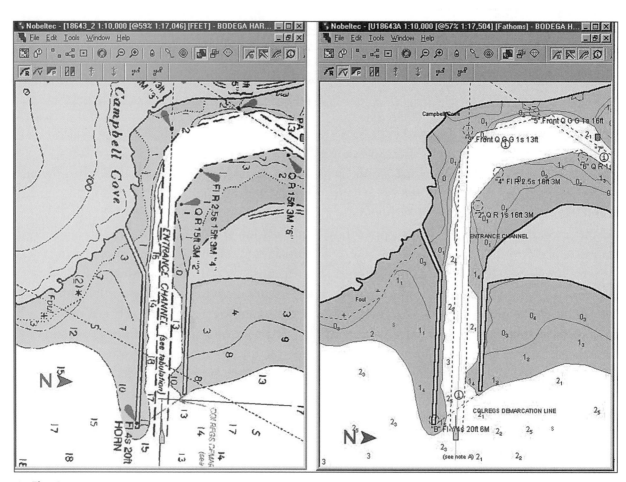

▲ **Fig. 8-23**
Raster vs Vector
Two ECS displays of a vessel entering Bodega Harbor, California, in Course-up mode. On the left is a raster chart display. Note that the soundings and other written notations have rotated with the chart and are difficult to read. On the right is a vector chart presentation of the same area. Note that the soundings maintain their proper orientation.

information only temporarily; otherwise you may forget that you have done so, and deprive yourself of a valuable source of information.

Most proprietary systems use vector charts of some type, usually in a cartridge format such as C-map or Garmin's G-charts, but CD-based formats are available as well.

PC systems can use both types of chart, depending on the software. Authorized government charts are available in both raster and vector format for these PC-based systems.

If you are comfortable with North-up display mode, feel free to use raster charts. However, if you feel more comfortable with the "Course-up" mode of display, give serious thought to purchasing an integrated system that uses vector charts. The price is a little higher than for raster charts, but the extra cost is worth it if it increases your peace of mind.

Colours and Transparency

One of the risks you take when you overlay a radar image on a chart image is that you may obscure important chart detail; this can be a problem if the sea clutter hides a charted object such as a buoy, or even worse, an isolated rock. Consequently, radar overlay software normally allows you to apply a degree of transparency to the radar image so that the charted details show through.

At times you will want the radar image to be opaque; for instance, when you need to see all the detail in the radar image. At other times you may wish to apply the highest transparency setting, so the radar image shows as a mere shadow against the chart background.

Normally, you should never turn the transparency completely off. Instead, if you want to view all the details in the radar image, switch to

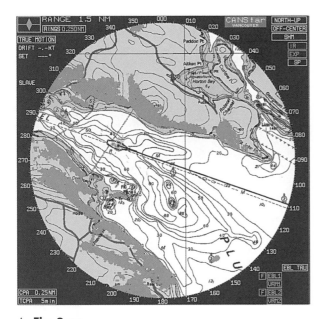

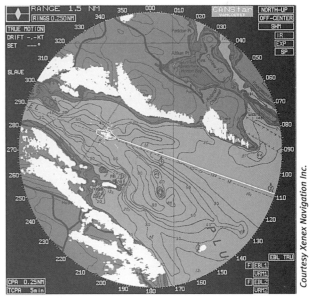

Courtesy Xenex Navigation Inc.

▲ **Fig. 8-24**
Image Intensity
Charts containing a lot of detail can interfere with the radar image, making it difficult to see weak radar tar-

gets (lower right). By adjusting the chart or radar intensity, you can de-emphasize the chart in relation to the radar image or vice versa.

a window that shows a pure radar image without any chart background at all. If you have a separate dedicated radar display, you won't need to switch to another window—just turn your head.

The software will undoubtedly give you the option of setting the colour of the radar image or the image intensity. You may even have the option of applying different colours to different strengths of radar echo. Here you must be careful.

Make sure you do not set a radar colour that is identical to any of the colours in the electronic chart. If you do, you may have difficulty determining whether a particular colour in the display is the result of a weak radar echo or a charted object.

The purpose of the radar/ECS integration is to enhance your navigation experience, not to add to your confusion. So be sure not to inadvertently complicate the issue by confusing the colours of chart and radar. You will usually be on safe ground if you apply various shades of red to the overlaid radar display—red isn't common on navigation charts.

Chapter Nine

Further Adventures in Collision Avoidance

Steering and Sailing Rules

At this point, let's briefly review the following excerpts from the steering and sailing rules for power-driven vessels from the *Collision Regulations*.

Rule 13: Overtaking

(a) ... **any vessel overtaking any other vessel shall keep out of the way of the vessel being overtaken.**

Rule 14: Head-on Situation

(a) When two power-driven vessels are meeting on reciprocal or nearly reciprocal courses so as to involve risk of collision **each shall alter her course to starboard so that each shall pass on the port side of the other.**

Rule 15: Crossing Situation

(a) When two power-driven vessels are crossing so as to involve risk of collision, **the vessel which has the other on her own starboard side shall keep out of the way and shall, if the circumstances of the case admit, avoid crossing ahead of the other vessel.**

Rule 19: Conduct of Vessels in Restricted Visibility

(a) This Rule **applies to vessels not in sight of one another** when navigating in or near an area of restricted visibility.

(b) **Every vessel shall proceed at a safe speed** adapted to the prevailing circumstances and conditions of restricted visibility. A power-driven vessel shall have her engines ready for immediate maneuver.

(d) A vessel which **detects by radar alone the presence of another vessel** shall determine if a close-quarters situation is developing and/or risk of collision exists. If so, she shall take avoiding action in ample time, provided that when such action consists of an alteration of course, **so far as possible the following shall be avoided**:

(i) **an alteration of course to port for a vessel forward of the beam, other than for a vessel being overtaken,**

(ii) **an alteration of course towards a vessel abeam or abaft the beam.**

You will notice that there are significant differences between the rules for vessels in sight of one another and the rules for restricted visibility; it is crucial that you understand the difference between the rules, and when to apply them.

Rules 13, 14, and 15 apply when vessels are in sight of one another—including the hours of darkness. At night, observers aboard each vessel can still see the navigation lights of the other, so

Fig. 9-1 ▶

Collision Avoidance — Restricted Visibility (Rule 19)

Avoid as far as possible:

◆ *Altering to port for a vessel forward of the beam*

◆ *Altering towards a vessel abeam or behind the beam*

(If necessary, slow down or stop to assess the situation.)

The reason you should not turn to port for a vessel forward of the beam is so you do not come into conflict with a vessel on an opposing course that has decided to turn to starboard. [See the sidebar on the *Andrea Doria* on the next page.] If you must turn to port because of a lack of sea room or due to the presence of other vessels to starboard, do so as early as possible.

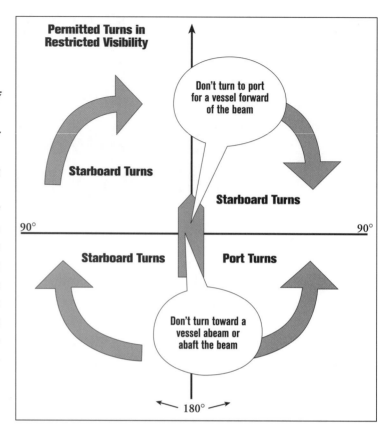

Circumferential Distortion

▼ **Fig. 9-2**

Circumferential Distortion

As a result of beam-width distortion, most small targets appear to be wider than they are deep. Also, because they are distorted in width but maintain the same distance from the center of the display, they appear slightly curved. This is a characteristic of all small targets, such as ships and small isolated rocks, especially on the

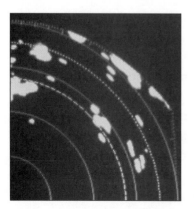

outer third of the display. The result is that ships appear to be oriented parallel to the range rings, no matter what direction they are actually headed. Only very large ships, viewed at close range with a short pulse length, will reveal their actual heading on the radar.

Due to circumferential distortion, you cannot tell the direction a target vessel is headed by radar alone. When you can view the other vessel directly out the pilothouse window, you can deduce the other vessel's direction of travel from the appearance of its navigation lights. But in restricted visibility, you have no way of knowing the heading of the other vessel, and thus cannot be sure whether you are in a crossing, passing or head-on situation.

they are considered to be in sight of one another.

- Under Rules 13 and 15, in any crossing or overtaking situation, one vessel is the "stand-on" vessel and is required to maintain its course and speed. This vessel has "right-of-way".

- The other vessel is the "give-way" vessel and must keep clear so as to avoid collision.

- Under Rule 14, in any head-on situation, both vessels are "give-way" vessels.

- You cannot make your decision about what action to take based purely on the relative bearing of a target; you must also consider the heading of the other vessel. For instance, a target in the forward port quadrant of your radar could be a crossing vessel (in which case you must maintain course and speed) or it could be a vessel being overtaken (in which case you must stay clear).

Rule 19 applies when a vessel is in or near an area of restricted visibility. The rule includes situations "near an area of restricted visibility" because it assumes that if one vessel cannot see the other, both should operate according to the same rule. **Remember:** ***Simple darkness is not considered "restricted visibility."***

The *Andrea Doria*

As mentioned in the Introduction, the *Andrea Doria/Stockholm* collision is facetiously referred to as "the first radar-assisted collision." This is not quite accurate—the collision was undoubtedly not the first of its kind. Neither was it "assisted by radar." Rather, the collision resulted from a failure to understand the need for systematic plotting and adherence to proven practices, which are embodied in the *Collision Regulations*.

On July 25, 1956, the two ships approached each other on almost opposing courses near Nantucket Lightship. Each had observed the other for 29 minutes prior to the collision and had drawn erroneous conclusions as to the identity and nature of the other. Neither was aware that a fog bank had settled in between the two vessels until it was finally too late.

Among the causes of the collision were the following:

- Neither vessel systematically plotted the other. *Rule 7 (b) Proper use shall be made of . . . radar plotting or equivalent systematic observation of detected objects.*
- The *Andrea Doria* made numerous small alterations of course which would not have been apparent to the *Stockholm* even if its crew had been plotting the target properly. *Rule 8 (b) a succession of small alterations of course and/or speed should be avoided.*
- The crew of the *Andrea Doria* could not see the navigation lights of the *Stockholm* because the *Stockholm* was in a fog bank. The captain of the *Andrea Doria* thought it was because the *Stockholm* was a small fishing trawler. He realized the size of the *Stockholm* only when it was too late to avoid a collision. *Rule 7 (c) Assumptions shall not be made on the basis of scanty information, especially scanty radar information.*
- The captain of the *Andrea Doria* did not realize he should be following the rules for vessels not in sight of one another. Consequently he intended to pass starboard to starboard, or "green to green."
- In order to increase the passing distance, he ordered the *Andrea Doria* to turn to port when at 3-1/2 miles distance; at the same time the Stockholm was turning to starboard, thus cancelling out the *Andrea Doria's* maneuver. *Rule 19—avoid turning to port for a vessel forward of the beam.*

In restricted visibility:

♦ You have no idea which direction the target is heading because you cannot see its navigation lights. Therefore you cannot tell if you are in a crossing, meeting or passing situation, and consequently, *neither vessel is the stand-on vessel—both vessels are expected to avoid the other, guided by Rule 19.*

♦ You cannot see the navigation lights of the other vessel, and so you cannot tell whether it is a fishing vessel, a sailing vessel, or any other "privileged" vessel. The rules do not recognize any special "privileged" cases in restricted visibility. *There is just the one rule because there is only one kind of target on the radar.*

♦ You must take avoiding action that is consistent with the avoiding action taken by the other vessel. If you follow the principles in Rule 19, you will be able to maneuver in confidence and safety.

The implications of these rules are profound. During simple darkness, when you can see the

---

Rule 8
Action to Avoid Collision

(a) Any action taken to avoid collision shall, if the circumstances of the case admit, be positive, made in ample time and with due regard to the observance of good seamanship.

(b) Any alteration of course and/or speed to avoid collision shall, if the circumstances of the case admit, be large enough to be readily apparent to another vessel observing visually or by radar; a succession of small alterations of course and/or speed should be avoided.

(c) If there is sufficient sea room, alteration of course alone may be the most effective action to avoid a close-quarters situation provided that it is made in good time, is substantial and does not result in another close-quarters situation.

(d) Action taken to avoid collision with another vessel shall be such as to result in passing at a safe distance. The effectiveness of the action shall be carefully checked until the other vessel is finally past and clear.

Rule 16
Action by Give-way Vessel

Every vessel which is directed to keep out of the way of another vessel shall, so far as possible, take early and substantial action to keep well clear.

Rule 17
Action by Stand-on Vessel

(a) (i) Where one of two vessels is to keep out of the way the other shall keep her course and speed.
(ii) The latter vessel may however take action to avoid collision by her maneuver alone, as soon as it becomes apparent to her that the vessel required to keep out of the way is not taking appropriate action in compliance with these Rules.

(b) When, from any cause, the vessel required to keep her course and speed finds herself so close that collision cannot be avoided by the action of the give-way vessel alone, she shall take such action as will best aid to avoid collision.

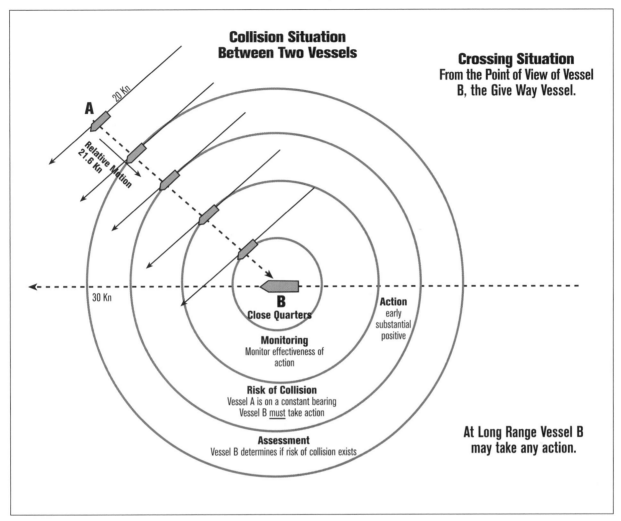

**Collision Situation
Between Two Vessels**

Crossing Situation
From the Point of View of Vessel
B, the Give Way Vessel.

A
20 Kn

Relative Motion
21.6 Kn

30 Kn

B
Close Quarters

Action
early
substantial
positive

Monitoring
Monitor effectiveness of
action

Risk of Collision
Vessel A is on a constant bearing
Vessel B must take action

Assessment
Vessel B determines if risk of collision exists

**At Long Range Vessel B
may take any action.**

▲ **Fig. 9-3**
Collision Avoidance

A crossing situation from the point of view of vessel B, the give-way vessel. Vessel A is shown as it appears to B, on a constant bearing and at steadily reducing range—in other words it is on a collision course. This is identical to the situation shown in Fig. 9-5 and 9-6 except that so far, B has taken no action to avoid a collision.

Note that the field of view (representing the radar display) is divided into four concentric circles.

◆ While the target is still in the outer circle, you should assess whether there is a risk of collision.

During this period you will maintain your course and speed, so that the other vessel can assess your movements.

◆ If your assessment indicates that the vessel is on a collision course or will pass very close to you, then you must take action in the "Risk of Collision" circle. The action you take will depend on whether you are in restricted visibility or not.

◆ In the "Monitoring" circle, you should monitor the progress of the target very closely to determine if your avoiding action has had the desired effect.

◆ The whole purpose of the avoiding action is to ensure that the target vessel does not enter the "Close Quarters" circle.

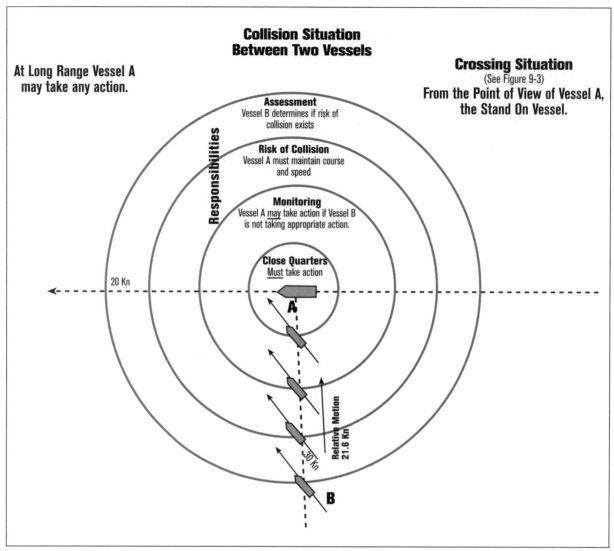

Collision Situation Between Two Vessels

At Long Range Vessel A may take any action.

Crossing Situation
(See Figure 9-3)
From the Point of View of Vessel A, the Stand On Vessel.

Responsibilities

Assessment
Vessel B determines if risk of collision exists

Risk of Collision
Vessel A must maintain course and speed

Monitoring
Vessel A may take action if Vessel B is not taking appropriate action.

Close Quarters
Must take action

A

20 Kn

Relative Motion 21.6 Kn

30 Kn

B

▲ **Fig. 9-4**

The same crossing situation from the point of view of vessel A—the stand-on vessel.

◆ While the target is in the outer circle, the skipper of vessel A must assess the situation to determine risk of collision. During this period both vessels should maintain their course and speed.

◆ If the target is on a collision course, or will pass very close, then the action that vessel A takes depends on the state of visibility. If vessel B is in sight, then rules 13 to 15 apply [see page 155] and vessel A is the stand-on vessel and must maintain course and speed. [Rule 17 (a) (i)] However, if visibility is restricted, there is no stand-on vessel and

therefore both vessels must take action according to Rule 19.

◆ If vessel B enters the "Monitoring" circle without appearing to have taken any action, vessel A may take avoiding action. [Rule 17 (a) (ii)]

◆ If vessel B enters the "Close-Quarters" circle, vessel A **must** take avoiding action. [Rule 17 (b)]

If this scenario took place during restricted visibility, the only difference would be the avoiding action required. However, you would still be expected to go through the same basic procedure of assessing risk of collision, taking action, monitoring, and avoiding a close quarters situation.

other vessel's navigation lights, the radar simply adds another dimension to your senses. But when the fog rolls in (during daytime or at night) you have only your hearing and your radar to help you avoid collisions. So you must follow Rule 19, which places the same responsibility on both vessels, since all targets are alike in fog.

According to Rule 8 of the *Collision Regulations*, any action you take should be taken **early** and **substantial** so that observers on the other vessel will be able to see that you have taken action, and you should monitor the situation until you are finally past and clear.

Most mariners agree—an alteration should be at least 20° to 30° for it to be readily apparent to observers on the other vessel. If you alter less than 20° to 30°, the other vessel may assume you have not taken avoiding action and may take action herself. The problem is that by doing so the other vessel may cancel out the effect of your alteration of course or speed. You won't know until both vessels have steadied up on their new courses, by which time it may be too late.

A series of small alterations may not be detectable at all!

The implications of this are profound. It means that *you should avoid small alterations of course or speed when other vessels are in the vicinity—even if you have the right of way! Other vessels may be assessing your movements!*

Systematic Observation of Other Vessels

Rule 7 (b) states "Proper use shall be made of radar equipment if fitted and operational, including long-range scanning to obtain early warning of risk of collision and radar plotting or equivalent systematic observation of detected objects."

In order to observe the behaviour of a target you must watch it for some time.

♦ The longer you observe a target, the better you will be able to predict its behaviour. In practice this means you must observe it for at least one minute. When plotting the course and speed of another large ship, captains typically try to observe another vessel for at least 6 minutes. This means they must try to obtain early warning of other vessels at 12 miles or more.

♦ In **Fig. 9-3** vessel A is approaching vessel B at a relative speed of 21.6 knots. This means that when observed on 3-mile range, it will cross the distance from the edge of the display to the center in just 90 seconds.

♦ During the assessment period, you must not alter course or speed yourself. Since the relative motion plot is defined by the combination of the course and speed of both vessels, any alteration on your part during the assessment period will invalidate any conclusions you draw from the observation.

♦ If you scan outward at too short a range scale, you will not have adequate time to assess, take action, and monitor the effectiveness of the action before the other vessel comes into a close-quarters situation.

♦ If you can see the other vessel, you will be able to see its heading (its aspect relative to your own heading). This will help you to understand if it actually presents a risk or not. For instance, you will be able to immediately rule out any vessel that is clearly headed away from you and which you will not be overtaking.

In taking action to avoid a collision, you should strive not only to avoid a collision, but also to avoid a close-quarters situation. In order to do so, you must estimate the distance of the other vessel at its Closest Point of Approach (CPA).

Obviously, both vessels must conduct some form of systematic observation in order to determine risk of collision. ***In a simple situation, you may be able to do this merely by placing the EBL over the target and observing its relative course.***

◆ ***If the target travels down the EBL to the center of the display, it is on a collision course.***

◆ ***If it deviates only a little from the EBL, a close quarters situation is developing.***

◆ ***If the target deviates significantly from the EBL, it will pass well clear.***

If the situation is complex, with a number of other vessels present, you will not have enough EBLs to track each of the other targets and, if the target is heading to a point near the center of the display, you may wish to track it more accurately. In other words you will have to resort to a more systematic method of observation.

> At long range the Collision Regulations do not apply. ***Try to maneuver when other vessels are at long range, in order to avoid setting the stage for a close-quarters situation.***

How Close is Too Close?

The answer depends on the size of your vessel, your speed, and the amount of sea-room. In the deep sea, captains of large ships are reluctant to let other ships approach closer than one nautical mile. For smaller vessels inshore, this is totally impractical.

◆ Your tolerance will depend on your experience and your comfort operating with radar.

◆ Generally you should try to scan three miles ahead and to the sides to get early indications of any situations that may develop into close quarters situations.

A Eureka Bar Story
by Don Douglass
from *Exploring the Pacific Coast, San Diego to Seattle.*

Late in the summer, friends of ours were leaving Humboldt Bay in heavy fog. They were proceeding slowly and, as they made their final turn southwest into the entrance channel, the skipper switched his radar to a very short range to keep track of his distance from the south jetty. (The north half of the entrance channel fills with sand.) The first mate headed down to the galley to get a coffee refill.

The skipper checked his radar, then looked out through the windows. To his horror, he saw a black shadow closing in a high speed directly in front. He jammed the helm to starboard and yelled to his wife, just as their boat glanced off a steel fishing vessel. He made a quick Mayday call on Channel 16, giving his position as the two boats drifted apart. The damage turned out to be mainly superficial and, with temporary repairs and a lot of duct tape, they made it down the coast for a serious fiberglass job.

Lessons learned: First, keep crewmembers on an alert watch when navigating in close quarters during limited visibility. Second, keep switching radar ranges to make sure no high-speed vessels are approaching from any direction. (Fixation on short range is false security. A quarter-mile or half-mile range does not give adequate advance warning for fast closing-vessels.) Third, make a security announcement on Channel 16 stating your position and intentions. ***In tight quarters, with limited visibility, listen for fog signals and sound your own horn frequently.***

- In confined waters, or where there are large amounts of traffic, you may not have the luxury of scanning that far ahead, in which case *set your radar to a range that allows you to assess the other vessels while they are still in the outer third of the display.*

- *In open water and foggy conditions, you may be able to tolerate other small boats approaching within 1/4 mile—but not much closer.*

- *In confined waters and foggy conditions, even if you have a small boat, you should attempt to maintain as large a CPA as practical.*

Head-Up, Course-Up or North-Up?

Each mode has its advantages and disadvantages for collision avoidance.

In Head-up mode:

- Echo trails operate well, but yawing of the vessel causes the images to "smear".

- What you see ahead of you (and to port and starboard) corresponds to what you see on the radar.

- It is easy to understand the actions of other moving targets in relation to your own vessel.

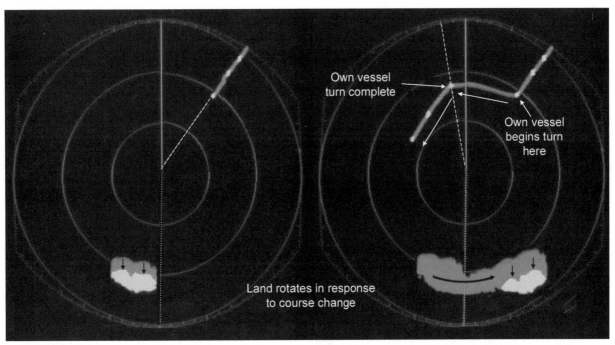

Own vessel turn complete

Own vessel begins turn here

Land rotates in response to course change

▲ **Fig. 9-5**
Collision Avoidance in Head-Up Mode
A vessel approaches from the forward starboard quadrant.

Left
After you have tracked the target vessel and determined it is on a collision course (represented by the three "pips" on the EBL), you alter course 35° to starboard.

Right
This brings your heading to the right of the target vessel. On the display, the target has rotated to the left of the heading marker, and then continues its relative motion. The land rotates counter-clockwise in response to the turn. At this point, you must move the EBL to place it over the target "pip" again.

The new relative motion line now leads to the left and astern of your vessel and the target is no longer a threat.

- When you alter course, targets rotate around the display in a direction opposite to the direction you have turned and begin a new Relative Motion (RM) line from that point. You must reset your EBL to track the new RM line.

In Course-up mode:

- The display is stabilized like North-up mode, so echo trails work well and do not smear.
- Like Head-up mode, it is easy to relate your point of view to the radar display.
- When you alter course, targets rotate around the display. You must reset the EBL in order to track the new relative motion line of the target.

- Unless your autopilot is interfaced to the radar you must remember to reset the course setting each time you alter course—at a time when the situation may be changing rapidly.

In North-up mode:

- Echo trails work well—when you alter course, it is the heading marker that rotates, not the target images, so echo trails will not smear.
- When you alter course in a collision-avoidance situation, the target does not rotate around the screen, it simply begins its new relative motion

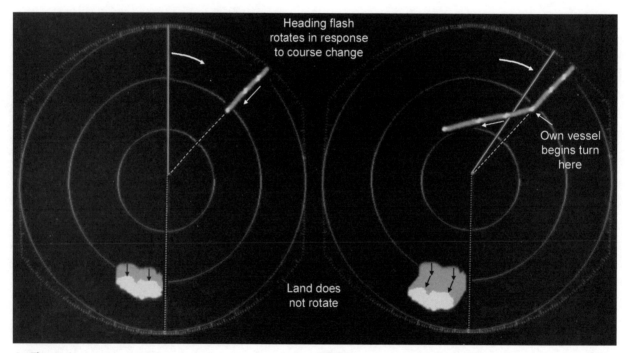

Heading flash rotates in response to course change

Own vessel begins turn here

Land does not rotate

▲ Fig. 9-6
Collision Avoidance in North–up Mode
The same situation—a vessel approaching from the forward, starboard quadrant.

Left
In this case, your vessel begins by steering 000°. After you have tracked the target vessel and determined that it is on a collision course (represented by the three "pips" on the EBL), you alter course 35° to starboard.

Right
Because your radar is in North-up mode, the targets do not rotate around the display. Instead, the heading marker rotates 35° clockwise. The target "pip" continues to follow an unbroken track but, after a few moments, you notice that its Relative Motion (RM) line has changed direction and crosses the heading flash well ahead of your vessel. The target is clearly no longer a threat. The land echo does not rotate, but with the change in course, it now follows a different RM line as

line from that point. You do not need to reset the EBL.

Inevitably, you must chose a mode of presentation with which you feel comfortable. Course-up requires a discipline that you may not wish to exercise. North-up and Head-up are the most useful for collision avoidance purposes. I strongly recommend using Head-up mode when in very short-range collision-avoidance situations.

Target Behaviour After an Alteration

Once you have observed the target's behaviour, you must respond to any target that presents risk of collision. Following are some examples of the changes in relative course and/or speed of an observed target (target behaviour), resulting from an alteration of your own course or speed. All examples are shown in North-up mode and, for simplicity, your own vessel is shown initially heading north (000°).

In **Figures 9-7 to 9-12** you can see that some actions result in the target vessel passing astern and some result in its passing ahead. You should be careful to avoid combinations of maneuver where one action cancels out another, such as turning to starboard **and** reducing speed for a target in the port forward quadrant. The *Collision Regulations* specifically advise that an alteration of course alone may be the best choice of action. There are two reasons for this advice. First—an alteration of course will be more apparent to the target vessel than a change in speed. Second—it is important that a vessel's actions be predictable. There is nothing worse than having to deal with a target vessel acting unpredictably in the fog. It merely adds to your level of anxiety.

Generally, if both vessels follow the procedures set out in the *Collision Regulations*, they will be safe; but if the other vessel fails to act appropriately (or fails to maintain course and speed when required to do so) you must continue to observe the situation and take further action if necessary.

To the do's and don'ts listed in the *Collision Regulations* we can add another—***be very careful about reducing speed for a vessel in your forward port quadrant***. Can you identify any other combinations of actions that would result in a collision?

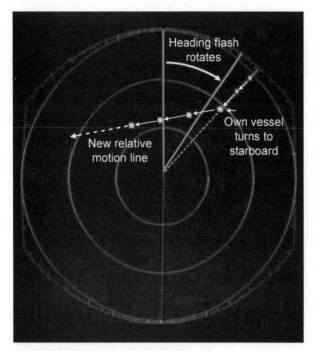

▲ **Fig. 9-7**
Own Vessel Turns to Starboard
Situation repeated from above—target approaching
from forward starboard quadrant

♦ **Own vessel turns to starboard**
♦ Target vessel passes ahead

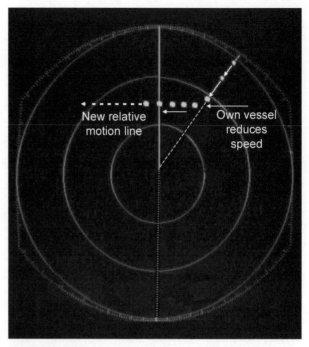

▲ **Fig. 9-8**
Own Vessel Reduces Speed
Target approaching from forward starboard quadrant

♦ **Own vessel reduces speed**
♦ Target vessel passes ahead

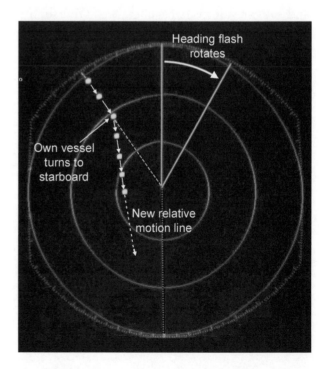

Fig. 9-9 ►
Own Vessel Turns to Starboard
Target approaching from forward port quadrant

♦ **Own vessel turns to starboard**
♦ Target vessel passes astern

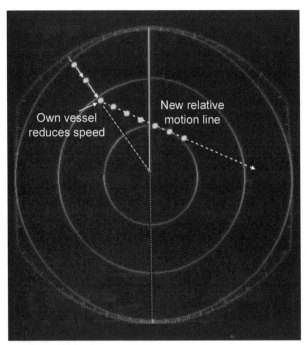

▲ Fig. 9-10
Own Vessel Reduces Speed
Target approaching from forward port quadrant
- ◆ **Own vessel reduces speed**
- ◆ Target vessel passes ahead.

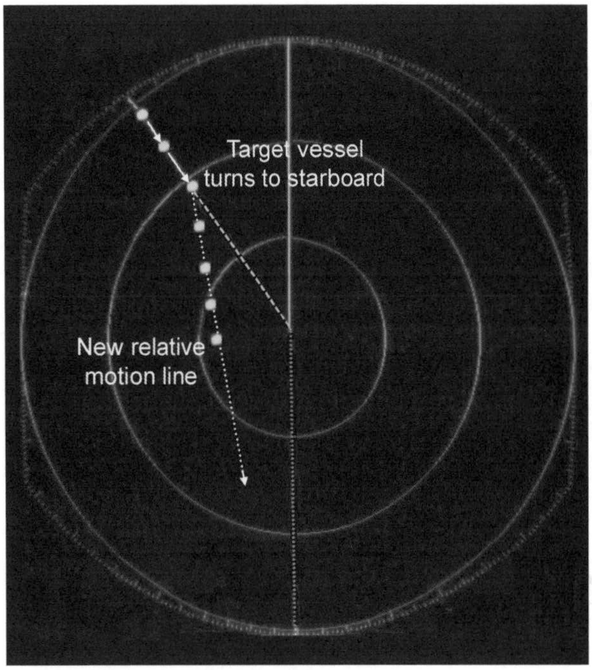

▲ Fig. 9-11
Target Vessel Turns to Starboard
Target approaching from forward port quadrant
Target vessel turns to starboard
- ◆ Own vessel maintains course and speed
- ◆ The same situation would result if the target reduced speed.

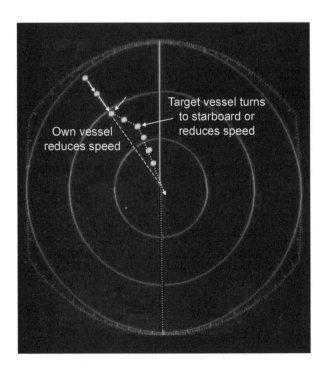

◀ Fig. 9-12
The Result of a Combination of Actions
Target approaching from forward port quadrant
- ◆ **A first, own vessel reduces speed**
- ◆ **A short time later, the target vessel turns to starboard or reduces speed**

The result is that the target vessel's maneuver has actually negated the effect of your own vessel's reduction in speed. The same situation would result if the target vessel maintained course and speed and your own vessel turned to starboard *as well as* reducing speed.

Handling Multiple Targets

In the radar display in **Fig. 9-13**, numerous targets are visible that could either be isolated rocks or other vessels. Your first and most important task is to identify every contact that is a probable vessel. You must do this by elimination—which means that first you must positively identify every rock and buoy.

In Good visibility:

- During daylight hours, you can confirm the identification of each target by eye and, since all the rocks and buoys will be visible, the job is much simpler.

- At night you must identify any lighted buoys by their light characteristics as described on the chart.

- Any target that remains unaccounted for must be "transient phenomena"—a vessel, a barge, or even a large tree-stump. But you can positively state that it is not a charted feature.

- Once you have eliminated the rocks and buoys, you must identify the outstanding targets. Again, this is relatively easy when you can see all the targets, but at night, you must identify each target by its navigation lights.

Tugs at Nelson Island

Heading northwest in Malaspina Strait, British Columbia, one rainy night, I saw a series of targets on the radar at 3 Nm range. They looked like a tug with two barges in tow near Cape Cockburn, which I confirmed visually. I could see three white lights in a vertical line that indicates a vessel with a tow more than 200 meters in length, and intermittently behind it I could see one or two faint green sidelights. Farther beyond, I could vaguely see another three white lights in a vertical line—another tug—but when I switched up to 6 Nm range, I couldn't see a target representing the distant tug. I assumed it was so close to the shore that its echo blended with the shore return.

Since my vessel and the first tug were approaching each other head-on, we would both have to take avoiding action. I reached for the VHF microphone and called on Channel 16 for "the tug heading southeast at Cape Cockburn." The tug answered and we agreed to switch to Channel 06. Since I had plenty of sea-room to port, I suggested a starboard-to-starboard passing. (We were far enough distant from each other that the COLREGS did not yet apply.) The skipper of the tug agreed, and so I altered to port.

I couldn't tell immediately if the tug had altered, but it actually seemed to be turning the wrong way—to starboard, across my bow. This continued; the more I altered to port, the more the tug altered to starboard. We were approaching one-half mile of each other, and I was growing concerned. Finally, I abandoned my proposed maneuver, and turned hard to starboard.

We passed well clear of each other, but I wanted to understand what had happened to make such a simple plan go so wrong. Again I made a VHF radio call for "the tug heading southeast at Cape Cockburn." This time a different voice answered. When I asked why he hadn't followed our "green to green" agreement, he answered that we were still several miles apart!

When I had made the green-to-green agreement with the tug, I was actually talking to the second tug and barge combination, not the first as I thought. Clearly, *you can never guarantee that the vessel you are talking to on a radio is the same vessel you observe on radar. If you make an agreement to depart from the rules, be prepared to alter your plans at a moments notice.*

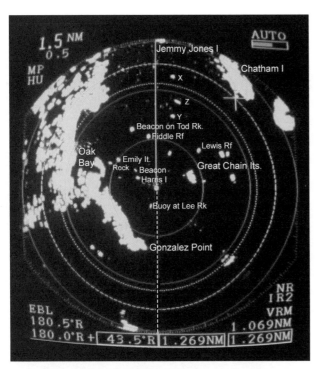

◀ **Fig. 9-13**
Identify Every Contact
The only unidentified contacts in this radar image are contacts X, Y, and Z. X is probably a vessel. Y is probably a tug towing a barge, Z. You must observe the behaviour of these targets closely and avoid them if necessary.

In this case, most of the rocks are marked by buoys and/or beacons. However, where buoys and beacons do not mark the navigational hazards, you must be prepared to account for only those that are exposed by the tide. For instance, Caroline Reef does not show on this radar image because it was submerged at the time. Under normal circumstances, submerged rocks do not return a radar echo.

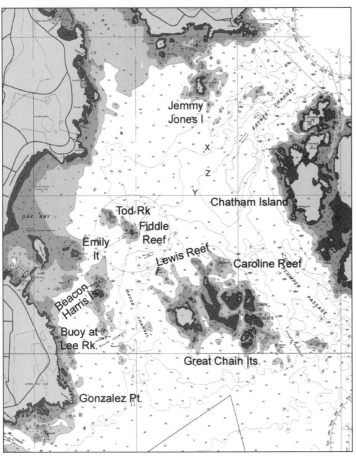

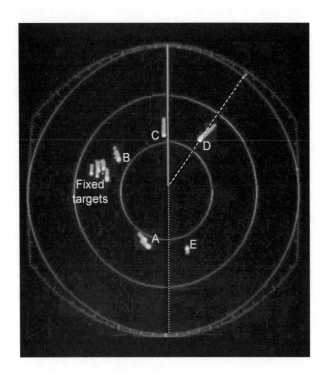

◀ **Fig. 9-14**
Multiple Targets
Echo trails can help you make a quick assessment of the most dangerous targets. If you do not have echo trails enabled, perform a quick plot using a dry erase marker.

- Abeam to port is a group of fixed targets, moving directly toward the bottom of the display.
- Targets A and B will clearly pass astern.
- Target C is approaching from directly ahead, on an almost opposing course.
- Target D is on a course that will result in a close quarters situation.
- Target E is overtaking. It will not be a problem for a while.

You must alter to starboard for Target D. This will also resolve the situation with Target C. However, it will put you in a crossing situation with Target E, which is overtaking. Once C and D have passed safely, you will have to alter again for E. You should resume your original course, because E still has the same responsibility to avoid you in an overtaking situation. This is also an appropriate maneuver for restricted visibility.

- Lighted targets may be difficult to identify in the presence of background lighting, especially in urban areas. For instance, you may mistake a red or green traffic light for the navigation lights of a vessel. Watch the lights closely to confirm that they are actually moving in front of the cityscape. You may also have some difficulty differentiating between flashing lights on buoys and flashing red and amber traffic lights.

- Once you have accounted for all the lighted targets, if there are any still unaccounted for, you must proceed very cautiously. Unlighted targets may be vessels with burned out navigation lights, but they could also be drifting derelicts, or large tree stumps, or other flotsam.

In Restricted Visibility:

- In restricted visibility, you must identify every target that you can.

- You must treat all others as vessels until you can confirm otherwise.

- Fixed targets will move across the display in a direction directly opposite to the direction of your heading marker. In a head-up display, they will move directly downwards.

- Targets on an opposing course will also move in the same direction as a fixed target, but they will move faster, because they are actually in motion.

- Overtaking targets will move in the same direction as your heading marker, but at a slower relative speed.

◆ All other moving targets will appear to move at an angle to the heading marker.

In the presence of multiple targets, you should identify the most dangerous targets first. These are normally the closest targets, but not always. In **Fig. 9-14**, the closest targets are clearly not a danger because they will pass well astern. Overtaking targets normally show a very low relative speed, and need not concern you immediately. The most dangerous targets are those on reciprocal courses, and crossing targets.

It is not always possible to maneuver to resolve all the developing interactions at the same time. You must deal with them one at a time or in groups. Other vessels will also need to avoid each other, so you should try to anticipate the maneuvers of other vessels in making your plans. In **Fig. 9-14**, Target C will probably slow down or alter starboard to avoid Target D. Your best move is to avoid them both by turning to starboard.

However, this will put you in a crossing situation with Target E, which is overtaking. Once C and D have passed safely, you will have to alter again for E by resuming your original course. Target E's obligation to stay clear of you does not disappear just because you have altered to avoid another vessel.

Rule 13(d) (Overtaking) Any subsequent alteration of the bearing between the two vessels shall not make the overtaking vessel a crossing vessel within the meaning of these Rules . . .

In restricted visibility, a turn to port to resume your course is consistent with Rule 19. (Avoid an alteration toward a vessel abeam or abaft the beam.)

If you need more time to assess the situation, reduce speed or come to a complete stop.

Switching Between Collision Avoidance and Navigation Modes

As a target approaches and you take avoiding action, you may have to switch to shorter-range scales in order to view the target properly. After all, it is difficult to tell exactly what a target is doing if it is too close to the center of the display. *In general, you should reduce range if the target comes within the central 1/3 of the display.*

You must remember that collision avoidance and navigation are fundamentally different processes. Each process requires different settings and different range scales for best results. As you reduce range scales, you may also find it necessary to reduce the gain or to increase the Sea Clutter suppression just to be able to see the target clearly. You may even switch from North-up to Head-up. For navigation mode, you may use long pulse/ long range, with the "anti-Rain Clutter" control disabled; whereas for collision-avoidance, in order to obtain a discrete image of each target, you may use short range/ short pulse, with the "anti-Rain Clutter" control enabled.

Obviously, as you change settings for the new range scale, these same settings may not be appropriate when you switch back to long range again. But remember when switching back to navigation mode, return to the settings you were using previously. If you find it necessary to switch back and forth frequently, you should use settings that are a compromise between the two different range scales.

If you are lucky enough to have two radars, set one to navigation mode—North-up, long range (3 to 6 miles depending on the circumstances) and the other to collision avoidance mode—Head-up, short range (0.5 to 1.0 mile).

Manual Radar Plotting [*See* Appendix A]

Ever since the early days of sail, it has been necessary to intercept other vessels, or in more extreme situations, to avoid them—perhaps to avoid a collision or a pirate attack. Thus it was necessary for old time sailors to know the other vessel's course and speed relative to one's own. While it may have been possible to assess this "by the seat of the pants," as soon as they wished to accurately intercept (or avoid) another vessel, they had to

Photograph courtesy of the Puget Sound Coast Artillery Museum

DIRECTING THE RANGE FOR THE MORTARS
AT FORT WRIGHT, FISHERS ISLAND, N.Y.
PHOTO © UNDERWOOD & UNDERWOOD, N.Y.

▲ **Fig. 9-15**

Coast Artillery Plotting Room c. 1910

Until aircraft carriers and modern missile systems rendered the Coast Artillery Corps obsolete, the coastal defenses of North America consisted of batteries of guns housed in major fortifications at harbour entrances.

In order to hit a target at sea, the gun layers needed to know the angle of elevation of the barrel, the direction to fire and (for mortars) the time of flight. Observation posts on high ground reported the changing range and bearing of targets to the plotting room where the plotting team laid out the firing solution on a semi-circular plotting board (actually a graphic representation of the battle field).

To obtain plunging fire on the unarmoured decks of target vessels, the mortars fired shells at a high angle. When firing at long ranges, the shells passed through the stratosphere before falling back to earth. The plotting teams made up to twenty-six different adjustments to derive the firing solution, including adjustments for temperature of powder, air temperature, barometric pressure and rotation of the earth. (At ten miles range, the earth would rotate almost 200 meters while the shell was in flight.) The result was a firing system so accurate that in 1937, a Coast Artillery Battery destroyed two targets measuring 24 feet by 8 feet each at more than ten miles range using only 13 rounds.

revert to more scientific methods, using a plotting (or maneuvering) board.

If the target vessel changed course the plot had to be started again. Still, the method worked very well if, for instance, the target had no idea that anything was about to intercept it, such as a torpedo or a high-explosive shell fired from over the horizon. *(This is why the zig-zag was adopted by both naval and merchant ships as the primary defense against torpedo attack.)*

The techniques of manual plotting are still practiced today and are actually fairly simple. You can learn the rudiments in a couple of hours. First, you record the target vessel's range and bearing as they change over time. From this point it is simple to calculate the other vessel's true course and speed and the Closest Point of Approach (CPA) and the time and distance to the CPA. Using the techniques of manual radar plotting you can even plot a planned maneuver and evaluate its effectiveness before you actually alter your own course or speed.

Simple Radar Plotting

Manual radar plotting is a useful skill, but to plot other vessels effectively, you must have immediate access to a chart table, or at least a small flat surface. Consequently, it is often not possible for operators of small recreational boats to perform radar plotting on a proper maneuvering board. However, you can construct an adequate plot directly on your radar with a dry erase marker. [See **Appendix A**.]

Automatic Radar Plotting Aid (ARPA)

One of the difficulties with the "echo trail" feature is that it is indiscriminate—every echo on the display leaves an echo trail and if the vessel makes a major alteration of course while in Head-up mode, smearing of the echoes renders the display almost useless for a while. If only we could stabilize the radar display *and* select specific targets to leave echo trails, the problem would be solved.

The modern radar plotter—Automated Radar Plotting Aid (ARPA)—was developed to perform this task, but the manner in which it presents the information is far more advanced than the "echo trail" feature available on most small radars.

Commercial ARPA units for use on large ships have been available for at least 20 years. At one time these ARPA units were valued at over $100,000 and were available only to wealthy ship owners.

Now, small mini-ARPA radars, which have many of the capabilities of the state of the art ARPA radars of the recent past, can be purchased for $5,000 to $10,000. Using the integrated ARPA or mini-ARPA circuits, the operator clicks the cursor onto any target on the display. The radar then begins to calculate the target's course and speed. Once the ARPA has calculated a preliminary solution, it attaches a vector arrow to each selected target, showing the course and speed of the target. All commercial ARPA units are now available with automatic target acquisition, as are many of the smaller consumer mini-ARPAs.

As the situation develops, the ARPA continuously recalculates the target course and speed and automatically updates the target vectors to reflect any changes in the target's course or speed. If the target is stationary, its relative vector will be the exact opposite of the operator's own vessel.

ARPA is normally offered only in North-up, stabilized mode.

▲ **Fig. 9-16**
A Large Commercial ARPA Radar

▲ **Fig. 9-17**
Mini-ARPA
A Raytheon mini-ARPA, displaying vectors for four targets selected targets. Each target has an associated vector drawn in the direction of relative motion. The end of the vector represents the "relative" position of the target at the end of the time period.

Data for each target is contained in the window at the side of the display. Notice that the display is in North-up mode, and that the "own ship" vector is the heading marker.

The operator can select vectors corresponding to any length of time—the ARPA will then display vector arrows drawn in the direction of the target's travel in proportion to its speed. At a glance, the operator can estimate the course and speed of the target based on the direction and length of the vector and immediately isolate the targets that are approaching his own vessel, thus focusing his attention on the targets that deserve the most attention.

The operator can select any time interval. A short plot interval is best at close range, or when tracking a high-speed target when a quick assessment of the situation is required. A longer interval is useful at longer ranges.

The operator can access data concerning any particular target simply by selecting the target and reading the data in a separate window. Data provided indicates not only the target's relative course and speed and CPA, but also the target's true course and speed. Clearly this is a great improvement over the echo trails laid down by simpler radar equipment.

The different radars offered with ARPA features approach target-acquisition in a manner that is generally unique to the individual manufacturer. Many small ARPA radars use the same controls to operate the cursor, VRM, EBL and to select targets. This may make the use of the EBL or the VRM somewhat complicated. It is always better to have a separate control for selecting or acquiring an ARPA target.

Radar plotting will surely be useful to a vessel that spends a lot of time in waters congested by other marine traffic or that operates often in dense fog. Those who have had some nasty sur-

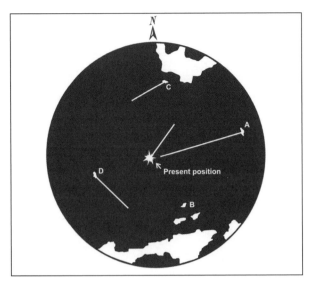

▲ Fig. 9-18
ARPA in Relative Motion Mode
At a glance you can tell that targets C and D pose no danger to your own vessel, but that target A is on a definite collision course.

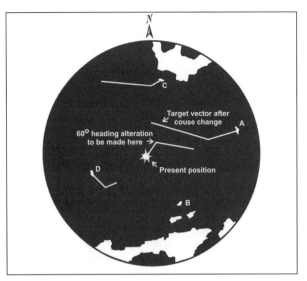

▲ Fig. 9-19
ARPA Trial Maneuver
Some ARPA equipment has "trial maneuver" capability. Using this feature, you can try out a maneuver to see what effect it will have on the relative vectors of plotted targets. This feature which is especially useful when there are numerous other targets in the vicinity allows you to observe the effect of a specific alteration of course or speed on the relative vectors of all the targets being tracked.

prises in the past, especially at night and in fog, may find the ARPA feature extremely valuable.

ARPA Errors

In all radar installations there is an unavoidable limit to accuracy of position which is determined by the physics of microwaves themselves. Instead of a definite point, a target displays a smeared "blip". Lines drawn between "blip" may have a fairly large error unless enough interval is allowed for the plotter to work out a good aver-

age solution. If the ARPA calculates a solution too rapidly, the solution will be suspect. Also, if the target vessel is following a variable course, the solution will be compromised. A large enough plotting interval must be used for the plotter to establish the target's average course and speed.

ARPA Heading and Speed Input

As with any stabilized radar display, the heading data should be supplied by a flux-gate or gyro-compass or by one of the new GPS compass sensors.

ARPA purists prefer heading supplied from a gyro-compass and speed-through-the-water data from a speed log. Since GPS provides "speed over the ground" not "through the water," it results in a "ground-locked" ARPA. Purists believe that "ground locked" ARPAs tend to give a false impression of the heading of the target vessel, but on small craft this should not be a problem.

When an ARPA tracks two separate targets, it assigns certain values, such as relative course and speed and heading vectors to each target. However, if the two targets come so close that their echoes merge on the PPI, when they separate again the ARPA may lose track of which target is which and assign the incorrect values to each of the targets. If this occurs, it may take a minute or two for the ARPA to recalculate the accurate values. In the meantime, *the target data will be erroneous.*

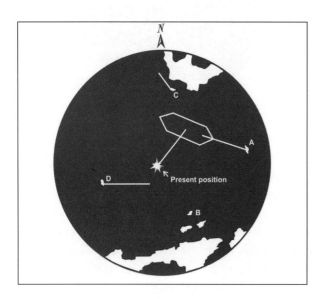

◄ **Fig. 9-20**

ARPA in True Motion Mode with Potential Areas of Danger (PADs)

The same situation, presented in True Motion ARPA. The vector of your own vessel ends in the PAD associated with target A, indicating a collision course.

Notice that the vector of A no longer points at the center of the display. It is extremely important that you be aware at all times, of the differences between true motion and relative motion and that you know exactly what mode you are in; otherwise, you may not be aware that target A presents a very clear danger.

Remember that the plotter circuits rely on data supplied by the radar itself. If tracking a weak echo (a small vessel at long range, for instance) the plotter may have trouble acquiring the target. Also, targets can be lost when they are submerged in heavy clutter. Adjusting the gain or clutter controls may resolve this difficulty. When encountering heavy seas, your own heading and speed may be very variable, or the platform itself may be too unstable and targets may be lost. When targets merge with the returns from shorelines or buoys or other vessels, the plotter may "lock on" to the new target and lose the original.

Under any of these conditions, targets may need to be re-acquired, and if this cannot be done, plotting may not be possible at all. In all cases, careful adjustment of tuning, gain and clutter controls to show clear discrete targets will greatly assist in reliable plotting.

ARPA in True Motion Mode

True motion display is another mode of display made possible by interfacing a radar with course and speed data. In a true motion display, stationary targets remain stationary and only moving targets are shown to be in motion. In this mode, your own vessel actually moves across the display, carrying with it the origin of the heading flash and all the range rings. In true motion, ARPA target vectors are shown as true, not relative vectors.

Generally, true motion is not offered on small-boat radars. But you may find it as an option on some ARPA-equipped radars.

It is vital to understand the difference between the two kinds of information available from this type of ARPA—relative course/speed and true course/speed.

Relative Motion

- A relative plot is easiest to interpret, since any target vector that passes through or near the sweep origin of the display is on a collision course.

- In order to develop a solution for true course and speed, further calculations must be performed.

True Motion

- Instead of relative vectors, the ARPA shows "true vectors." Target vectors that point at the center of the display do not indicate a collision course. Further calculations must be performed to develop relative information, including CPA and time to CPA.

- True vectors heighten situational awareness by revealing the aspect of the other vessel. Thus, you can understand the true behaviour of the other vessel—including its aspect—not just its relative behaviour. Understanding the aspect of the other vessel is almost a good as being able to see its navigation lights!

> Aspect of the target vessel is the relative orientation of the target vessel from the observer's point of view.

In true motion mode, vessels on a collision course will not appear to travel toward the sweep center of the display.

Instead, a true motion plot can show a Potential Area of Danger (PAD) at the end of any target's true vector. If your own vessel's vector arrow passes through the PAD, then risk of collision exists. If you alter course and or speed your own vector will shift away from the PAD thus eliminating the risk.

Not only does the plotting radar assist in collision avoidance, but it can also be used to assist interception of another moving target. By steering directly toward a (PAD) associated with another specific moving target, you can achieve a least time course to interception, without resorting to any calculations at all.

> **Because true motion and relative motion ARPAs show very different target vectors, you must be aware of the type of ARPA information being presented. Failure to do so may result in your not realizing that a target is on a collision course.**

The Use of Collision Alarms for Offshore Sailors

Offshore sailors often set a circular Guard Zone on their radars to warn them of oncoming ships. This technique is not foolproof, but it does allow a short-handed crew to manage a watch at night, especially outside normal shipping lanes.

In order for the Guard Zone to serve as an effective collision alarm, you must pay attention to the following:

1. Set the Guard Zone at enough distance that it provides several minutes warning of an approaching ship. When you consider that large ships often make 20 to 25 knots, you should set the Guard Zone at a minimum of 3 Nm.

2. Sea Clutter, birds and other weak echoes can cause the guard alarm to sound unless

you turn up the "anti-Sea Clutter" control. By setting the Guard Zone at 3 Nm and turning up the "anti-Sea Clutter" control, whatever sea return does occur will take place within the Guard Zone, and won't set off the alarm.

3. Because you have turned up the "anti-Sea Clutter" control, you may not be able to detect weak target echoes, such as other small boats. The Guard Zone is a tool primarily used to provide warning of large ships, not of other small boats. You will gain the maximum effectiveness if you can set the "anti-Sea Clutter" levels while there are both large targets and small boats in the vicinity.

The Use of Radar Overlay in Collision Avoidance

A radar image overlaid on an electronic chart is a wonderful tool for helping you develop situational awareness. While viewing the images of other vessels and observing their relative motion, at the same time you can directly view their course and speed in relation to the chart itself. It may help you to make sense out of the movements of other vessels if you can see the charted background and identify exactly where the other vessels are headed.

But when there is risk of collision with another vessel, what you need most is an uncluttered radar display. This is the time you must be able to switch quickly back to that dedicated radar display or window and observe the movements of other vessels without distraction.

This does not mean that you should ignore the chart overlay display. In fact, you should refer to all your information sources as often as possible. But your primary navigational aid in a collision avoidance situation is your radar, not your chart. The chart merely shows you where you cannot go. So be sure to set up a radar window that you can return to at the flip of a switch or the click of a mouse.

Chapter Ten

Heavy Weather

The effect of heavy weather on your radar is dependent on the height of the radar scanner, the vessel's inherent stability and the power of the radar.

Scanner Height

▲ **Fig. 10-1**
The Effect of Scanner Height
Above

In heavy seas, when the wave height approaches a significant percentage of the height of the scanner, the sea returns will simply overwhelm the radar. Not only will returning echoes be so strong that they will be impossible to remove with the "anti-Sea Clutter" control, but the waves will physically block the radar beam before it reaches any distance.

At times, when a small boat is on top of a wave the radar may reveal some useful information, but when the boat is in the trough it becomes essentially blind. This figure shows an extreme example, when it would have been prudent for the small boat to have stayed alongside the dock.

Below

When the radar scanner views the same scene from a higher vantage point, the sea clutter is troublesome, but not impossible to deal with.

Vessel Stability

When your boat pitches forward, the radar momentarily views the surface of the sea, and when it pitches upward, it scans the sky. Only when the radar is on an even keel, does its beam attain the greatest efficiency. However, most boats seldom pitch more than 20°, which is why manufacturers have chosen 20° as a standard vertical beam-width. If the weather is so violent that your boat pitches more than this amount, you should consider seeking shelter as soon as possible.

Since your vessel rolls side-to-side with far more freedom than it pitches fore-and-aft; the side-to-side roll has a significantly greater effect on the efficiency of your radar beam. You needn't be concerned with the longitudinal (fore-and-aft) stability of your vessel, but if you can improve your vessel's lateral stability in heavy weather, you will also improve the efficiency of your radar.

▲ **Fig. 10-2**
Fishboat Overtaken by a Wave
Even though this vessel is labouring in heavy seas, the radar beam still scans horizontally some of the time. This is enough to ensure that it will scan ahead and astern and pick up other vessels and land returns at least once out of three rotations.

Larger, more stable boats provide a more stable radar image in heavy weather, especially if their radars are mounted higher.

The effect of instability is accentuated if the vessel has a significant list to one side or the other—*even in calm seas.* In fact, if the vessel has a significant list, it will always scan the sea surface to one side and the sky on the other. *Thus loading your boat evenly is not just safe seamanship, it is important for navigation and collision avoidance as well.*

Sailboats normally operate at a constant angle of heel, and this presents special challenges for the sailor. There is much debate in the sailing community as to whether or not a radar scanner should be mounted on gimbals, to ensure that it stays level, no matter how much the boat itself heels over in response to wind pressure.

There is no easy answer to this question. Retailers can supply mounting hardware for hanging your radar scanner on a backstay or on the mast. There are obvious advantages to a hanging radar scanner that stays level at all times, but there are also disadvantages:

- More hardware in the rigging creates more opportunities for interference with the sails and rigging.

- More moving parts means more opportunity for hardware failures.

- Unless the swing of the gimballed mount is adequately damped, it may actually lead to more movement of the radar scanner, resulting in a less stable radar image.

Some inshore sailors do not sail at night or in fog, and when they do, they do not have the power available to operate a radar. They find that they need their radars most when they are motoring, and their boats are not heeled over in the wind. So they do not need to hang their radars on expensive and potentially failure-prone hardware.

If you own a sailboat, you should examine your own patterns and habits before you make the decision to buy a gimballed radar mount.

Transmitted Power

Scanners are rated by the width of their main radiating element. The wider the element, the narrower the radar beam. The narrower the beam, the more focused is the radar energy in that beam. However, radar scanners also vary in their actual radiated power.

A four kW radar packs twice the punch of a 2 kW radar and, if the more powerful radar also has a wider radiating element, the radar beam will be even more intense over its cross-section.

Since fog, snow, and rain droplets actually absorb the energy in the radar beam, a higher-power radar stands a greater chance of being able to push through the intervening moisture and to obtain a readable return. Thus a higher-power radar will be able to see further and detect smaller objects during heavy weather.

"Anti-Sea Clutter" Control (STC)

When using the "anti-Sea Clutter" control during heavy weather, do not expect to remove all the clutter from the display. The sea returns at close range will be so strong that, when you tune them out (if you are able to do so), you will also tune out the echoes from any vessels or isolated rocks in the neighbourhood—not a very good idea.

Instead, you must accept a significant amount of clutter on the display, possibly hiding small boats in the sea return; in these circumstances you must exercise special caution.

If you have the opportunity to pass another small boat at close range, you may want to adjust your STC very carefully to the point where you can identify the other vessel, but without over-

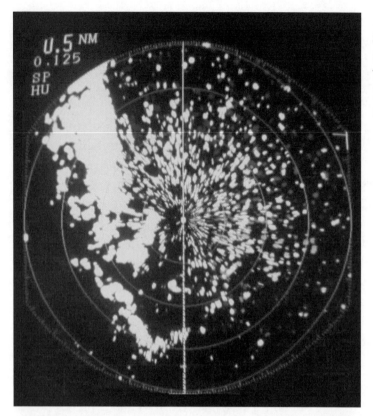

◄ **Fig. 10-3**
Sea Clutter
Sea clutter at close range in Haro Strait near Victoria, British Columbia, during moderately heavy weather (25-30 knots); Cadboro Point to port.

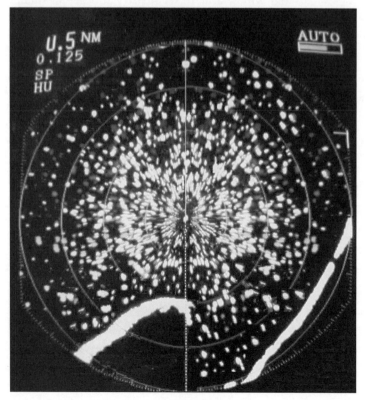

◄ **Fig. 10-4**
Sea Clutter Free Areas
The area behind the image of Sidney Spit (bottom of the display) is free of clutter, partly because it is protected from the weather, but also because this image was taken at low tide, and the mudflats behind the spit do not reflect radar energy well. Depending on the height of your radar, the sand-spit itself may cast a radar shadow.

suppressing the sea return. If you can fine-tune your set in this way, it will give you confidence in your ability to identify other vessels—provided the sea conditions do not worsen.

When the rest of your display is full of sea clutter, blank areas may indicate

- protected channels or areas,
- low-lying mudflats, or
- radar shadow.

And when you finally turn out of the weather into that protected channel, remember to readjust your "anti-Sea Clutter" control, to reestablish your radar's sensitivity to close range targets.

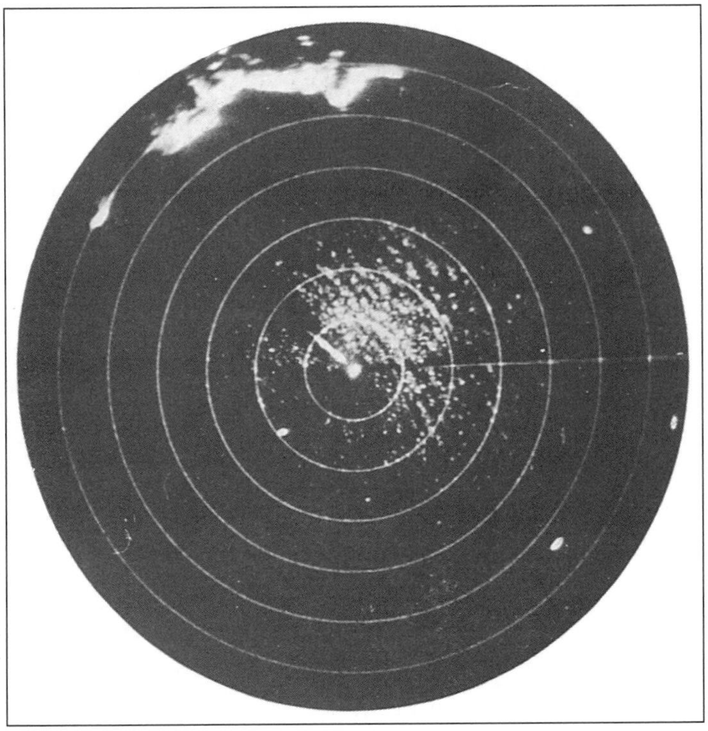

Courtesy of the Royal Institute of Navigation

▲ **Fig. 10-5**
Lines of Rollers
Large seas and swells produce a characteristic echo pattern.

Large Waves

Sea clutter is caused by the radar beam reflecting off the angled surfaces of waves. Smaller waves lead an ephemeral existence; on every revolution of the scanner, each small wave echo winks into existence, and then disappears. The pattern of sea clutter constantly changes—predictable only in the general area it covers.

However, big seas and swells are large enough and regular enough to produce a characteristic echo. Normally these large wave echoes are visible only in the upwind direction—their steep downwind faces reflect radar energy quite efficiently. Each large wave appears as a discrete entity and moves slowly across the display, only to disappear as it passes the center.

Do not try to suppress the echoes of these large waves—they return an echo that is far stronger than sea clutter.

Identifying Submerged Hazards

A number of different types of submerged hazards may create a characteristic image or pattern of images on your display. The type of pattern is dictated by the manner in which the submerged hazard affects the surface of the water and the types of waves that are formed.

Shoal Areas

Shoal areas may cause waves over them to steepen and to break—the shallower the shoal, the more pronounced the effect. However, be aware that as the tide rises, the increased water depth over the shoal may stop the waves from breaking at high water. Of course, during calms there will be no breaking waves; look for this effect to occur when

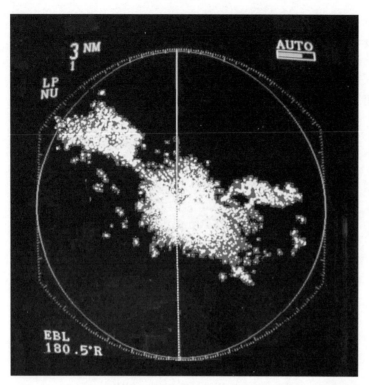

◄ **Fig. 10-6**
Waves Breaking Over Shoals
In this North-up radar image, the normal sea clutter pattern is clearly visible at close range. But you can also see more areas of what appear to be sea clutter to the north-west and to the east. This is a special kind of sea return, caused by seas breaking over shoals—a clear indication that something is not right at that location. In this case, you should continue on your current heading, thus passing *between* the shoals.

the wave height is more than 1½ times the depth of water over the shoal.

During heavy weather, waves over the shoal will attain significantly greater heights and steeper downwind faces than the waves over deep water, thus becoming visible to your radar at greater distances than normal sea clutter.

Isolated Hazards

Isolated hazards, such as rock pinnacles may have a similar effect to large areas of shoals, but the pattern on the radar will be decidedly different. In a large shoal area, numerous waves break all the time, so at least some are always available to return a radar echo; but waves breaking over an isolated hazard may appear, disappear and reappear intermittently.

An isolated pinnacle may even cause large, but gentle, ground swells to break. When these swells do break over such an object, depending on the depth of the rock and the height of tide,

the sequence of events will create several opportunities for the rock or the swell to be visible to local radars. However, these events may each last for only a short time and, thus, if your scanner is not pointing in the right direction at the right time, you may have to wait for a number of swells to pass before you can detect the rock.

These types of isolated dangers (or their effects) will appear only intermittently to your radar. In order to navigate safely around the area, you must first recognize (by reading your chart) that the isolated rock is present and then search for it visually or by radar. Once you have detected the wave disturbance, or the rock itself, you will find it much easier to navigate with confidence in the area; you may even choose to use it as a reference target to find your position. In any case you will know your position relative to the danger.

Those who are equipped with electronic charting systems and radar overlay, will notice

◄ **Fig. 10-7**

Swells Breaking Over an Isolated Rock

A—A submerged rock is totally covered by the crest of a large swell. This swell is high enough to allow it to pass over the rock undisturbed.

B—As the next trough approaches from the right, the rock is exposed. At this point, the rock will return an echo to a radar located to the right.

C—The next crest is not high enough to remain undisturbed by the rock, so it begins to break. At this point the rock and the breaking face of the swell will be visible to a radar located to the left.

D—As the crest moves across the rock, the water rushes in from both sides, finally slapping together and shooting spray to a height of several meters. This final exuberant wave will be visible to a radar in any direction.

immediately that the radar image of the disturbed swells appears only intermittently over the danger.

As the weather worsens, and the waves increase in height, you will be able to see the target more frequently, but at the same time the sea clutter will increase. At first, the disturbance over the rock will appear stronger than the sea returns but, at some point, the sea clutter will totally obscure the area. At this point you must exercise extreme caution when navigating in the area.

Breakers

Be careful around breakers—from seaward their gentle rear slopes may be invisible, whereas from the shore, their steeply sloping front faces may present ideal radar targets. Unfortunately, in most circumstances, you will not have a chance to view their forward faces by radar.

However, when seas break over shoal areas, you may be able to view their steep forward faces from downwind of the shoal.

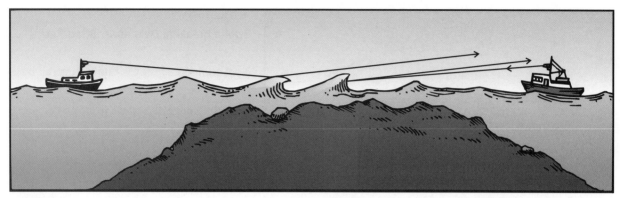

▲ **Fig. 10-8**
Breakers
Breakers created by a submerged shoal reflect radar pulses from their downwind faces. This makes the breakers visible to a vessel downwind. The same breakers are invisible to a vessel upwind of the shoal.

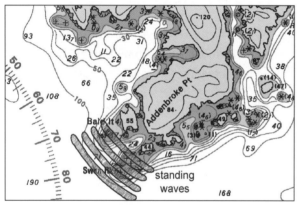

▲ **Fig. 10-9**
Standing Waves
Certain locations produce characteristic wave patterns. When the prevailing swells from the southwest approach Addenbroke Point at the entrance to Rivers Inlet in British Columbia, they steepen over Swan Rock. In addition, the reflected waves from Addenbroke Point interact with these steep waves and set up a pattern of standing waves off the point. This effect is so pronounced that a radar can detect these waves from seaward, and so predictable that you can navigate by their images on a radar. So long as there are at least four wave sets visible between yourself and the point, you are far enough off the point to avoid grounding on Swan Rock.

Effective Use of Crew

On occasion, you may find your navigational and collision avoidance skills severely tested by heavy weather. On small boats, skippers frequently do not have a suitable chart table available, and they must navigate while using a chart hastily folded and stuffed into the most convenient (or least inconvenient) location.

At such times, you can obtain great advantage from a radar image overlaid on an electronic chart. This functionality relieves the skipper from having to match the radar image to a chart or, in fact, from referring to the paper chart at all. While hydrographic agencies world-wide abhor the use of electronic charting systems instead of paper charts, they are secretly relieved that the boater actually has *any* charts of the area at all.

But this presupposes that you actually possess the electronic charts for the area. If you do not, you must resort to more familiar and traditional methods of navigation.

During heavy weather you should not try to manage both the radar and the steering yourself. You will find that you can handle only the steering—the radar will have to look after itself (or vice-versa). At such times, you will need an additional crew member just to help you steer while you manage the radar. If you do not trust your crew's steering skills, you must ask him or her to manage the radar while you steer. A little

Fig. 10-10 ▶
A Small Growler
This chunk of ice will reflect radar pulses only from its vertical surfaces. As a result, it will reflect a very weak radar echo. In any kind of sea conditions, the ice return will be overwhelmed by sea clutter. After a while, the sea washing the ice surfaces will melt them smooth. Smooth ice may reflect radar energy well, but not necessarily back to the direction of origin.

Be very careful when navigating around ice that you keep a good lookout for these smoothly-washed chunks, called "growlers." Because of their low profile, they may go completely unnoticed by your radar—yet these growlers are solid enough to cause devastating damage to a small boat.

Ice that is composed of pressure ridges, hummocks, or any other extremely rough surface is much more easily detected by radar.

advance training and practice will pay off in a big way. If you can teach the crewmember to perform simple functions with the radar—such as changing ranges, and adjusting the gain, and the "anti-Sea Clutter" and "anti-Rain Clutter" controls—you will be able to steer the boat yourself, comfortable that your crew's skills are being applied to the right task.

Ice

Ice is merely frozen water and, as such, the radar treats it much as it would water. Ice reflects radar pulses only when its vertical or nearly vertical components present a reasonable reflective surface.

Pack ice is normally riddled with hummocks and pressure ridges as a result of the intense horizontal forces generated by colliding floes. These forces cause portions of the ice surface to thrust above or below the other surfaces, creating

◀ Fig. 10-11
Ice in the St. Lawrence River at Quebec City
Extensive brash ice, composed of the remnants of other ice (including small growlers as in **Fig. 10-10** above) is visible as a sort of clutter, reminiscent of sea clutter. In the presence of even small waves, the ice echoes will be indistinguishable from sea clutter.

Fig. 10-12 ▶
Pack Ice
Pack ice, frozen solid, shows to the northwest between two stretches of land. To the southeast lies open water with occasional drift floes.

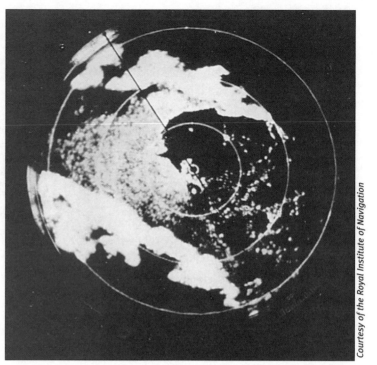

extremely rough boundaries between relatively flat floe surfaces. The flat, undisturbed surfaces do not reflect radar energy well, but the pressure ridges and hummocks return a noticeable echo. When observing a pack, it is the hummocks and ridges that make it detectable.

Icebergs

Icebergs often present vast vertical surfaces, making them visible on radar at 3 to 6 Nm; but they often produce moderate to weak echoes because of some unique features.

- Icebergs often have smooth surfaces, created by melting and sea-wash. The result is that, lacking any small-scale roughness, these smooth surfaces may reflect the radar beam away from its source.

- You should be able to detect most icebergs within 3 to 6 Nm but their images may be poorly defined.

- Even if it does not return a strong echo, a large iceberg will definitely cast a radar shadow, so it may be recognizable by the absence of sea clutter beyond it.

- Of all icebergs, a recently calved iceberg will return the strongest echo, due to the roughness of the broken surface.

Chapter Eleven

What Can Go Wrong and What You Can Do About It

Radar is a remarkable tool—more robust and dependable, probably, than most electronic equipment. You may operate a radar for years and never encounter any problems and, as a result become too dependent on it, unprepared for the time when it does let you down.

The fact that electronic equipment can fail is hardly news. You have undoubtedly experienced the failure of some electronic instrument, probably at the most inconvenient time. If you live each day knowing that this might be the day the radar will fail, then you'll be prepared for any eventuality.

The purpose of this chapter is to help you identify when a failure has occurred—not all failure modes are obvious—and to help you recover from, or compensate for the failure.

Failure Modes

Radar failures and error can be roughly classified into the following categories:

- Total failure—the radar ceases to give any meaningful information—usually the result of blown breakers, fuses, or other hardware items, though sometimes the result of corrupted software. You will probably need assistance to

resolve this kind of failure unless you carry a variety of spare fuses and other parts.

- Partial failure—the radar continues to operate but gives erroneous or degraded information —usually the result of faulty software or incorrect settings. It could also be the result of physical causes such as stripped gears in the scanner which cause the scanner to slip out of synchronization with the display. The most important aspect of recovering from this type of failure mode is to learn to recognize that it has occurred.

- Human error—the most common source of radar problems is human error—and *the most common type of human error is simply failing to pay attention to the events unfolding on the display*.

Protecting Yourself

The moment you first recognize that your radar is failing you must begin to protect yourself from the results of that failure. If this is the first time you've thought about this subject, then it is probably too late. You must prepare yourself ahead of time to deal with instrument failures.

Dead Reckoning

The first and most important thing you can do to protect yourself is to maintain backup information about your position on a regular basis by recording your position on the chart with the time noted beside it. From this mark, draw a line in the direction of your heading and project your position along the line according to the distance travelled in the elapsed time; this will generate your **Dead Reckoning position**. When you alter course, note your new position on the chart, and project your position along the course line to a new Dead Reckoning position. Should your navigational equipment fail at a critical moment, you can revert to your Dead Reckoning and figure out approximately where you should be at that time. **By law, all commercial vessels must maintain their plotted position on their charts.**

To obtain a fairly accurate **Estimated Position**, simply project your **Dead Reckoning posi-**

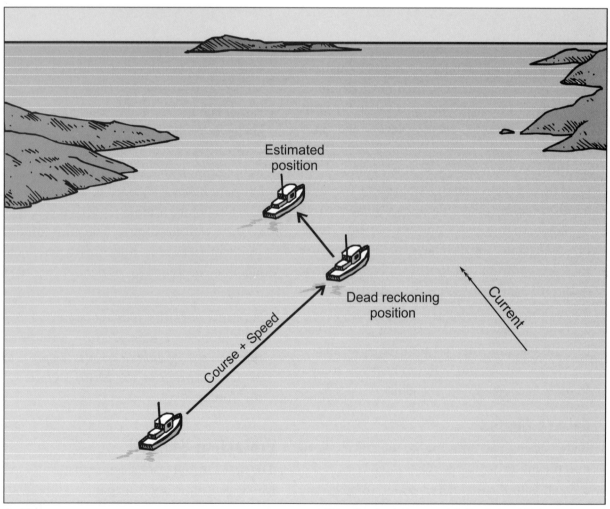

Estimated position

Dead reckoning position

Course + Speed

Current

▲ **Fig. 11-1**
Finding Your Estimated Position

◆ Project your course and speed forward from your last known position. This will give you your Dead Reckoning Position.

◆ Then apply the set and drift of the tide to find your Estimated Position

tion in the direction of the set of the current for a distance proportional to the speed of the current. In most cases, the ***Estimated Position*** that results will be tolerably accurate.

If you are navigating along a twisted, narrow channel, you may not be able to record each change of course, but you can record your progress along the channel. When your radar fails you at night, use your spotlight to keep you safely off the shore, and estimate your progress according to the speed you are making through the water. The effects of current in a narrow channel usually occur along, rather than across the fairway, so you can develop an ***Estimated Position*** with very little trouble, as long as you have a rough idea of the force of the current.

Two conditions are essential for effective Dead Reckoning. First, you must maintain steady course and speed. If your speed varies, you will have no idea how far you travel in 15 minutes and, if you do not steer as accurately as possible, you won't not be able to predict the direction of future positions. Second, you must have an accurate compass. A compass with unknown deviation will not help you when you are forced to rely on it for heading information.

Be sure to check the accuracy of your compass regularly: get it swung by a professional if necessary. Check it again whenever you reposition any large metal items on the vessel, or when you add new electrical or electronic equipment.

Radar Should be Your Primary Tool

If you are equipped with radar and electronic charts, your radar should be your primary navigation and piloting aid (other than your compass). With proper interpretation of the image, a radar set can show you exactly what is out there in the real world. In fog, rain, sleet or hail, it will show you a picture of everything it detects. Radar is the only navigation system that will do so.

An Electronic Charting System is wonderful, but it will tell you ***only where you are, not where everyone else is***. Nor will it tell you where the land masses actually are—only where they are ***supposed*** to be. Radar may provide degraded information, but it is highly unlikely to lead you astray.

Maintaining Situational Awareness

Situational awareness is an understanding of your boat's position in relation to its environment, other vessels and your boat's interaction with its environment. Put simply, it's knowing what is going on around you. You will enhance your situational awareness by paying attention to all the cues coming from your environment, and not letting your attention lapse.

As you can see from the U.S. Coast Guard figures, loss of situational awareness can have serious consequences. But if you maintain situational awareness, you will know where you are and what to do in the event of an equipment failure. In order to maintain situational awareness:

Placing Too Much Reliance on the Radar

Remember, if your radar fails, you will have to revert to some other form of navigation. If you placed all your navigational eggs in one radar basket and the radar fails, it will be much more difficult to recover from equipment failure.

- Always use at least two sources of navigational information. The second source could be GPS or simple visuals but, in any case, you must always have another system of navigation to fall back on in case of emergency and to verify the accuracy of your primary source.

- ***Without a second source of navigational information you may not even recognize that the first source has failed.***

"United States Coast Guard analysis of navigational mishaps for cutters and boats revealed that 40% were due to a loss of situational awareness."

—from the Director of the U.S. Coast Guard Auxiliary, 7th District, website on Situational Awareness at www.dirauxwest.org/situational_awareness5.htm

♦ Know where you are at all times.

♦ Form a mental picture of your environment and know how and where your vessel fits into the picture.

♦ Become familiar with your radar and its operation. **Use your radar both day and night** to build your comfort levels with the instrument; do not just turn it on when you need it the most.

♦ Pay attention to other cues, and other systems of navigation, such as GPS, compass, sounder, etc.

♦ Continually assess and reassess your situation and the relative position of other vessels, lights, buoys and navigational hazards.

When the weather is fine, and all your equipment is working well, it is easy to maintain situational awareness. But when night falls or the weather closes in, maintaining situational awareness becomes more difficult. If the weather continues to deteriorate, you may lose so many clues that you lose your situational awareness. This is the point where you begin to doubt your own understanding of the navigational situation and you may be tempted to ask yourself "Am I going crazy?" [See **Sidebar** on next page.] **When that happens, you have totally lost your situational awareness, and must make every effort to regain it.** There are clues you probably ignored that would have indicated your situational awareness was slipping.

Clues to loss of situational awareness:

♦ **Confusion** or a "gut feeling" that "This cannot be right." **Trust your gut feelings!**

♦ You realize that you are **not watching or looking for hazards.**

♦ **Unresolved discrepancies** in information from two or more sources.

♦ **Ambiguity** in the information you have obtained. If it is unclear or ambiguous, you must resolve the ambiguity before proceeding.

♦ **Fixation or preoccupation.** If you are fixated on one aspect of the situation, you cannot hope to understand all the forces affecting your vessel.

In order to resolve a discrepancy or an ambiguity, you must learn how to recognize when you have a problem. Constantly and continuously use navigational information from at least two sources; never base your navigational decisions on information from a single source. Even your compass can be incorrect.

The four most common causes of boating accidents are:
· Lack of knowledge
· Complacency
· Carelessness
· And last, but not least—alcohol

Improving Your Own Visibility

Now that your boat is equipped with radar, you will probably be boating more often at night or in fog. As a result you must ensure that other vessels can detect your vessel as easily as you can detect them, by installing a good radar reflector. The *Collision Regulations* require that non-metallic

Am I Going Crazy?

I have always believed that I should trust my compass over all other instruments. But my attitude changed one day when I was navigating a 50-meter converted minesweeper in the new Gwaii Haanas National Park in B.C.'s Queen Charlotte Islands.

I was steering 162° Magnetic in order to avoid a series of submerged reefs to starboard. All seemed to be going well when, suddenly, the compass read 216°M—more than 50° off course to starboard. It was at this point I thought I was going crazy, because I could plainly see that the visual markers to which I was steering were still dead ahead.

In this case, the radar and my visual references confirmed what my eyes were telling me—that I was not off course at all. All the islands and transits were in the right place. My view ahead had not changed at all. Instead, it was my compass that was in error. And, sure enough, as if to confirm my suspicion, when I looked at my chart it plainly showed the iron mines at Jedway Bay—less than 3 miles from my current position. I had experienced a magnetic disturbance, not a mental disturbance.

This temporary loss of navigational sanity (loss of situational awareness) can happen to any of us on occasion. Most professional navigators are reluctant to admit it, because their livelihood depends on knowing exactly where they are at all times. The key to resolving a loss of situational awareness is to instantly take steps to resolve the situation. When confronted with conflicting information, or when a "gut feeling" tells you that something is not the way it should be, ***stop your vessel and reassess the situation.*** Post additional look-outs and review all your sources of information to regain situational awareness. ***Proceed only when you have determined it is safe to do so.***

▲ **Fig. 11-2**

Losing Situational Awareness

Before and After. The only difference between the two situations was that the compass had swung to a new heading, but the radar image and the visual picture had not changed. This was a rare case of the compass being wrong!

Total Electrical Failure

In the spring of 1999, I was operating a 20-meter vessel at night in the Gulf Islands area of British Columbia, when both the main and auxiliary generator failed. The vessel was equipped with a split 24-volt electrical system supplying the bridge electronics. When the battery voltage dropped below a certain value, the non-vital bus kicked out, leaving only the most vital 24-volt electronics connected—in this case, a single 24-volt VHF radio. Though the non-vital bus drop-off delay gave me time to switch off sensitive electronics, someone had forgotten to connect the GPS to the vital bus. Consequently, the sum total of my navigational aids on the bridge were a magnetic compass and a VHF radio. Suddenly I was back to the basics and, when the engineer reported that the problem would take some time to fix, I was faced with navigating at night in confined waters with minimal assistance.

However, since I had been maintaining a Dead Reckoning plot I was able, with the assistance of various lights and lighted buoys, to bring the vessel to a safe harbour, while we fixed the problem. Had I not maintained my log and plotted my position on the chart, I could have been in big trouble. Equipment failures can occur at any time and only the most credulous or apathetic navigator will fail to make some contingency plans.

From GPS Instant Navigation, 2nd Edition, *by Kevin Monahan and Don Douglass*

---

vessels and other vessels less than 20 meters in length carry a radar reflector.

Radar reflectors come in many different shapes and sizes. Some are simple open corner reflectors similar to the buoy-fitted reflector in **Fig. 4-7**. Others are housed in rubber or plastic housings, in order to protect them from the weather and from becoming tangled in sails and lines. Another style of reflector is contained within a thin piece of tubing that can be attached to any vertical structure on your boat, including mast stays and radio antennas. The *Collision Regulations* set a minimum standard for radar reflectors. Any radar reflector that meets these standards will show an adequate "radar cross-section" and significantly increase the visibility of your boat to someone else's radar.

Do not come too close to a large ship while it is maneuvering because you may be in its blind zone and may not appear on its radar at all.

> *Do not install a radar reflector with the planes of its reflecting surfaces parallel to or vertical to the horizon.*

◄ **Fig. 11-3**
A Housed Radar Reflector
A housed radar reflector mounted on the mast below a radome antenna.

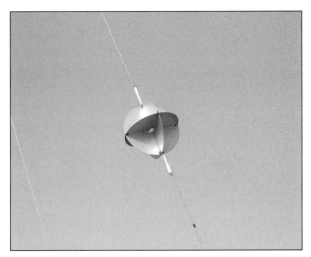

▲ Fig. 11-4
A Corner Radar Reflector
An open radar reflector mounted on the backstay of a sailboat. This radar reflector is mounted properly— the planes of its reflecting surfaces are not mounted parallel or vertical to the horizon. This type of mounting provides an ideal radar cross-section.

▲ Fig. 11-5
Blind Zones
The cruise ship *Maasdam* alongside Centennial Place in Vancouver, BC.

Be careful not to approach within one ship's length of the side of this ship. You will enter a blind zone (below the line) in which even the side lobes of the ship's radar beam are unable to find you due to masking by the ship's own superstructure.

Do not confuse this with a blind sector, though the effect is the same.

Radar Reflectors Work

On the Coast Guard Cutter **Robson Reef**, I was having difficulty in the fog observing my inflatable workboat as my crew moved from fishing vessel to fishing vessel inquiring about catches. The small inflatable boat was virtually invisible to my radar when it was more than a couple of hundred meters away. We needed to manufacture a quick radar reflector so I could track their movements by radar and guide them safely home by radio.

The next time they returned to the mother ship, the crew fashioned a crude reflector in the best traditions of jury rig seamanship. They scavenged a couple of meters of aluminum foil from the galley, loosely crumpled it up, and stuffed it in a plastic garbage bag. They held the garbage bag aloft with a boat hook lashed to the workboat's transom. I was dubious about its effectiveness, but was willing to give anything a try.

As the workboat proceeded away from the mother ship, I was able to track it to a half-mile, then to a mile. As the boat receded into the fog, the radar reflector made a fine trace on my radar. I finally lost track of the little boat at 3 miles. Until we obtained a proper radar reflector, we continued to use the garbage bag and tin foil. I wondered what the fishermen thought of the strange object held up by a boat hook, but I didn't care because it provided an element of safety for my crew.

Human Error

When it is in a partial failure mode, a GPS/Electronic Chart System may continue to provide information that appears correct because it is so unambiguous, but which may actually be significantly in error.

On the other hand, radar normally requires a significant amount of interpretation. A radar that is not operating optimally provides ***degraded quality of information***, requiring even more interpretation. At some point its performance will be so degraded that no useful information can be obtained, no matter how well it is interpreted. Since radar requires so much interpretation, there is plenty of opportunity for human error to creep into the situation.

The following human errors are among the most common:

- The tendency to watch the radar exclusively, at the expense of observing the real world outside your wheelhouse windows (Situational Awareness). [**Chapter 11**]

- Confusing Magnetic and Relative bearings when in head-up mode. Remember, "R" stands for "**R**elative to the vessel's heading." [**Chapter 7**]

- Failure to recognize that the heading flash is out of alignment. [**Chapter 4** and **Chapter 11**]

- Failure to select an appropriate range scale or to switch to the appropriate range scale as the situation develops. If you operate at too great a range scale all the features of interest may be jammed into the center of the display. If you operate at too short a range scale, you may not receive adequate warning of the approach of other vessels. [**Chapter 1**]

- Forgetting to pay attention to the range scale. [**Chapter 1** and **Chapter 2**]

- Improper set-up of the radar. [**Chapter 2** and **Chapter 5**]

  - Setting the gain too low, or the "anti-Sea-" or "anti-Rain Clutter" controls too high. Any of these mistakes will tune out the echoes of targets at close range.

  - Gain and "anti-Sea Clutter" values can drift, so you should reset them on a regular basis.

  - Gain and "anti-Sea Clutter" values can effect the image differently on different range scales. When you change ranges you should perform a quick check to ensure the settings are optimum.

- Incorrectly identifying a radar-conspicuous target. You must learn to think "***If***" and "***Then***". In other words, you must consider that "***if***" this is the point you think it is, "***then***" the next target must be the next point. If you doubt your assessment of the situation, continue to examine the image until everything makes sense. [**Chapter 1**]

- Failing to make allowance for the tide level when ranging on a particular target. [**Chapter 1** and **Chapter 2**]

- Choosing objects for fixing position that are closely grouped. Learn to select targets that will give you a reliable position. [**Chapter 2 and Chapter 7**]

- Mis-reading the VRM or EBL. [**Chapter 2**]

- Failure to note the heading when taking relative bearings. [**Chapter 7**]

- Failure to recognize that another vessel is on a collision course. [**Chapter 2**]

- Forgetting or failing to follow the *Collision Regulations*. [**Chapter 2**]

◆ Taking ranges or bearings from an object below the horizon. You may think you are measuring a coastal feature when, instead, you are measuring the distance to a hill-top. [**Chapter 4** and **Chapter 7**]

Safe Speed

Conventional wisdom states that a safe speed permits a vessel to stop within half the visibility distance. This means that to avoid collisions with others, a vessel must travel very slowly in severely restricted visibility. However, since virtually all commercial vessels are equipped with radar, many skippers feel they can approximate normal operating speeds in restricted visibility and still maintain safety.

The concept of safe speed was developed in order to prevent collisions between two or more vessels. This theory applies only if both vessels are equipped with radar and are using it properly. If one of the vessels is not equipped with radar and is proceeding slowly in fog, while the other vessel is maintaining normal speed, the slower vessel must depend on the other vessel's radar skills for its own safety. This situation is guaranteed to provoke anxiety in the skipper who does not have radar.

If your vessel is equipped with radar, slow down so that other vessels without radar can respond appropriately when you come into view. *Conventional wisdom still applies—slow down in fog!*

High Speed Operation

If you operate a high-speed vessel you may have to reconsider some of the essential truths you have learned in this book. Many modern power boats are capable of travelling at 30 to 40 knots. At this speed, you will travel one mile in two minutes. When you are approaching another vessel travelling at 30 knots on a reciprocal course, the relative speed of closure is 60 knots. If your radar is set to 3 mile range, the "pip" of the other vessel will move from the edge of your display to the middle in 3 minutes. If both vessels are making 40 knots, the target "pip" will

Vessel A speed	Vessel B speed	Relative angle of approach	Relative speed of closure	Time to close from edge to center of display	
				3 mile range	1 mile range
10 knots	30 knots	head on	40 knots	4 min 30 sec	1 min 30 sec
10 knots	30 knots	45° ahead	37 knots	4 min 52 sec	1 min 37 sec
10 knots	40 knots	head on	50 knots	3 min 36 sec	1 min 12 sec
10 knots	40 knots	45° ahead	47 knots	3 min 50 sec	1 min 17 sec
30 knots	30 knots	head on	60 knots	3 min	1 min
30 knots	30 knots	45° ahead	42 knots	4 min 15 sec	1 min 25 sec
30 knots	40 knots	head on	70 knots	2 min 34 sec	51 sec
30 knots	40 knots	45° ahead	54 knots	3 min 20 sec	1 min 7 sec
40 knots	40 knots	head on	80 knots	2 min 15 sec	45 sec
40 knots	40 knots	45° ahead	57 knots	3 min 9 sec	1 min 3 sec

cover the same distance in two minutes and 15 seconds. This does not give much time to assess the movements of the other vessel and to make the necessary alteration.

The new IMO (International Maritime Organization) standard for high-speed commercial vessels requires that scanners on high-speed craft must rotate much faster than a normal radar scanner.

A sample of closing speeds is shown in the table on the preceding page.

As you can see, **when you are operating at high speed, or if you are in the vicinity of other vessels travelling at high speed, you do not have much time to make decisions, especially if you have set your radar to 1 mile range scale.** Notice that when the target vessel's true speed is 40 knots, approaching from 45° ahead, it does not matter much whether you are making 10 knots or 40 knots; the time for the target to cover a one-mile range scale is only 77 seconds or 63 seconds, respectively—a difference of just 14 seconds.

The message is clear—you must scan in all directions at longer range on a regular basis to ensure that high-speed vessels do not approach undetected. If you are travelling at high speed, **you must scan ahead diligently** and be prepared to make decisions very rapidly, or **slow down to better assess the situation.**

Raster Freeze

On occasion, certain "raster scan" radars have been known to "freeze." When a raster scan radar freezes, it no longer updates the display with the latest information from the scanner. Instead, it continually updates the display with the same previous scan from stored memory.

The result is a displayed image that does not change or even fade, as it would normally, and the time base (the rotating region of continually updating information) disappears. Also, the controls cease to have any effect on the display. **These are your cues for identifying that your display has "frozen."** The effect is subtle. If you do not frequently pay attention to the behaviour of the display, you may not notice anything wrong until your visual cues are seriously out of synch with the "frozen" radar image.

Fortunately, the solution is simple. Power off your radar, then power it up again. This reboots the software and gets the instrument back on line. If the problem occurs again, obtain technical assistance; the manufacturer may have developed a software fix.

The Effect of Heavy Precipitation

At times, your radar may simply be overwhelmed by heavy rain, hail or snow. When you try to clean up the image by increasing the "anti-Rain Clutter" control, you may find it ineffective because the precipitation is so heavy.

If your radar is in auto-gain mode, you may be able to further improve the situation by switching to manual gain mode. The auto-gain function limits the degree of "anti-Sea Clutter" (STC) and "anti-Rain Clutter" (FTC) that can be applied to the incoming signal. By switching off

---

Just because you are operating at displacement speeds, you should not be complacent; a collision situation can still develop rapidly. If you are making 7 knots and approaching an 18-knot cruise ship head-on, it takes just 7 minutes 12 seconds to close from 3-mile range. If, however you are on 1/4 Nm range, the cruise ship will close from the edge of the display in just 36 seconds.

the auto-gain function, you may be able to apply higher levels of "anti-Sea Clutter" and "anti-Rain Clutter" to further clean up the image. But be careful you do not apply so much "anti-Sea Clutter" control that you tune out close range echoes.

If you have done everything you can, and the display is still overwhelmed by clutter, you may simply have to wait it out. If necessary, bring your vessel to a stop or heave-to for a while—rain and snow rarely continue at such intensity for very long. The precipitation may also temporarily smooth out the seas, allowing you to heave-to in relative comfort.

Ice on the Scanner

Whenever you experience ice build-up on board, it is cause for concern. Excessive amounts of ice on the superstructure and rigging raises the vessel's center of gravity and reduces the vessel's stability. In extreme cases, icing on the superstructure can cause a vessel to capsize, especially if it is labouring in heavy seas.

Ice build-up on a scanner does not have nearly such dramatic consequences. However, ice can **interfere with free rotation of an open array scanner** [see below], and it can block microwave signals. You may notice that no matter how much you adjust the gain and "anti-Sea Clutter," the radar seems to be **losing sensitivity to distant targets**. If the temperature is below freezing, you should immediately check for frost or

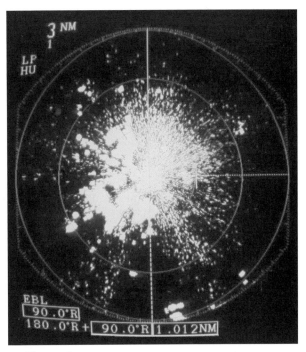

▲ **Fig. 11-6**
Intense Rain Clutter
A radar display completely overwhelmed by intense rain clutter. If you cannot eliminate the clutter, you may have to wait for the intense shower to pass.

ice on the radiating surfaces of the scanner.

Very carefully chipping the ice off the scanner or washing it off with warm water should resolve the problem.

Heading Flash Error

Heading flash error [**Chapter 4**] is a result of a failure of synchronization between the rotating time base and the actual physical orientation of your scanner. It may be due to a software glitch, but it is most likely due to a physical cause. When a buoy or other object, that you have sighted directly ahead, appears to the side of the heading flash instead of directly under it, you should immediately suspect heading flash error.

Some rain squalls may be so intense that they block your radar beam entirely, casting a radar shadow that hides any target beyond. If this is the case, no amount of "anti-Rain Clutter" control will remove the clutter and reveal the hidden targets.

This is an indication that the entire radar image has rotated to port or starboard by a small amount.

If you do not remember when the problem started, you can assume that it is the result of the scanner not having been installed exactly fore and aft on its mounting bolts. Luckily, radar manufacturers have provided a software fix for this hardware problem. Depending on the model of your radar, you may be able to adjust this yourself, by accessing the diagnostic menus on your set, or by manipulating a small set of miniature controls under the main control panel. These controls will permit you to rotate the entire radar image to where it should be. However, some radar manufacturers have made this a "technician-only fix".

If you feel comfortable attempting this solution, read your manual carefully, and follow the instructions precisely. Otherwise, you will have to wait until you can get some expert help.

If this problem happened spontaneously, it is most likely a physical problem, not a software glitch. Somewhere in the scanner unit, a detector is triggered each time the scanner rotates to a forward position. If your radar has spontaneously developed a heading flash error, it could mean that a gear in the scanner is stripped or a detector has come loose. In either case you will probably be unable to fix the problem yourself. Instead, you should watch keenly for any indication that the heading flash error is changing and have your scanner serviced as soon as possible.

Whatever the cause, you can temporarily set your Electronic Bearing Line to indicate the direction that is actually dead ahead and try to ignore the heading flash until you can have your set repaired.

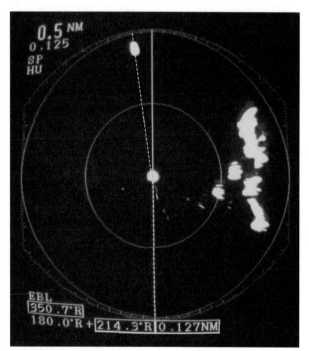

▲ **Fig. 11-7**
Heading Flash Error
You have determined that the buoy is directly ahead, but it shows at 351°Relative. Until you get the radar realigned, just set an EBL on the buoy and use it as a heading indication. In the meantime, try to ignore the heading flash.

Obstructions to Scanner Rotation

When halyards or other lines in the rigging come loose and blow around in the wind, they can catch on a rotating open array scanner and rapidly wind themselves tight. Once this occurs, there are only two possible results—either the line will break (unlikely) or the scanner will stall.

If the scanner stalls, a fuse or a breaker in the radar will blow. Depending on the specific model of radar, the entire radar will shut down, or the time base will cease to rotate. In either case, immediately shut down the radar before you attempt anything further.

◆ Once you have shut down the radar, check the scanner. Are there lines wrapped around it or any other obstruction to free rotation? If so, free the lines and ensure that the scanner rotates freely. Secure the lines or other obstruction and ensure that this problem cannot repeat itself. If necessary reposition the offending lines.

◆ Next, check the fuses or breakers.

◆ Your owner's manual will tell you whether your radar is equipped with a breaker or a fuse, and where to find it. If it is a circuit breaker, then you need only reset the breaker and restart your radar.

◆ If a fuse has blown, you must replace it. If you do not have the correct size and amperage of fuse for the job, do not use a substitute and never try to bypass a fuse; you may jeopardize your radar, and possibly your entire vessel to risk of fire.

◆ Next, check the ship's fuses or breakers. The main power to the radar may have failed, rather than the radar's own fuses .

◆ Once you have restored power, power up the radar again. Carefully check to see that you have not developed a heading flash error. Whenever anything obstructs free rotation of the scanner, you should check for heading flash problems. If everything seems okay, proceed on your way.

To protect your scanner, regularly check any lines in the vicinity and ensure they are well secured. If this does happen, to reduce down-time, be sure to carry a set of spare fuses for the radar. Consult your owner's manual and purchase the proper fuses for the job.

> Caution: *Radar sets generate high internal voltage. Never remove a panel unless your owner's manual specifically indicates that it is safe to do so.*

Heading Input Error

In order to operate in North-up mode, a radar set must be supplied with a reliable form of heading information from either a flux-gate compass, a gyro-compass, or one of the new GPS compasses (heading sensors). A GPS compass is a specific type of equipment—do not confuse it with a regular GPS, DGPS or WAAS navigator. You should never provide heading data from a regular GPS, DGPS or WAAS unit.

A GPS does not measure heading directly; instead it calculates the course followed from a series of position fixes. Because GPS positions are never static—they wander around within prescribed limits—even a stationary GPS will provide a series of different positions over a short period of time. The GPS will then *calculate the course that it thinks it must have travelled during this period*, and it will display this direction as the "course" travelled, even if the vessel is stationary. This "heading" error is obviously less pronounced when the vessel is moving. At high speeds the effect is not significant at all but, at less than one or two knots, the effect becomes significant and, when the vessel is stopped, the indicated heading may rotate "completely around the clock."

In order for your radar to display waypoints, you must supply it with navigational information from a GPS, DGPS or WAAS. Be sure you do not get confused and extract the heading data from the GPS—the GPS provides position, course, speed, and waypoint information, but not heading data.

However, there may be occasions when the heading input feed from your compass fails. The radar may then default to another available source of "heading" data—your GPS. If this occurs in North-up mode, you won't notice anything when the vessel is moving at a reasonable speed; but when you slow down or come to a stop, the heading flash may freeze and fail to respond to helm movements at all—or even worse, ***the entire radar image may rotate erratically in response to the wandering heading input.*** This depends on the GPS—some units refuse to output any course data at all at slow speeds; these are the units that cause your heading flash to freeze in place.

Switching to Head-up mode should solve your problems. By doing so, you are essentially rendering the heading input irrelevant. However, if switching to Head-up mode does not solve the problem ***you should physically disconnect the radar from the GPS unit.***

If you are experiencing this problem with a radar overlay on electronic charts, you will find that the radar overlay will rotate out of alignment with the charted landforms. The only solution is either to fix the problem or disable the radar overlay.

Zeroing Error

Imagine for a moment that the rotating time base is actually a distance scale, with zero at the center of the display. Also imagine that various distances on this scale are marked by bright points of light. As the time base rotates, the bright points draw the range rings on the display.

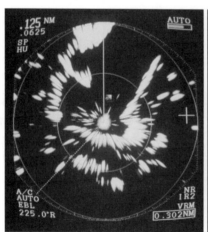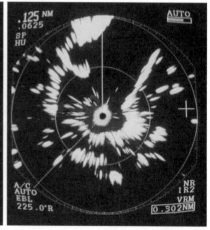

▲ **Fig. 11-8**
Zeroing Error
A radar in proper adjustment. The time base accurately represents distances in the real world. The sea wall below the vessel appears straight. The corner of the dock to starboard is a right angle.

A radar with negative zeroing error. At close range you can clearly see that all targets have been sucked in toward the center of the display. The sea wall below the vessel shows a clear "hour-glass" effect. The corner of the dock to starboard is pointed toward the center and the returns from other vessels have been sucked toward the center.

A radar with positive zeroing error. In this image, all targets have been pushed away from the center of the display. A blank circular area is clearly visible adjacent to the center of the display and the sea wall appears to have a pronounced bulge. Returns from nearby vessels have been pushed away, and the corner of the dock is blunted. The zero point of the distance scale is actually located some distance from the center of the display.

If the rotating time base is a distance scale, any slippage in this scale will shift the radar image toward or away from the center of the display. If the time base scale slips inwards, it will cause all the echoes on the display to shift inwards. Images close to the center may completely disappear into the central "black hole." If the time base scale slips outward, it will carry all echoes away from the center. Thus the zero point of the time base will actually appear at a distance from the center of the display.

To check the zeroing error on your radar, bring your vessel close to a long, straight linear target such as a sea wall, or a log boom. Switch to the shortest range possible, and adjust gain and "anti-Sea Clutter" for the clearest picture. If the distance scale has slipped, you should easily be able to tell by the appearance of the center of the display.

Zeroing error is generally not a critical error—not only has the distance scale slipped along the time base, but also *all the range rings, VRMs and detected targets are shifted toward or away from the center by the same amount, so any range or bearing taken from the center of the display will still be accurate.* However, a zeroing error will cause an offset VRM or EBL to measure inaccurately.

Once you have determined whether you have a zeroing error and whether it is positive or negative, you may be able to adjust the radar to eliminate the bulge or the "hour-glass" in the image of the sea wall. [See **Fig. 11-8**.] Read your owner's manual first to determine exactly how to find out if this is an owner-adjustable feature or not. You may be able to make a menu-driven adjustment, or you may have to adjust a physical micro-control under the front panel. If your owner's manual does not cover the subject, you should obtain technical assistance.

PC Problems

Of all the electronic instruments in a pilothouse, a PC is the most likely to cause trouble. PC hardware is generally not very robust, and software can become non-cooperative, especially a long distance from assistance.

PC-based navigation systems require extraordinary amounts of computing power. The new navigation software systems available today would not have been possible ten years ago—computers were just not up to the task. The complexity of modern software is accompanied by a potential for software conflicts, which can lead to crashes. The more software your run on a single computer, the more prone the system is to failure.

- If you are going to use a PC-based system, you should take some precautions to reduce the likelihood of computer failure or to ensure recovery **when—not if**—it occurs:

- If possible, dedicate the computer solely to navigation tasks. If you want to use your PC for other purposes as well, think about acquiring another PC.

- Obtain the most rugged computer you can afford. The marine environment is rough on computers.

- Consider your PC navigation system to be a secondary navigation aid. Expect that it will fail, and ensure that you have another method of navigating that does not depend on the PC.

- If you can afford it and you have the space available, install a stand-alone radar that feeds the radar image to the PC. Then, if the PC fails, you still have the dedicated radar display.

- Do not place all your eggs in one basket. If all your sensing modules feed to a single computer, a failure of that PC will render all your instruments useless. Set up your system to prevent a single failure from disabling all your electronic instruments.

♦ Be sure to meet or exceed the system requirements recommended for the software. If your computer is under-powered for the task, you will face slow response, inability to access charts, crashing software and a host of other problems.

Radar Overlay Problems

Positioning Issues

If the radar overlay does not match up to the charted outlines of the coast, it may indicate that the software has placed your boat in the wrong position in relation to the chart. This could be due to a number of causes:

1. A horizontal datum problem

Check your GPS. Make sure it is set to display your position in WGS84 or NAD83 horizontal datum.

2. An error in the GPS positioning input

Check the positioning input from the GPS. Normally, the GPS position of a stationary object varies to some degree due to inherent errors in the system. When reading out in three decimals of a nautical mile, the last decimal point represents 1.8 meters. Even in a Differential GPS the third deci-

---

Memory Overload

In March 1999, I approached Porlier Passage in British Columbia in a 20-meter Coast Guard Cutter. Rocks and shoals abound in Porlier Passage, and wicked turbulent currents are set up as the Strait of Georgia waters roar through the passage under the influence of the tides. Porlier Passage is unforgiving to poor navigation, so it is essential to stay on the ranges as you make the approach and follow the course line between Race Point and Romulus Reef.

As soon as I input the waypoints at Race Point and Virago Point, the software began to flash incomprehensible warning messages at me and refused to follow any instructions. My only choice was to shut down the program and restart it—and once I had done so, everything seemed to be working fine. But after having had trouble inputting the waypoints, I was reluctant to place much faith in the computer until I had an opportunity to verify its behaviour.

As I passed Virago Point, I glanced at the electronic chart display. At first I thought it was behaving properly, but when I looked closer (the next time the turbulent water gave me the opportunity), I realized that it showed my position alongside Race Point, approximately 0.25 Nm astern of my actual position! That quarter-mile represented one and a half minutes—quite an update delay! Had I not plotted my courses on the paper chart and worked out transits, radar ranges and bearings to prominent points I could have been in serious trouble.

It didn't take me long to figure out the problem. I had been running for over 200 miles with the navigation program recording the vessel track history all the way. I had forgotten that the program was set to record position every 10 seconds, and it had been doing so for over two days. That represents a huge amount of information. It was this track history data that had jammed up the computer's RAM and caused it to slow to a crawl. In the end, all I had to do was delete the vessel track history, and the computer leapt back into life again and operated beautifully.

The most important lesson I learned was not just that computers can fail—this is nothing new—but that the system can fail and yet appear to be operating normally.

The horizontal datum describes a system on which the latitude and longitude are based. The same latitude and longitude coordinates can indicate different positions relative to the surface of the earth depending on the datum they are based on. In northern British Columbia and Southeast Alaska, the difference between datums (datum shift) may be as much as 200 meters. In North America, NAD83 is equivalent to WGS84.

mal will vary when the vessel is stationary. When moving, the GPS position reading will change continuously. If the reading is static, it is a good bet that the GPS is not functioning correctly.

The most common cause of GPS failure is corroded or broken antenna connections, so you should thoroughly examine the antenna wire and its connection to the GPS. Beyond that, it is out of the scope of this book to delve into trouble shooting your GPS. Instead, read the trouble shooting section of your owner's manual, or refer to Chapter 12 of *GPS Instant Navigation, 2nd Edition* by Kevin Monahan and Don Douglass (available from nautical booksellers or from www.fineedge.com).

3. A chart error

The chart may be in error. If you are using an electronic chart at a scale greater than its natural scale, significant errors will become apparent, including a lack of detail and—in raster charts— a high degree of pixelation. Older charts may have significant errors because they were surveyed at a time when the hydrographer's tools were not as accurate as your modern GPS.

You may also find that certain electronic charts are not registered accurately to the proper horizontal datum. In this case, try to switch to another chart. If that does not solve the problem, the cause is probably not a chart error.

4. Failure of the chart and the radar to synchronize range scales

If there is a mis-match between the range scales of the chart and the radar, you may be able to manually adjust the scale of the chart to match the scale of the radar. However, this is a fundamental error in the integrated system, and you should seek expert help as soon as possible.

5. Heading input error [see above]

If the radar is mistakenly reading the course data as heading in North-up mode, then the radar image will rotate around the display, while the chart remains properly oriented. In this case, try to determine why the heading input has failed. If you can't fix the problem, disable the radar overlay, and operate the radar in head-up mode.

6. Heading flash error

If the heading flash is misplaced, the radar image will be rotated in relation to the chart. If you cannot fix the heading flash error, you may still be able to use the radar overlay if you switch to course-up mode and manually input the appropriate heading until the radar and chart match up properly. By doing this you will be able to assess the exact degree of heading flash error for reference later when you try to fix the heading flash problem.

7. Zeroing error

If both sides of the channel are visible on the display and appear to be shifted either outward or inward a uniform amount, your radar probably has a zeroing error. This kind of error is internally consistent and does not cause problems for a stand-alone radar—except when you use an offset

VRM or EBL, the readouts of ranges and bearings are still accurate. But when interfaced with ECS, a zeroing error becomes a critical issue because it causes a mis-match between the radar image and the chart.

When you first integrate your radar with an ECS, you may discover a zeroing error, of which you were previously not aware.

If you cannot find the cause of the problem, or are unable to fix it (e.g. a broken antenna connection) you cannot merely shift the charted image to match the radar image; instead you will have to live with it. ***Probably the best thing you can do is disable the radar overlay function.***

Colour Issues

Certain colour radars display weak echoes in a shade of yellow. On occasion, you may confuse this weak yellow echo with a yellow that actually belongs to the electronic chart. In most charting software, various shades of yellow indicate land above high water.

When using a radar overlay, you may not be sure if a small isolated target is actually a small vessel or an isolated island—both typically appear as yellow. Even if you can observe contour lines surrounding the target, it may indicate that a small boat is fishing at the top of a submerged pinnacle; or it may indicate an island. The only way to confirm the nature of the target is to:

- refer to a stand-alone radar
- temporarily switch off or reduce the intensity of the radar overlay so you can view the electronic chart
- or refer to a paper chart.

When you first set up your radar overlay, you may be able to choose the colours to apply to various strengths of echo. You may even be able to choose colours for the electronic chart system (especially if you use vector charts). If you can, be sure that the colours of the radar and the electronic charts are different enough so there is no confusion.

Radar Plotting

Simple Radar Plotting

Fig. A-1 ►
A Simple Radar Plot

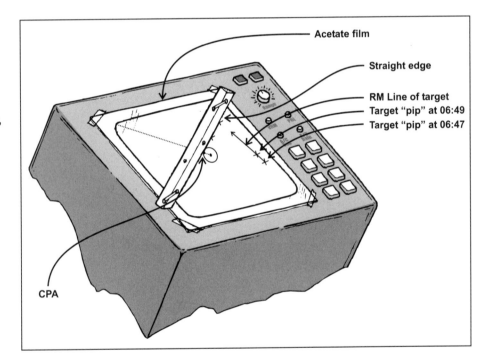

- Acetate film
- Straight edge
- RM Line of target
- Target "pip" at 06:49
- Target "pip" at 06:47
- CPA

- If you own a CRT radar, you may be able to plot directly on the glass of the cathode ray tube. However, if your radar has an LCD display, you should tape a sheet of clear acetate film over the display screen, and make all your marks on it.

- Using a dry-erase marker, place a mark on the acetate directly over the target that concerns you. If there are numerous targets of concern, place a mark over each one. (To avoid confusion, use a different mark for each target.)

- Allow a precise amount of time to expire, then place another mark over each target. (If you have used different marks, make sure you match the right mark to the right target.)

- Using a straight edge, connect the two marks associated with any target, and extend this line past the center of the display. This Relative Motion (RM) line will indicate whether the other vessel will pass ahead or astern.

- Using the Variable Range Marker (VRM), measure the distance from the center of the display to the RM line. This is the distance at the Closest Point of Approach (CPA)

- Using the Electronic Bearing Line (EBL), measure the bearing to the CPA. When the EBL is positioned properly, it will be exactly perpendicular to the RM line, at the point where the VRM is tangent to the RM line.

Fig. A-2 ►

Measuring the Time to the Closest Point of Approach (CPA)

- Using a set of dividers, measure the distance between the two marks that define the Relative Motion (RM) line.
- Step off this distance from the second mark along the RM line to the CPA. (The EBL is perpendicular to the RM line at the CPA.)
- Multiply the number of steps you obtain by the time interval between the marks.
- If you chose a simple time interval such as one minute or two minutes, you can easily estimate the time to the CPA. In this case, if the chosen interval was two minutes, the CPA will occur at approximately 06:51.

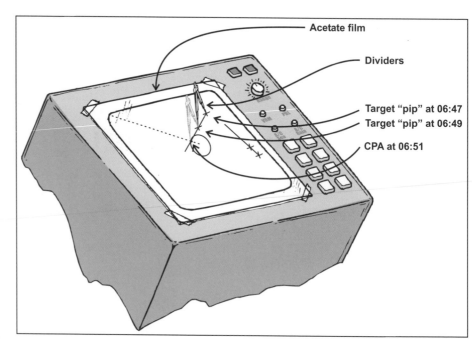

Acetate film

Dividers

Target "pip" at 06:47
Target "pip" at 06:49

CPA at 06:51

Fig. A-3 ►

Radar Plotting

At 12:30 you observe target "A" on radar 45° on the starboard bow, distant 5.8 Nm.

At 12:36 the same target has approached to 3.8 Nm while maintaining its relative bearing. During this period you have been maintaining the same course and speed so you could observe the behaviour of the target.

Clearly, the target is on a collision course.

Let's assume that at 12:30, someone on target "A" threw a radar reflective marker overboard, at the exact same time you first plotted the relative position of the target. In a head-up display, stationary targets travel down the display at the same speed as your own vessel.

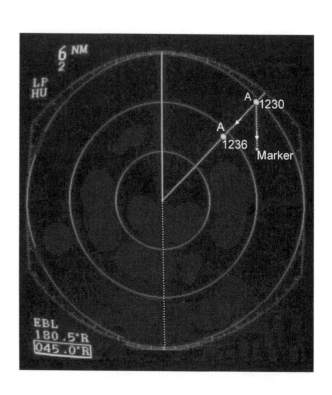

Fig. A-4 ▶
Radar Plotting (continued)
When you look at the screen at 12:36, the only two targets you would observe are target "A" and the reflective marker.

Since the marker has not actually moved, you can assume that the position it is in now represents the actual position of target "A" at 12:30.

Therefore a line drawn from the 12:36 position of the marker to the 12:36 position of target "A" represents the true course and speed of target "A".

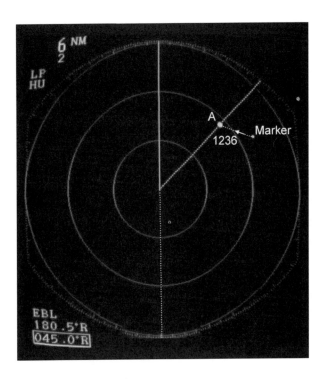

Manual Relative Motion Plots in Head-up Mode

Sometimes it is not adequate to perform a simple plot as in **Figs. A-1** and **A-2**. Instead you must be more systematic about evaluating another vessel's movements.

When you operate a small maneuverable vessel, you may not need to be more precise about another vessel's movements. But if your vessel is larger and, consequently, less maneuverable, or when the other vessel is also very large, systematic plotting becomes essential. As shown in Chapter 8, there are radars that plot targets automatically, (Automatic Radar Plotting Aids—ARPA for short), but if you do not possess an ARPA you will still need to perform the plotting manually.

First, let's look at how you can derive the true motion of a vessel from its relative motion.

To construct a plotted representation of the same situation, you will need plotting sheets. The United States Defense Mapping Agency Maneuvering Board—publication 5090 [**Fig. A-5**] is the most commonly used, but you can use any similar sheet. **Fig. A-6** is such a simplified maneuvering board, which you can photocopy and use for radar plotting.

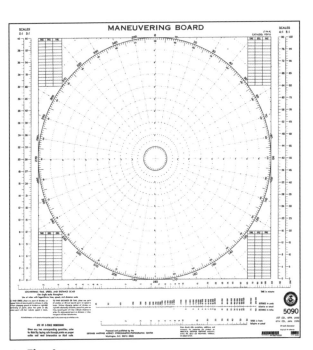

▲ **Fig. A-5**
Maneuvering Board
DMA publication 5090—Maneuvering Board comes in pads of 50 sheets and is available from most reputable marine chandleries.

A maneuvering board is simply a graphic representation of the sea surface and the other vessels around you. When you note the relative position of a target on your radar display, simply note the range and bearing and transfer the position to the maneuvering board.

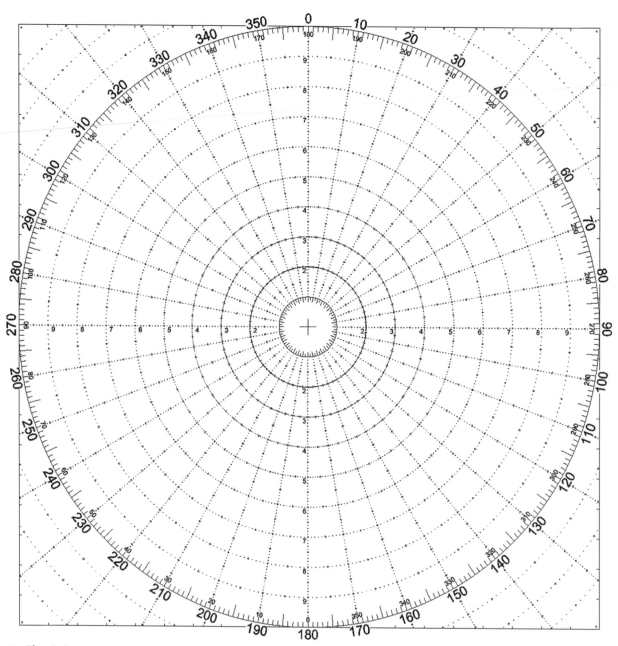

▲ **Fig. A-6**
A Simplified Maneuvering Board

Fig. A-7 ►

Collision Course

To plot this potential collision situation:

♦ Transfer the 12:30 position of the target (A) and the 12:36 position (A').

♦ Also plot some intermediate positions.

♦ Draw a line between the A and A' and extend it toward the center of the display. This is the line of relative motion (RM).

♦ Note that the intermediate positions do not necessarily fall directly on the RM line. This is due to small variations in your own heading and (possibly) of the target.

♦ Project the position of A vertically down the board a distance proportional to the distance your own vessel travels in 6 minutes. (In this case your own speed is 21 knots. Therefore you will travel 2.1 Nm in 6 minutes.)

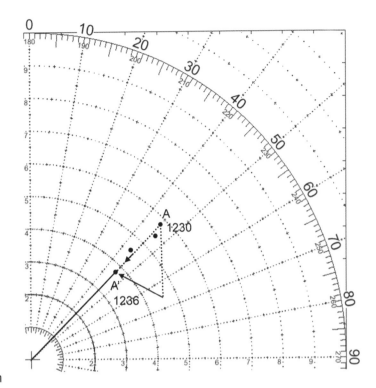

♦ Draw a line between this point and the target position at 12:36 (A'); this is the True Motion Line (TM).

♦ This line represents the true course and speed of the target.

♦ Use a parallel rule to determine the actual course—(298°R). Since this is a head-up plot, the target course is relative to your own heading. If your own vessel is heading 089°T, then the target true course is 298° + 89° = 387°T = 027°T.

♦ Use dividers to determine the length of the True Motion Line. In this case it is 1.6 Nm. Since this is a 6 minute plot, this represents a speed of 16 Knots.

Using the procedure outlined in **Fig. A-7**, you can determine the actual course and speed of the target. You can also learn some other information about the target—such as its aspect. **Aspect** of the target vessel is the relative orientation of the target vessel from the observer's point of view.

Fig. A-8 ▶

Variability of the RM Line

Note that the RM line could have been drawn slightly differently—the four observations of the target could just as easily describe a near miss. Slight variations in the course and speed of both vessels could render this plot slightly in error. Remember, too, that the bearing error of the radar could be several degrees depending on the scanner length. The actual relative motion (RM) line could be anywhere within the shaded area. This is why you should treat all such situations as potential collision situations even if the bearing of the other vessel does change by a small amount.

Collision Regulations—Rule 7 (d)

In determining if risk of collision exists the following considerations shall be among those taken into account:

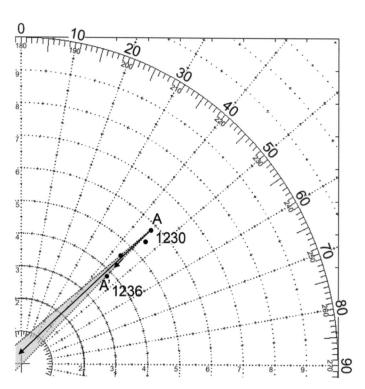

(i) such risk shall be deemed to exist if the compass bearing of an approaching vessel does not appreciably change,

(ii) such risk may sometimes exist even when an appreciable bearing change is evident, particularly when approaching a very large vessel or a tow or when approaching a vessel at close range.

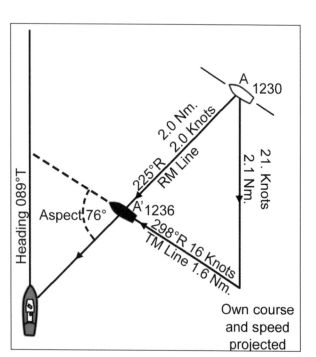

◀ **Fig. A-9**

Aspect

Now that you have laid out the plot, closer examination reveals the aspect of the other vessel as well. In this situation you are viewing the target from 76° on the target's port bow. This reveals the interaction as a crossing situation.

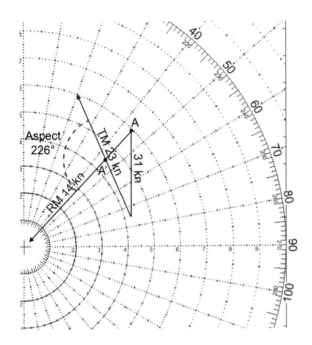

◀ **Fig. A-10**
Overtaking Situation
In this situation, the target maintains a steady bearing of approximately 45° to starboard, as in the previous example. However, it travels only 1.4 Nm in 6 minutes; therefore, its relative speed is 14 knots. Also, in this plot, your own speed is now 31 knots.

The plot reveals a significantly different situation. The target vessel true speed is 23 knots, but most important, it's aspect is 226°R. *You are now an overtaking vessel, and must behave accordingly.*

Fig. A-11 ▶
Closest Point of Approach
Target is observed at 12:30 at 7.0 Nm, 045°R
12:36 at 4.5 Nm, 037°R
Own vessel speed is 21 knots
Relative speed is 26 knots
True speed of target is 24 knots
Aspect of other target is 70°, making this a crossing situation.

To find the Closest Point of Approach (CPA)
◆ Project the RM line past the center of the board.
◆ From the center, draw a line perpendicular to the RM line. This will identify the CPA.
◆ In this case, the CPA is 1.5 Nm and occurs when the target bears 31° to port.

To find the time to the CPA
◆ Measure distance from A' to the CPA. Here it is 4.2 Nm.
◆ Relative speed of target is 26 knots.
◆ Therefore the time to CPA = distance / speed x 60
= 4.2 Nm/26 knots x 60
= 9.7 minutes = 9 minutes 42 seconds
◆ Therefore the time of CPA is 12:36 + 9' 42" = 12:45 42"
◆ In a collision situation you can use the same method to calculate the time to collision.

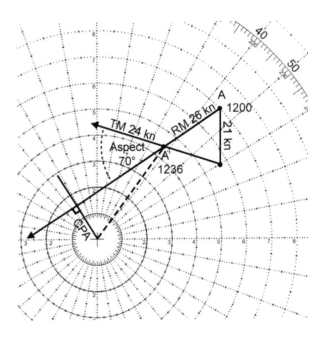

Fig. A-12 ▶

A Current Plot

You can use the plotting technique to find the strength of the current.

- Identify an isolated target that you know is stationary. This could be a buoy or an isolated rock.
- Plot the movements of this target on the maneuvering board.
- In this case the target is observed at

  A 12:30 at 8.0 Nm, 45°R

  A' 12:36 at 6.5 Nm, 55°R

  Own vessel speed   20 knots

  Own vessel heading   89°T

- Project the distance covered by your own vessel but, apply it backwards (toward the bottom of the maneuvering board), just as you did in the previous plots.
- Connect this projected position with the actual position of the target at A'. This line represents the relative set and rate of the current. In this case the current is setting 111°R (200°T) at 3.0 knots.
- The relative motion line (reversed) represents your own vessel's Course and Speed Made Good—010°R (099°T) at 19 knots.

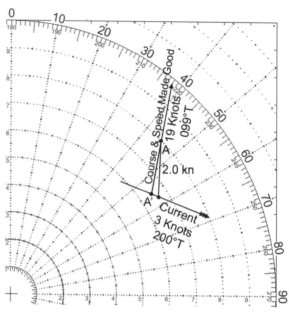

Note: the examples above all use a 6-minute interval. But you could just as easily use a 3-minute or a 12-minute interval. The reason a 6-minute interval is so convenient is that, being 1/10 of an hour, the distance covered in Nm in the 6-minute interval is equal to 1/10 of the speed in knots.

Trial Maneuver

You can also plot the effect on the target of an alteration of your own course or speed.

Fig. A-13 ▶

To Observe the Effect of an Alteration of Speed

Target "A" is observed at 12:30 at 6.8 Nm at 45°R
12:36 at 4.8 Nm at 45°R

Own vessel speed is 21 knots.

To observe the effect of a change of your own vessel's course at 12:39 that will result in a 1.0 Nm CPA:

1. Plot the 12:30 and 12:36 position of the target—A and A'

2. Plot the projected 12:39 position of the target—A"

3. Project your own vessel vector reversed from the 12:30 position of A [**Fig. A-7**]. Mark this point O.

4. From the target's projected 12:39 position, draw a line that is tangent to the 1.0 Nm range circle. This will be the new RM line that will result in a 1.0 Nm CPA. (If you wanted a 0.5 Nm CPA, you would draw a line tangent to the 0.5 Nm range circle.)

5. Using parallel rules, draw a line from the 12:30 position of target A in the opposite direction. This line should be parallel to the new RM line. At the point where this new RM line crosses the line OA, place a mark—X.

6. Note—the distance OX is 1.5 Nm, which represents a speed of 15 knots. This is the speed you should reduce to in order for the target to pass with a 1 Nm CPA. If you measure the new RM line, from X to A' you will find it is 1.7 Nm, which represents the new relative speed of 17 knots.

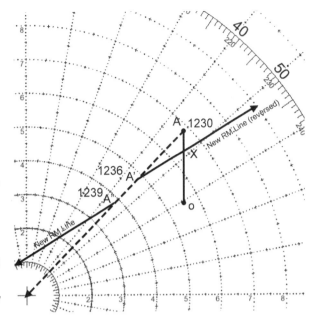

Fig. A-14 ▶

To Observe the Effect of an Alteration of Course

Instead of completing step 6 in the illustration above:

1. Place the point of your compass on point O and draw an arc through point A to the new RM line (reversed). At the point where this arc crosses the reversed RM line, mark O'.

2. Draw a line from O to O'.

3. Measure the angle between the line OA and OO'. The angle is 21°. This is the amount you should alter course to starboard at 1239, for the target to pass with a CPA of 1 Nm. If you measure the new RM line, from O' to A' you will find it is 2.6 Nm, representing a relative speed of 26 knots.

4. To determine the time of the new CPA, calculate it based on the new relative speed. [See **Fig. A-11**.]

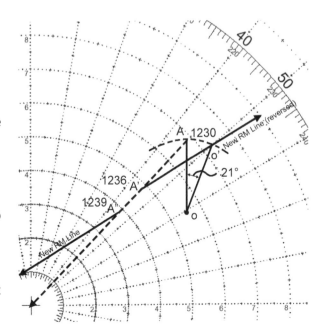

Technical Specifications

Basic Microwave Frequencies

There are two types of radar in common use:

S-Band

- Frequency = approximately 3 gHz
- wavelength = approximately 10 cm
- used in large commercial applications

X-Band

- Frequency = approximately 9.6 gHz
- wavelength = approximately 3 cm
- Commonly used in recreational and small commercial applications

The remainder of the specifications in this appendix apply only to X-Band radars.

Pulse Repetition Frequency (PRF) and Pulse Length

Most radars employ a number of different pulse repetition frequencies, depending on the range in use and/or the pulse length selected.

The Furuno 7000 Series uses the following:

	Pulse Repetition Frequency (PRF)*	Pulse Repetition Interval (PRI) **		Pulse Length *		Range Scales
Short Pulse	2100 Hz	476 μsec	77 Nm	0.08 μsec	24 m	0.125 – 1.5 Nm
Medium Pulse	1200 Hz	833 μsec	135 Nm	0.3 μsec	90 m	1.5 – 3.0 Nm
Long Pulse	600 Hz	1667 μsec	270 Nm	0.8 μsec	240 m	3.0 – 72 Nm

* *μsec* = micro-seconds   Hz = cycles per second
   m = meters   Nm = nautical miles

** Formula used:
   Where the speed of light (C) = 300,000,000 m/sec
   Speed of light (m/sec) = Frequency (Hz) x Wavelength (m)
   Then, substituting PRI for wavelength;

   PRI (m) =   C(m/sec) ÷ Frequency (Hz)

Remember:
Long Pulse – better long range detection
Short pulse – better range resolution

Maximum Range

The theoretical maximum range of a radar is limited by its Pulse Repetition Interval. The radar can only detect objects that return an echo during the receive window for that pulse. During this time period the pulse must travel from the antenna to the maximum limit and return, covering twice the maximum distance.

Therefore the maximum range = 1/2 the Pulse Repetition Interval (Nm)

Minimum Range

The theoretical minimum range to a target for the target to appear as a separate image is dictated by the pulse length in use at that particular range scale. During the broadcast phase, the antenna cannot receive or "listen to" the returning pulse. Consequently the target must be far enough away that the leading edge of the reflected pulse returns to the antenna after the antenna has finished broadcasting the pulse.

Therefore the minimum range = 1/2 the pulse length (m)

Specified minimum range for Furuno 7000 Series = 25 meters

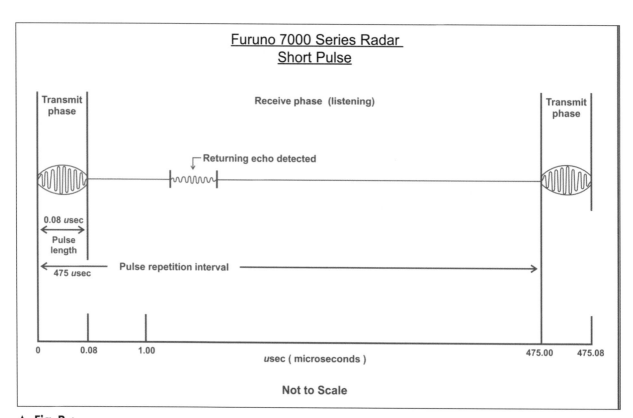

▲ **Fig. B-1**

The Pattern of Transmit and Receive Phases in a Furuno 7000 Series radar.

Note that when using short pulse, the receive phase is six thousand times the length of a single pulse. This provides ample time for the pulse to reach extremely long distance targets and return before the radar broadcasts the next pulse.

Minimum Range Resolution

The theoretical minimum distance apart for two targets to be seen as separate targets is also a function of the pulse length in use. If the echoes of the pulses from the two targets overlap, the radar will display them as a single target.

Therefore, the minimum range resolution = 1/2 the pulse length (m)

Specified range resolution for Furuno 7000 Series = 20 meters

Bearing Resolution

The minimum angular separation for two targets to be seen as separate targets is dependent on the horizontal beam width, which is dictated by the length of the scanner radiating surface.

Some specified beam widths are as follows:

72-inch scanner — 1.2º
48-inch scanner — 1.9º
36-inch scanner — 2.5º
24-inch scanner — 3.9º
18-inch scanner — >5º

Radar Horizon

The radar horizon is slightly further away than the optical horizon, because the microwaves are longer and thus more subject to diffraction in the atmosphere than are visible light waves.

Where h is the height of eye, the distance to the optical horizon in Nm
$$= 1.15\sqrt{h(ft)} \text{ or } 2.08\sqrt{h(m)}$$

Where h is the height of the scanner, the distance to the radar horizon in Nm
$$= 1.22\sqrt{h(ft)} \text{ or } 2.21\sqrt{h(m)}$$

If the scanner is mounted at
45 ft, the radar horizon = 8.2 Nm
10 ft, the radar horizon = 3.9 Nm
5 ft, the radar horizon = 2.7 Nm

Glossary

Abeam—Directly to one side of a vessel, perpendicular to the vessel's heading.

Accuracy—A measure of the difference between the position indicated by measurement and the true position.

Analog radar—An old-style radar which "paints" the returning echo directly on the CRT. The signals are not processed by any type of software.

"Anti-Rain Clutter" control (FTC)—A control which "clips" off the trailing edge of all target echoes. Since rain and snow return thousands of short echoes, this control eliminates the clutter caused by rain or snow at all ranges.

"Anti-Sea Clutter" control (STC)—A control which reduces the sensitivity of the receiver at short range. The "anti-Sea Clutter" control reduces the echoes of sea clutter, which is strongest near the center of the PPI.

ARPA—Automatic Radar Plotting Aid

Aspect—The relative orientation of the target vessel from the observer's point of view.

Attenuation—The decrease in strength of the radar pulse with distance as a result of the spreading of the beam, as well as from absorption and scattering by the atmosphere.

Auto-gain—Software that automatically sets the appropriate gain level for the existing conditions.

Autopilot—A device used for automatically steering a vessel.

Beam—The directed flow of microwave energy broadcast by the radar antenna.

Beam width—The width of the beam, both horizontally and vertically, measured in degrees.

Beam-width distortion—The distortion of displayed images resulting from the inherent width of the beam.

Bearing—The direction of a line joining any two points on the surface of the Earth. May be expressed in degrees True or Magnetic, the same as for any measurement of direction.

Bearing resolution (discrimination)—The minimum angular distance between two targets at the same range which will allow both to appear separately.

Blind piloting—The art of staying on your intended track, relying only on your instruments.

Blind sector—A sector on the display in which echoes cannot be received due to an obstruction (usually part of the vessel's structure).

Brilliance—The control that regulates the brightness of the echoes on the display.

CCG—Canadian Coast Guard.

CD (CD-ROM)—Compact disk data storage medium.

CEP—Circular error of probability—the radius of the circle containing 50% of the measurements being made.

Chart datum—Horizontal datum—the basis for calculations of positioning in surveying. Charts drawn to one datum may not be consistent with those drawn to another.

Chart plotter—A plotter which has the capability of displaying rudimentary charts.

CHS—Canadian Hydrographic Service.

Circumferential distortion—*See* **Beam-width distortion**.

Clearing range—A range set on the radar display that indicates the minimum safe distance to approach a hazard.

Clutter—Unwanted echoes from waves, rain or other transient phenomena.

CMG—Course Made Good—The average direction travelled from the vessel's point of departure to the current position of the vessel (sometimes confused with **COG**).

Cocked hat—When you use three circles (or lines) of position, they will form a triangle known as a "cocked hat." Your position is in the center of the "cocked hat." (The triangle gets its name from the resemblance to the three-cornered hats that gentlemen and captains wore in the eighteenth century.)

COG—Course Over the Ground. The direction of travel along the Actual Track at any moment. COG is sometimes confused with **Course Made Good (CMG)**. The difference is subtle. **CMG** is calculated over a period of time. ***COG is an instantaneous value.***

Collision avoidance—The systematic practice of avoiding collision with other vessels.

Collision course—A course which, if followed, will result in a collision.

COLREGS—The *International Regulations for Preventing Collisions at Sea* or other similar regulations enacted by various jurisdictions.

Coordinates—A set of measurements that define the position of a point. Coordinates are usually given in degrees, and minutes of latitude and longitude.

COP—Circle Of Position—A circle drawn on a chart. If the vessel is known to lie somewhere on the circle, it is known as a Circle of Position.

Course—The direction in which a vessel is intended to travel along the **Intended Track**. Some electronic navigators confuse this with COG.

Course line—The line laid down on the chart to represent the intended track on the chart.

Course steered—*See* Course.

Course to steer—The specific Course or Heading to steer to ensure that the vessel will counteract the current and follow a particular Course to Make Good.

Course-up—When the direction of travel is represented at the top of a radar or EC display, the display is said to be Course-up.

CPA—Closest Point of Approach as defined by the Relative Motion line on a radar plot.

Crash—When a computer fails, it is said to crash.

CRT (Cathode Ray Tube)—A large vacuum tube in which an electron beam "paints" an image on the inner surface of the face of the tube.

Cursor—The arrow, or other indicator that the operator moves around the screen with a mouse, trackball, or arrow keys.

Datum shift—The difference between co-ordinates of the same point made according to two separate horizontal datums.

Degree—An angular measure equal to 1/360 of a circle.

Depth sounder—An electronic device that emits sound waves to determine the depth of water beneath a vessel.

Deviation—The difference in degrees between a magnetic direction and the direction indicated by a magnetic compass.

DGPS—Differential GPS. An enhancement to the Global Positioning System that compensates for errors in positioning.

Diameter—The distance from one side of a circle to the other across the circle's center. Diameter is equal to twice the radius.

Display—The graphical representation of target echoes and other information on the radar screen.

Display unit—The component of a radar system that displays images and other information.

DMA—United States Defense Mapping Agency (now called **NIMA—National Imagery and Mapping Agency**).

DR—Dead Reckoning—Projecting a course and speed ahead in time to estimate the position of a vessel at the end of that time period.

DR position—The point at which the vessel would have arrived had there been no current or wind. Projected by advancing the vessel's position along the **Course Line** a distance equivalent to the distance that would be travelled by the vessel at its speed through the water in the direction of its heading over a specific time period.

Drift—The distance, parallel to the direction or **Set** of the current, that the vessel has been carried from its **DR (Dead Reckoning) position**. May also refer to the total movement caused by current and wind.

EBL (Electronic Bearing Line)—A radial line, originating in the sweep origin of the PPI, that may be rotated through 360°. Used to precisely measure the bearing of a target.

EC—Electronic Chart

Echo (Return)—The reflected radar pulse that is detected by the radar. Also refers to the image of the target on the radar display.

Echo trail—The persistent image of past positions of an echo on the PPI.

ECS—Electronic Charting System—a combination of GPS, computer, navigation software and Electronic Charts, which permits the operator to view the position of the vessel in real time against a background chart.

Estimated position—The most probable position of a vessel obtained by applying wind and current to the **DR position**.

Fix—A position determined by a human or an electronic navigator.

Frequency—When referring to radio or microwave radiation, the number of cycles of the radio energy per second. Measured in kilohertz or megahertz.

FTC (Fast Time Constant)—*See* **"anti-Rain Clutter" control**

Gain control—A control used to increase or decrease the sensitivity of the receiver, and thus the intensity of the displayed images.

Ghost echo—An unwanted image appearing on the display caused by echoes reflected off other structures. An echo of unknown origin.

Give-way vessel—In the *COLREGS*, a vessel that must stay out of the way of another.

GPS—Global Positioning System—Also used to refer to GPS receiving and navigation equipment.

GPS receiver—An electronic receiver which decodes GPS satellite broadcasts and displays solutions for position, course and speed. Now also used colloquially to indicate a GPS with a built in chart-plotter.

GPS sensor—A GPS receiver that has no display capability or controls. A GPS sensor is designed to output raw GPS data to another unit such as a PC or chart-plotter.

Grass—Transient electronic "noise" which must be tuned out by reducing the receiver **gain**.

Growler—A piece of ice less than 1 meter high and less than 6 meters long. A growler is large enough to be a hazard, but small enough to escape detection by radar.

Guard zone—An area of the display established by the user. When activated, the entry of an echo into the Guard Zone causes an alarm to sound.

Harbour chart—A large-scale chart intended for use in harbours and small channels.

Heading—The direction a vessel's bow is pointing as

indicated by a compass. Not necessarily the direction of travel.

Heading flash—The illuminated line visible on a radar display which indicates the direction the vessel is heading.

Head-up—When the vessel's heading is represented at the top of a radar or EC display, the display is said to be Head-up.

Horizontal datum—**Chart datum**—the basis for calculations of positioning in surveying. Charts drawn to one datum may not be consistent with those drawn to another.

Hydrography—The science of measurement and description of the oceans, particularly for navigation purposes.

Iceberg—A massive piece of ice extending more than 5 meters above sea level. Icebergs may be afloat or aground.

Icon—A symbol on the computer display that represents something.

IMO—International Maritime Organization.

Intended track—*See* **Course**. Sometimes may also refer to the Course to Make Good when counteracting the current.

kHz (kilohertz)—1000 cycles per second.

kn (knot)—A speed measurement of one nautical mile per hour.

Kilometer—1000 meters.

kW (kilowatt)—1000 watts.

Latitude—An angular measurement indicating how far a position lies north or south of the equator.

LCD (Liquid Crystal Display)—A display that uses the Liquid Crystal technology common to flat screen computer monitors and laptop computers.

Leeway—A measure of how far a vessel is pushed off its heading by wind only.

Lollipop—A visual indication of the position of a waypoint on a radar display.

Longitude—An angular measurement indicating how far a position lies to the east or west of the prime meridian. Lines of longitude are all great circles and include both the north and south poles of the earth.

LOP (Line of Position)—A line on a chart. If the vessel is known to lie somewhere on the line, it is known as a Line of Position.

Magnetic direction—Directions in 360-degree notation referenced to the magnetic pole rather than the true pole.

Magnetic north—the direction to the north magnetic pole, located in the Boothia Peninsula of northern Canada.

Magnetron—An electronic tube used to generate the microwaves used in marine radar systems.

Maneuvering board—A representation of a PPI printed on paper, and used by radar observers to track the movements of radar targets.

Menu—A word or icon visible on the display which, when selected, gives the user a choice of many different functions. These menu items may each provide further choices.

Meter—A unit of distance equal to 3.28 feet.

mHz—megahertz—one million cycles per second.

Microwave—Electromagnetic frequencies which are at higher frequencies than radio bands. Microwaves are employed by radar and GPS satellites.

Micro-second—(*msec*)—One millionth of a second.

Mile—In this publication, refers to the Nautical Mile of 6076 feet (1852 meters).

Minute—One sixtieth of a degree (also one sixtieth of an hour).

Mouse—A device used to move a cursor on a computer display.

NDI—Nautical Data International. The initials of the Value-Added Reseller that distributes CHS (Canadian) electronic charts. Also taken as the name of the Canadian chart format.

Nm (Nautical mile)—A nautical mile is equal to one minute of latitude (1852 meters or 6076 feet).

NIMA—National Imagery and Mapping Agency (formerly known as Defense Mapping Agency).

NMEA—National Marine Electronics Association.

NMEA 0183—An electronic language used between navigation electronics to allow various equipment to be interfaced. The latest version of this language is NMEA2000.

North-up—When north is represented at the top of a radar or EC display, the display is said to be North-up.

Offset EBL—An EBL that originates at some other point than the sweep origin of the PPI.

Offset Mode—When the operator shifts the center of the PPI (the sweep origin or time base origin) away from the center of the display, the radar is operating in "offset mode".

Offset transit—A transit which is parallel to the vessel's heading.

Open array antenna—An antenna with rotating elements that are exposed to the weather.

Parallel indexing—The practice of following a course parallel to a line that passes through a radar conspicuous feature. The primary mechanism of **Blind Piloting.**

Parallel index cursor—A series of parallel lines on a radar display that can be rotated through 360°.

Parallel rule—A tool for transferring a line across a chart in such a way that it will remain parallel to the original line.

PC—Personal computer.

Perpendicular—When two lines meet at a 90-degree angle to each other they are perpendicular. When referring to a perpendicular distance from a line, the distance has been measured at 90º to the line.

Persistence—The retention of a radar image, during which time the image fades.

Piloting—The art of staying on course and monitoring your progress along your intended track.

Pip—The smallest target echo. Usually the echo of a buoy, vessel or a small isolated rock.

Pixel—A picture cell—the smallest unit of the image.

PPI (Plan Position Indicator)—The representation of target echoes in a map-like format. The PPI represents the images as if seen from above, with the radar's own vessel represented at the center. The PPI need not be centered on the display; it can be shifted off-center when the radar operates in **offset mode**.

Plotter—An electronic display which presents a plan view of the movements of a vessel by displaying a continuous series of position fixes.

Plotting—The systematic recording of the relative positions of targets over time.

Port side—The left side of a vessel when facing forward toward the bow.

Potential Area of Danger (PAD)—An area on a true-motion **ARPA** display which represents an area in which risk of collision is extreme.

Precision—A position given to several decimals of a minute is said to have a high degree of precision; not to be confused with accuracy. A position given to a high degree of precision may not be accurate at all.

Program—The instructions which tell a computer to perform certain actions. A navigation program is the software which allows the computer to manage navigational data and electronic charts.

Pulse—A short burst of microwave energy broadcast by the radar.

Pulse length—The length of the pulse. Usually expressed as the amount of time it takes the pulse to pass a specific point in space.

Pulse Repetition Interval (PRI)—The length of time between pulses emitted by a radar. Most radars use different pulse lengths when transmitting on different **range scales.**

Pulse Repetition Frequency (PRF)—The number of pulses transmitted per second.

RACON (R̲adar Transponder Bea̲con)—A radar **transponder** that broadcasts a series of omni-directional pulses when triggered by a marine radar.

Radar—RAdio **D**etection **A**nd **R**anging—Equipment that uses microwaves to determine range and bearing to various objects.

Radar-conspicuous target—A target that generates a discrete echo a navigator can clearly identify on a chart. The best radar-conspicuous targets are well-defined points of land and small isolated targets. Points of land with a large radius or extensive foreshore are not considered to be radar-conspicuous.

Radar cross-section—The equivalent area of a target that will reflect an echo of a given intensity. Thus a stealth bomber is said to have the radar cross-section of a small bird.

Radar horizon—The point where the earth's curvature begins to mask low-lying targets.

Radar overlay—An image of the radar display overlaid on an electronic chart.

Radar reflector—A highly reflective device used on small boats to return an efficient radar echo.

Radar shadow—An area which is hidden from the radar beam by higher ground.

Radius—The distance from the center of a circle to its outer edge.

Radome—A radar antenna and transceiver housed in a single weather-tight enclosure.

Rain clutter—Unwanted echoes reflected by rain drops or snow.

Range—A distance to a preselected target.

Range resolution (discrimination)—The minimum distance between two targets on the same bearing which will allow both to appear separately.

Range ring—Fixed circles centered on the sweep center of the PPI at preselected distances.

Range scale—The distance from the center to the edge of the display when it is not operating in **offset mode**.

Raster chart—A chart that is stored as an image. Raster charts cannot be manipulated and form a passive background to an electronic charting system.

Raster-scan radar—A radar display that displays images after digital analysis of the range and bearing of each echo.

Real-time—Implies that information is made available without appreciable processing delays.

Refraction—The deflection of a propagating radio wave as it passes through a medium of non-uniform density.

Relative bearing—A bearing measured clockwise from the vessel's heading.

Relative course—The apparent course of a target measured relative to the heading observer's vessel.

Relative speed—The apparent speed of a target measured relative to the observer's vessel.

Relative motion—The representation of the motion of a target or a group of targets relative to the observer's vessel.

Relative Motion line (RM line)—The projected course line of a target vessel measured relative to the observer's vessel.

Restricted visibility—According to the Rule 3 (l) of the *COLREGS*: "The term 'restricted visibility' means any condition in which visibility is restricted by fog, mist, falling snow, heavy rainstorms, sandstorms or any other similar causes."

S-Band—Radars using 10 cm (3000 mHz) microwaves.

Scale—A ratio of distances on a map or chart to the distances in the real world. Often expressed as in 1:50000. A chart is said to be large scale or small scale. *"Large scale covers a small area; small scale covers a large area."*

Scanner—A combined radar transceiver / antenna.

Sea clutter—Unwanted echoes returned by smaller waves and chop.

Second—One sixtieth of a minute of arc or of time.

Set—The direction toward which the current is moving.

Sidelight—The red or green navigation lights used to indicate the aspect of a vessel at night.

Side lobe—The areas of low power radar transmissions to either side of the main radar beam.

Side lobe echo—Reflections of a side lobe from objects outside the main radar beam. Side lobes reflections often cause **ghost echoes**.

Situational awareness—A holistic understanding of your boat's position in relation to its environment and to other vessels and the nature of your boat's interaction with its environment. Put simply, it's being aware of the "big picture."

SMG (Speed Made Good)—The speed of the vessel along the **Course Made Good**; i.e. along the straight line joining the point of departure and the present position.

Soft Key—A key with multiple functions depending on the software window open at the time. Soft keys are located immediately beside the screen. The function of the key is indicated on the screen adjacent to the key itself.

Software—Programs or operating systems which instruct a computer to perform certain tasks.

SOG (Speed Over the Ground)—The speed of the vessel at any instant along its Actual Track over the ground. The SOG may differ significantly from the Speed through the water. Sometimes SOG is confused with SMG. The difference is subtle. SMG is calculated over a period of time. *SOG is an instantaneous value.*

Soundings—Measurements of depth of water. On a chart the soundings are corrected to lowest low water (U.K.) or Mean Low Water (U.S.).

Speckling—Transient electronic "noise" which must be tuned out by reducing the receiver **gain**.

Speed—The speed of the vessel through the water as measured by a speed log.

STC (Sensitivity Time Control)—*See* "anti-Sea Clutter" control

Stabilized display—A radar display that is stabilized by input from a gyro compass, flux-gate compass or a GPS heading sensor. Stabilized displays are either **North-up** or **Course-up**.

Standby—The condition in which a radar is warmed up and is prepared to transmit.

Standing wave—A stationary wave generated by the interaction of separate wave trains or by a wave travelling against a current.

Stand-on Vessel—In the *COLREGS*, a vessel which must maintain its course and speed.

Starboard side—The right side of a vessel when looking toward the bow.

Sweep origin (time base origin)—The point at the center of the **PPI** about which the **time base** rotates, and which is the origin of the **VRM** and **EBL**.

Tangent bearing—A bearing taken from the edge of a target.

Target—An object detected by radar.

Target-acquisition—In an ARPA radar, the process of locking on to a target and beginning to track it.

Time base—The rotating line that updates the images on the PPI. In an analog radar, the time base is directly linked to the returning pulses.

Trackball—A ball mounted in a mouse or on the panel which, when rotated, moves the cursor.

Transceiver—A radio (or microwave) transmitter and receiver contained in the same physical unit.

Transit—When two landmarks are in line visually, they are said to form a transit.

Transponder—A radar transceiver that broadcasts a signal when triggered by radar beams.

True direction—Directions in 360° notation referenced to the true north pole.

True motion—The representation of the motion of a target or a group of targets relative to the surface of the earth.

True north—The direction to the true North Pole.

Tuning—Adjustment of the intermediate frequency in order to optimize the radar's performance. Most small vessel radars tune automatically.

USCG—United States Coast Guard.

Variation—The difference in degrees between Magnetic north and True north at any particular location.

Vector—A line that possesses direction and quantity, i.e. length or speed.

Vector chart—A vector chart is stored as data in a database. This data can be manipulated to a surprising degree.

VHF (Very High Frequency)—The type of radio most commonly used in inland and nearshore waters. VHF has a limited effective range of approximately 40 Nm.

VRM (Variable Range Marker)—A range ring which can be adjustable from zero to maximum range; used to precisely measure the distance to a target.

WAAS (Wide Area Augmentation System)—A system of satellite based differential GPS.

WGS 84—A universal chart datum used by all modern navigation systems and referenced to the earth's true shape rather than to a local datum. WGS84 and NAD83 are virtually the same for marine applications.

Waveguide—The resonant cavity between the magnetron and the antenna. When the antenna and magnetron are separated, the microwaves must be channelled through a waveguide to the antenna.

Waypoint—A position recorded in the memory of an electronic navigator that represents a position on the surface of the earth.

Windows—An operating system which use images instead of text to communicate with the operator.

X-Band—Radars using 3 cm (9600 mHz) microwaves.

XTE—Cross Track Error. The perpendicular distance of the vessel at any time from the Course Line. This value is displayed on the steering diagram.

Zeroing Error—The error caused by a failure in timing between the triggering of the pulse and the beginning of the receive phase. This causes inaccuracies in the representation of ranges on the PPI.

Zoom Mode—An operating mode in which the radar image has been magnified.

Zooming—Magnifying a chart image on the display.

Bibliography

Bartlett, Tim. *Radar Afloat*. 3rd Edition. Arundel, U.K.: Fernhurst Books, 2001.

Bole, A. G. and Jones, K. D. *Automatic Radar Plotting Aids Manual, A Mariner's Guide to the Use of ARPA*. Centerville, Maryland: Cornell Maritime Press, n.d.

Brogdon, Bill. *Boat Navigation for the Rest of Us*. Camden, Maine: International Marine, 1995.

Canadian Coast Guard. *Ice Navigation in Canadian Waters*. Ottawa, 1999.

Canadian Coast Guard Auxiliary. *Search and Rescue Crew Manual*. Victoria B.C., 2002.

CHS Notices to Mariners. Ottawa: Canadian Hydrographic Service, Department of Fisheries and Oceans.
"Horizontal Datum Unknown—Chart 7193." No. 546, 1996.
"Important Notice to Mariners." January, 1997.
"Horizontal Datum of Chart." Annual Notices to Mariners, No 45, 1996.

Cockroft, A.N., and Lameijer, J. N. F. *"A Guide to the Collision Avoidance Rules."* Fourth Edition. Oxford, U.K: Heinemann Newnes, 1990.

Contour Magazine, Canadian Hydrographic Service, Department of Fisheries and Oceans, Ottawa:
"The Digital Chart: Raster or Vector." (Spring 1993.)
Casey, M. J. "Hey! Why is My Ship Showing up on the Dock." (Number 8, Fall 1996.)
Grant, S., and Casey, M. "Updating Charts: High Priority for all HOs." (Winter 1994.)
Holroyd, Paul N. "S-57 Implementation." (Number 6, Summer 1995.)

Kraikiwsky, Dr. Edward, and Casey, Michael J. "Intelligent Ship Navigation Systems: What's Available and What Do They Do?" (Number 6, Summer 1995.)
Pace, Captain John D. "ECDIS at Sea: Come On In—The Water's Fine." (Winter 1993.)

Dahl, Bonnie. *The User's Guide to GPS—The Global Positioning System*. Richardson's Marine Publishing, 1993.

Furuno Operator's Manual. Nishinomiya, Japan: Furuno Electric Co., Ltd.

Hoffer, William. *"Saved! The True Story of the* Andrea Doria*—the Greatest Sea Rescue in History."* Bantam, 1979.

Hydro International Magazine, GITC bv, Netherlands

Rodrigues, Ian, "ECDIS: The Role of Training Institutions." (April 2001.)

Schwarzburg, Peter, "An ECDIS Pioneer: Interview with Helmut Lanziner." (January/February 2001.)

Van der Marel, H., "U.S. Discontinues Intentional Degrading of GPS". (October 2000.)

Lanziner, Helmut, "Progress in the Great Lakes." (May/June 1999.)

Hecht, Horst, "What is an ENC?—Revisited." (May/June 1999.)

Spaans, Jac A., "The Unsafe Use of (D)GPS as Sole Source Information in Maritime Navigation." (April 2000)

Mori, Adriano, "GPS-based Heading and Attitude Sensors." (April 2003.)

The Institute of Navigation. "*The Use of Radar at Sea.*" 2nd Edition. London: Hollis & Carter, 1954.

IMO (International Maritime Organization), "*Merchant Ship Search and Rescue Manual.*"

Lanziner, Helmut and Alexander, Lee. "ECDIS-Radar Integration: Why, What and How." St. Petersburg, Florida: Records of the 1995 RTCM Annual Assembly, May 1995.

Lanziner, Helmut. *The Manufacturer's Difficult Path to ECDIS.* CANStar Navigation Inc., 1996.

Lanziner, Helmut. "Impact of Radar Integration with Electronic Charting." International Hydrographic Review, Vol 2, No. 1 (New Series, June 2001)

Maddocks, Melvin. *The Great Liners.* Alexandria, Virginia: Time-Life Books, 1982.

Madon, Sam. *Radar Plotting—Step by Step.* North Vancouver, B.C.: Pacific Marine Training Institute, 1980.

Maloney, Elbert S. *Chapman's Piloting, Seamanship and Boat Handling.* 63rd Edition. New York: Hearst Marine Books, 1994.

Meeker, Ezra. *Pioneer Reminiscences of Puget Sound.* Lowman and Hanford, 1905.

Monahan, Kevin and Douglass, Don. *GPS Instant Navigation, 2nd Edition.* Fine Edge Productions, Anacortes WA, 2000.

Monahan, Kevin. "Electronic Charting Systems." *Westcoast Fisherman Magazine*, Vancouver: Westcoast Publishing, April 1994; reprinted in *The Fisherman's News*, Seattle, June 1994.

Monahan, Kevin. "GPS; Errors and Insights." *Westcoast Fisherman Magazine*, Vancouver: Westcoast Publishing, January 1994.

Navstar Global Positioning System, Joint Program Office. *GPS Navstar User's Overview.* Prepared by ARINC Research Corporation for the Program Director, 1991.

Raytheon Users Manual. Raytheon Inc., 1995.

Simrad RA40C/RA41C/RA42C *Marine Radar Instruction Manual,* 4th Edition, March 2001.

Tetley, L., and Calcutt, D. *Electronic Aids to Navigation: Position Fixing.* Edward Arnold, 1991.

Transport Canada, Marine Safety, Ship Safety Bulletins:

#01/1992—"Potential 'Lock-up' on Raster-Scan Radar Displays."

#05/1998—"Operation of Marine Radar for the Detection of Search and Rescue Transponders."

#14/1998—"Radar Reflectors on Small Vessels—Fittings and Limitations."

U.S. Defense Mapping Agency Hydrographic/Topographic Center. *American Practical Navigato— Bowditch,* Publication No. 9, 1995.

United Sates Defense Mapping Agency—Hydrographic/Topographic Center, *Radar Navigation Manual,* Publication 1310. Washington, D.C.: 4th Edition, 1985.

Internet

www.alcommarine.com/marine_radar.htm—Alcom Electronics, marine radar basics

www.c-map.com—C-Map: electronic charts

www.dirauxwest.org/situational_awareness5.htm—Director of the US Coast Guard Auxiliary, 7th District, Situational Awareness pages

www.fineedge.com—FineEdge.com, publisher of this book and other titles.

www.fugawi.com—Fugawi navigation software

www.furuno.com—Furuno Electric Ltd. USA—manufacturer of a complete line of marine electronics

www.hydro.gov.uk—United Kingdom Hydrographic Office home page—source of Notices to Mariners and the Admiralty Raster Chart Service

www.ion.org—The Institute of Navigation

www.maptech.com—Maptech—Chart Navigator software and source of authorized U.S. government NOAA electronic charts

www.nautinst.org/index.html—The Nautical Institute—The world's leading institute for professional mariners

www.navionics.com—Navionics: electronic charts

www.ndi.nf.ca—Nautical Data International: source for authorized Canadian Hydrographic Service electronic charts

www.noaa.gov—United States National Oceanic and Atmospheric Administration: producer of official US navigation charts—among numerous other functions

www.nobeltec.com—Home of Nobeltec Visual Navigation Suite and Passport World Charts

www.otenet.gr/sailor/radar.htm—Captain Ioannides radar pages

pollux.nss.nima.mil/index/index.html—National Imagery and Mapping Agency Publications Page—includes The American Practical Navigator (Bowditch) and the Radar Navigation and Maneuvering Board Manual.

www.raymarine.com—Raytheon Marine Electronics

www.rin.org.uk/—The Royal Institute of Navigation—for those with an interest in navigation in its broadest terms

www.shipwrite.bc.ca —Nautical publications and consulting—specializing in the Pacific Northwest and electronic navigation. Visit the Shipwrite web-site to download errata and corrections for all Shipwrite Productions' books and maps.

www.simrad.com—Simrad Marine Electronics

www.transas.com—Transas—World-wide vector charts based primarily on NOAA, British Admiralty and Russian Hydrographic Service charts

www.wa6pby.com—Navigation-L, a page of useful resources including links to electronic versions of the now out of print Defense Mapping Agency Maneuvering Board

www.wa6pby.com/nav/mb8x11.pdf—A free PDF maneuvering board form without the nomographs in 8.5" x 11" format, courtesy of Mike Wescott.

www.xenex.com—PC-based high performance radar and electronic charting systems.

About the Author

Kevin Monahan

Captain Kevin Monahan is a Canadian Coast Guard officer with over 20 years experience navigating the British Columbia coast as a small-vessel captain. Born in London England in 1951, Monahan—now a resident of Victoria, B.C.—emigrated to Vancouver and attended the University of British Columbia. His articles have appeared in various magazines including *Monday Magazine*, *Fine Homebuilding* and the *Fisherman's News* as well as in *West Coast Fisherman* which published a series of his articles on electronic navigation. Captain Monahan was a fisherman for 12 years, after which he worked on ferries and coastal transports, before joining Canada's Department of Fisheries and Oceans as a patrol vessel captain. Captain Monahan is now an officer with the Canadian Coast Guard Pacific Region. He has testified in court as an expert witness in the navigational uses of GPS and is the principal author of *GPS Instant Navigation, 2nd Edition* and *Proven Cruising Routes, Volume 1—Seattle to Ketchikan*.

Index

Enjoy these other publications
from FineEdge.com

Exploring the Pacific Coast—San Diego to Seattle
Don Douglass and Réanne Hemingway-Douglass

All the places to tie up or anchor your boat from the Mexican border to Victoria/Seattle. Over 500 of the best marinas and anchor sites, starting from San Diego to Santa Barbara—every anchor site in the beautiful Channel Islands, the greater SF Bay Area, the lower Columbia River, and the greater Puget Sound.

Exploring the San Juan and Gulf Islands—2nd Edition
Cruising Paradise of the Pacific Northwest
Don Douglass and Réanne Hemingway-Douglass

Describes the most scenic and accessible marine area in the world—a cruising paradise of 300 tree-covered islets and islands surrounded by well-sheltered waters, comfortable resorts, quaint villages, secure moorings and anchorages.

Exploring Southeast Alaska
Dixon Entrance to Glacier Bay and Icy Point
Don Douglass and Réanne Hemingway-Douglass

Almost completely protected, these waters give access to a pristine wilderness of breathtaking beauty—thousands of islands, deeply-cut fiords, tidewater glaciers and icebergs.

Proven Cruising Routes, Vol. 1—Seattle to Ketchikan
Kevin Monahan and Don Douglass

With our 34 routes you have the best 100 ways to Alaska! We've done the charting! This route guide contains precise courses to steer, diagrams and GPS waypoints from Seattle to Ketchikan. Check www.FineEdge.com to view or sample download-able routes.

Also available: Companion 3.5" IBM diskette to directly download routes into electronic charts.

Exploring Vancouver Island's West Coast—2nd Ed.
Don Douglass and Réanne Hemingway-Douglass
With five great sounds, sixteen major inlets, and an abundance of spectacular wildlife, the largest island on the west coast of North America is a cruising paradise.

Exploring the North Coast of British Columbia —2nd Ed.
Blunden Harbour to Dixon Entrance—Including the Queen Charlotte Islands
Don Douglass and Réanne Hemingway-Douglass

Describes previously uncharted Spiller Channel and Griffin Passage, the stunning scenery of Nakwakto Rapids and Seymour Inlet, Fish Egg Inlet, Queens Sound, and Hakai Recreation Area. Includes the beautiful South Moresby Island of the Queen Charlottes, with its rare flora and fauna and historical sites of native Haida culture.

Exploring the South Coast of British Columbia —2nd Ed.
Gulf Islands and Desolation Sound to Port Hardy and Blunden Harbour
Don Douglass and Réanne Hemingway-Douglass

"Clearly the most thorough, best produced and most useful [guides] available . . . particularly well thought out and painstakingly researched." — *NW Yachting*

Exploring the Marquesas Islands
Joe Russell

Russell, who has lived and sailed in the Marquesas, documents the first cruising guide to this beautiful, little-known place. Includes history, language guide, chart diagrams, mileages and heading tables and archaeology. "A must reference for those wanting to thoroughly enjoy their first landfall on the famous Coconut Milk Run."
—Earl Hinz, author, *Landfalls of Paradise—Cruising Guide to the Pacific Islands*

Pacific Coast Route Planning Maps
South Portion—San Diego to Fort Bragg

North Portion—Cape Mendocino to Seattle/Victoria

The perfect complement for the *Exploring the Pacific Coast—San Diego to Seattle* book. In beautiful color and full topographic detail, each 24' x 60" map includes the GPS waypoints for the three popular routes for cruising the coast, the Bluewater Route, the Express Route and the Inshore Route. Also included are over 500 places to tie up or anchor. Inset maps are included to show harbor approaches with local waypoints for the entrances to major harbors and coves. Plan your own custom itinerary and prepare for the trip of a lifetime. Both maps are available folded, rolled, or laminated rolled.

Inside Passage Maps *North and South portions*
The Inside Passage to British Columbia and Alaska is one of the most sheltered and scenic waterways in the world. Now, for the first time, our maps include an index to all harbors and coves in this superb wilderness allowing you to customize your own routes.

GPS Instant Navigation, 2nd Edition
A Practical Guide from Basics to Advanced Techniques
Kevin Monahan and Don Douglass

In this clear, well-illustrated manual, mariners will find simple solutions to navigational challenges. Includes 150 detailed diagrams, which illustrate the many ways you can use GPS to solve classic piloting and navigation problems.

Cape Horn
One Man's Dream, One Woman's Nightmare—2nd Ed.
Réanne Hemingway-Douglass

His dream: To round Cape Horn and circumnavigate the Southern Hemisphere. Her nightmare: Coping with a driven captain and the frightening seas of the Great Southern Ocean. "This is the sea story to read if you read only one."
—McGraw Hill, *International Marine Catalog* "Easily the hairy-chested adventure yarn of the decade, if not the half-century."
—Peter H. Spectre, *Wooden Boat*

Trekka Round the World
John Guzzwell

Long out-of-print, this international classic is the story of Guzzwell's circumnavigation on his 20-foot yawl, *Trekka*. Includes previously unpublished photos and a foreword by America's renowned bluewater sailor-author Hal Roth.

For all nautical titles, visit our website: www.fineedge.com

Sea Stories of the Inside Passage

Iain Lawrence

A collection of first-person experiences about cruising the North Coast; entertaining and insightful writing by the author of *Far-Away Places*.

The Arctic to Antarctica *Cigra Circumnavigates the Americas*

Mladen Sutej

The dramatic account of the first circumnavigation of the North and South American continents, continuing around Cape Horn via Easter Island and then to Antarctica before returning to Europe. Told through the words of a notable circumnavigator with beautiful photographs throughout.

Arctic Odyssey

Dove III *Masters the Northwest Passage*

Len Sherman

Len Sherman was the third crew member on the epic Northwest Passage voyage of the *Dove III,* one of the first west-to-east single-year passages on record.

Sailboat Buyer's Guide *Conducting Your Own Survey*

Karel Doruyter

This book guides you and provides you with an essential checklist of what to know and look for *before* you buy a sailboat! "Armed with this book a buyer can confidently inspect a new or used boat."—John Guzzwell, custom boat builder

Destination Cortez Island

A sailor's life along the BC Coast

June Cameron

A nostalgic memoir of the lives of coastal pioneers—the old timers and their boats, that were essential in the days when the ocean was the only highway.

The Final Voyage of the *Princess Sophia*

Did they all have to die?

Betty O'Keefe and Ian Macdonald

This story explores the heroic efforts of those who answered the SOS at first to save, then later to recover, the bodies of those lost.

Up the Lake with a Paddle

Volume 1: Sierra Foothills and Sacramento Region

Volume 2: Lake Tahoe & Sierra Lakes

Volume 3: Tahoe National Forest–West, Lakes within the Yuba River Drainage

William Van der Ven

The essential paddling books on all the great places to paddle in the foothills and mountains of California's Sierra Nevada.

For all nautical titles, visit our website: www.fineedge.com